PEACE, LOVE & HEALING

Also by Bernie S. Siegel, M.D.

LOVE, MEDICINE AND MIRACLES

PEACE, LOVE & HEALING

Bodymind Communication
and the Path to Self-Healing:
An Exploration

Bernie S. Siegel, M.D.

HARPER & ROW, PUBLISHERS, New York
Grand Rapids, Philadelphia, St. Louis, San Francisco
1817 London, Singapore, Sydney, Tokyo

Copyright acknowledgments begin on page 287.

FIRST EDITION

Designed by C. Linda Dingler

Library of Congress Cataloging-in-Publication Data

Siegel, Bernie S.
    Peace, love & healing : bodymind communication and the path to self-healing : an exploration / Bernie S. Siegel. — 1st ed.
      p.   cm.
    ISBN 0-06-016077-2 : $
    1. Medicine and psychology. 2. Healing. 3. Mind and body. 4. Control (Psychology) I. Title.
    R726.5.S55 1989
    615.5—dc19   88-45906
                                                            CIP

---

89 90 91 92 93 CC/RRD 15 14 13 12 11 10 9 8 7 6 5 4 3 2 1

I dedicate this book:

To all the loving, courageous people we have met whose lives have been healed by their disease. You are all winners. Thank you for being my teachers.

To my younger sister, Dossie. It was she who first taught me about responsibility and how to deal with adversity as we trudged the streets of Brooklyn to and from P.S. 226. And to her husband, Len, and children, Sarah, David, Cynthia and Daniel.

To Beth Rashbaum, editor and writer, for her work and perseverance. To Carol Cohen, my editor at Harper & Row, and to my agent, Victoria Pryor, for their continued support. (They now know how hard it is to be a scrub nurse in the o.r.)

To Julie Foley and Lucille Ranciato, who have sat by me and guided me.

To all my exceptional associates, friends, co-workers and patients.

To all of the ECaP staff and board.

And to those who most of all continue to accept, love and forgive me—my parents, Si and Rose, my wife, Bobbie, and our children, Jon, Jeff, Stephen, Carolyn and Keith, and Bobbie's parents, Merle and Ado.

I also want to acknowledge the work and words of my friend Dr. Karl Menninger, who knew it all decades ago, as shown by his dedication in *Man Against Himself* (1938):

To those who would use intelligence in the battle against death—to strengthen the will to live against the wish to die, and to replace with love the blind compulsion to give hostages to hatred as the price of living

Peace, love and healing to you all.

—BERNIE SIEGEL

Contents

PEACE, LOVE & HEALING

Introduction

Since writing *Love, Medicine and Miracles,* I've received an outpouring of letters and calls from people thanking me for helping them find the path to healing. I hope what I've learned in the intervening years will help you, too, to find that path. My emphasis in this new book and in *Love, Medicine and Miracles* is on self-healing, that ability given to us by our Creator and too long neglected by medicine. That does not mean that I am advocating turning one's back on the medical profession—but I also do not believe in relying on it alone. Modern medicine and self-healing need not and should not be mutually exclusive. I advise using all your options, which include your innate ability to heal, as well as what science can offer you. Drawing on my experience and that of the many exceptional people I have encountered, I explore the role of the self-healing system, explain the science behind it, and show why love is physiologic.

Woody Allen tells us that human beings are divided into mind and body: The mind embraces all the nobler aspirations, like poetry and philosophy, but the body has all the fun. I believe, however, that the body and mind are a unit, bound together via nerves and messenger molecules. Love, hope, joy and peace of mind have physiological consequences, just as depression and despair do. That's what the science of mind-body communication is all about.

Researchers are now studying the relationships among consciousness, psychosocial factors, attitudinal healing, and immune function. Gradually the medical profession, too, is relearning what once it knew so well—that we cannot understand disease unless we understand the person who has the disease. Recently my wife, Bobbie, was reading *Kinflicks,* a novel by Lisa Alther, in which a retired doctor speaks his mind:

> It's a notion that is out of favor among the medical profession at present. . . . But when you've been at it as long as I have, when you've treated people under all circumstances, when you've treated their parents and their children, you begin to see patterns. Illness doesn't strike randomly, like a thief in the night. Certain types of people at certain points in their lives will come down with certain kinds of ailments. You can almost predict it after a while. A disease can serve the same function for an alert doctor as a Rorschach inkblot for a psychologist; it's like a form of existential self-expression for a patient if you like. I know this may sound a little farfetched, my dear, but disease is not arbitrary; and it does not attack. But goodness, you're not interested in an old man's pet theories.

When appearing as a medical expert in a court case relating illness and stress, I was asked, "When did this new theory originate?" My response was, "Hundreds of years ago." Why? Because that was when physicians had little in the way of drug treatments with which to treat their patients—instead they had to *know* their patients and the circumstances of their lives in order to heal them.

The contribution of life-style and the emotions to the health of the individual was a concept easily accepted centuries ago. Today feelings have to be shown to create chemical alterations in our bodies in order for us to accept them as physiologic. Fortunately, we now have the science to document those changes.

Psychologists have shown that the effects of love on the body can be measured: An unloved infant will have retarded bone growth and may even die; a stroked infant grows faster. The effects of peace of mind are measurable too: People who meditated, as well as those who confided traumatic experiences to diaries rather than repressing them, were shown to have enhanced immune function. Love and peace of mind do protect us. They allow us to overcome the problems that life hands us. They teach us to survive . . . to live now . . . to have the courage to confront each day and utilize our pain and suffering as motivators and redirectors.

As children, however, most of us did not grow up in an environment with sufficient love and hope. It is time to move beyond that legacy of lovelessness, to forgive and be reborn. The energy for this rebirth often comes when we see and accept our own mortality. When we are willing to encounter our shadow and change, we can, as Freud tells us, convert neurotic conflicts into normal problems.

There will always be loss and grief. I know, however, that out of pain new love and true healing can occur. One must learn to use one's pain for personal transformation, or longevity will be no gift. The path is difficult but it will lead to moments of great beauty.

Peace, Love and Healing is about the very special people who have taken this path and the lessons we can learn from them. The dreams, stories and drawings of exceptional people are shared here to show how emotions can heal lives as well as cure diseases. I talk about people with cancer and AIDS frequently, because they are a large part of my experience. I will also share the stories of people with neurological problems, arthritis, diabetes, collagen diseases and heart disease. The healing mechanisms are the same for all diseases and for all patients as well as their doctors. We must all confront the reality that no one lives forever. Illness and death are not signs of failure; what is a failure is not living. Our goal is learning to live—joyously and lovingly. Disease can often teach us to do that.

When I speak to five hundred people with AIDS about the value of their illness, the gift and challenge it represents, and nobody tries to remove me from the stage, I know how courageous they are and how much they have learned about healing. When I discuss survivors I am interested in how they embrace life, not how they avoid death. Those who have learned to take on the challenge of their illness and share responsibility for their treatment have chosen the path that leads to peace of mind and healing on a spiritual level. This profoundly affects their ability to be cured physically, as the energy formerly involved in conflict is set free, and the body's immune system receives a dramatic "live" message.

However, those of you who feel guilt because you believe you have caused your own illnesses, or who feel like failures if you cannot cure them, are giving your healing system a destructive message. You must let go of feelings of guilt and failure so that, unencumbered by these negative messages, you can utilize to the fullest your innate healing capacities.

Our Creator has given us five senses to help us survive threats from the external world, and a sixth sense, our healing system, to help us survive internal threats. There is much that we can do, as individuals, to activate or impede this healing system, just as we can choose to confront danger or close our eyes and ears to it.

It took me many years to learn that our ability to mobilize our healing capacity means that survival statistics do not apply to individuals. Individuals who change in response to their illness can exceed expectations or achieve results doctors consider miraculous. When talking to these exceptional patients the words love, faith, living in the moment, forgiveness and hope come up again and again. The inner peace these people have acquired on a psychospiritual level leads to healing and often to cures as well. Self-healers are all the same. The results they achieve are no coincidence. Every doctor can share anecdotes about these people, though few doctors understand what they have witnessed. We must begin to acknowledge that these miraculous healings are scientific and can be taught to others, thereby creating more anecdotes and eventually a scientific understanding of these events.

It is my feeling that no longer should medicine be only a mechanistic specialty that deals with the unexplained by calling it miraculous. Now is the time to reopen our study of the healing process and alter the way medicine approaches it, to turn our attention from disease and death to health and life.

If we do not make this change in the theory and practice of medicine we cannot move forward. Every generation has and always will have its threatening illnesses. If we find a cure for one, another takes its place. If we find a wonder drug for one, we must search for another wonder drug for the next. We need therefore to focus not just on finding new wonder drugs, but on teaching people how to utilize the naturally occurring "wonder drugs" that exist within each of us. I predict that in the next decade, through genetic engineering, these internal wonder drugs will be cloned by scientists and used therapeutically. How much better it would be if we could stop science from being only a mimic and let it teach us to be our own genetic engineers.

That is what I am trying to get people to do in *Peace, Love and Healing.* I have remained a surgeon for two reasons: One is that most people refuse this challenge and I can still help them, but more importantly I would like to combine my mechanical skills with your healing skills to achieve the greatest potential. If I can make all of this credible, we can accomplish the incredible.

Still, there is no denying that not every physical illness can be cured. We can, however, make use of all illness to help us redirect our lives. I suppose, in the broadest sense, my book shows how illness or suffering can heal not just the individual but society. As the threat of nuclear disaster and famine can lead us to love and healing in our global relationships, so illness can do the same for our personal relationships.

Accepting our mortality as a motivator and not denying it, looking into the shadows of our unconscious, developing self-love and self-esteem—this is what I want to share with you. As a surgeon I know incredible things can happen when energy is freed for healing. We are looking beyond quantity (the province of medicine) to quality of life.

True healers know the value of afflictions and of adversity. They know that within the symbolic experience of disease lies a path to change and self-healing and a healthy bodymind. Let us start on that path. Allow the disease to heal your life. Begin your journey and become your authentic self. Now.

"That's the most interesting thing of all. The balance depends on the man's *frame of mind!* Understand? Which means that if he's cheerful and firm in spirit, there will be more sodium in the barrier; and no sickness, none whatever, will bring him to his death. But as soon as he loses heart, the potassium gains the upper hand and he might as well order himself a coffin. . . ."

"The physiology of optimism. The idea is sound. Quite sound. . . ."

"So I wouldn't be surprised . . . if they discovered some sort of cesium salt in about a hundred years, one that spread out in the organism if there was a clear conscience and didn't if there wasn't. And it will depend on that cesium salt whether the cells of the tumor will grow or whether the tumor will clear up."

Aleksandr Solzhenitsyn, *Cancer Ward*

Peace, Love and Healing is factually accurate, except that names, locales and individual traits have been altered to preserve coherence while protecting privacy.

1

*I have the conviction that when physiology will be far
enough advanced, the poet, the philosopher and the
physiologist will all understand each other.*

—CLAUDE BERNARD

The Physiology of Love, Joy and Optimism

In January of 1983 John Florio, a seventy-eight-year-old landscape gardener, was contemplating retirement. He developed
abdominal pain and underwent a GI series, which showed an
ulcer. He was treated for one month and re-x-rayed to see if
the ulcer had healed. This time, however, it was larger and
looked malignant. A biopsy revealed cancer of the stomach.

I first met John in late February when he was referred to
my office for surgery. I suggested to him that we get him into
the hospital right away since I was going on vacation, and I
thought that with a rapidly advancing cancer he ought to have
surgery immediately. He looked at me and said, "You forgot
something." "What did I forget?" I asked. "It's springtime. I'm
a landscape gardener, and I want to make the world beautiful.
That way if I survive, it's a gift. If I don't, I will have left a
beautiful world."

Two weeks after my vacation, he returned to the office,
saying "The world is beautiful, I'm ready." He looked incredibly well the night after his surgery, with no pain or discomfort.
The pathology report revealed: "Adenocarcinoma, poorly dif-
ferentiated, invasive through gastric wall and into perigastric
adipose tissue. Proximal margin involved by tumor, seven of
sixteen lymph nodes positive for tumor." That simply meant
he still had a lot of cancer left in him after the operation. I
explained to him that he ought to consider chemotherapy and

x-ray therapy to deal with the residual cancer. "You forgot something," he said. "What did I forget this time?" "It's still spring. I don't have time for all that." He was totally at peace, healed rapidly and was out of the hospital well ahead of schedule. (His granddaughter, an oncology nurse at Yale, was fully aware of the findings and his choice.)

Two weeks later he was back in my office, complaining that his stomach was upset, and I thought, "Aha, it's the cancer again." It turned out to be a virus, which I treated symptomatically, and he left my office.

In March of 1987 I arrived at my office and saw John's name in the chart rack. "You must have the wrong chart," I said to the nurse. "No, that's the right chart," she said. "Then there must be two people with the same name." "No, no," she insisted, "he's sitting in there." Then I showed her his pathology report to explain why I assumed she had made a mistake. If you think pathology reports predict the future for an individual, it wouldn't seem possible that I could be seeing John four years after his operation. But that's who I saw when I walked into my examining room.

I again feared that his visit would be related to cancer. Before I could ask him anything, the first words out of his mouth were "Don't forget, this is only my second postoperative visit." I think he wanted to make sure the insurance would cover it. "But why are you here?" I asked. "I have a question," he said. "I'd like to know what you can eat after a stomach operation." "Four years after, *anything!* But tell me, why are you here?" "I have a hernia from lifting boulders in my landscape business." Since he refused to be admitted to the hospital, I repaired it under local anesthesia on an outpatient basis, and he was off and running again. If he rested at all I'd be surprised, even though he promised to have two young men do his normal work the first few weeks after surgery.

John is one of those exceptional patients who seem to most clinicians to defy understanding. But I have learned that all of these exceptional patients have stories to tell and lessons to teach. It's not just a matter of being lucky or having "well-behaved" diseases (slow-growing tumors, "spontaneous" remissions and so forth). What you have to understand is that there is a biology of the individual as well as a biology of the disease, each affecting the other. On the day of diagnosis we don't know either well enough to use a pathology report to predict the future.

It is now six years after his surgery, and John celebrated his eighty-third birthday recently. You have to wonder—what has happened to his cancer?

I don't know if his immune system eliminated it or if it's still in there, enjoying John's life so much that it's going along for the ride. What I do know is that when you look at John what you see are signs of his ability to live and love. Still passionate about his life's work, he sends me letters with clippings about the therapeutic value of the outdoors and an article about himself in the local newspaper that quotes him as saying "If I find a little marigold just lying there, I feel so sorry for it I just put a hole in the ground with my finger and plant it." The article ends by saying "Today . . . John is still on the job, planting and pruning. He loves it. And like the legendary cowboy who proudly professes he wants to die in the saddle with his boots on, he says when his turn comes 'I always pray that I'll die at work, gardening.' "

Working outdoors, John maintains what I call a celestial connection, and, like patients in the hospital who have been shown to heal faster when their room has a view of the sky, he is healthier because of it. John is too busy living to be sick. That's his real secret. But how, in scientific terms, do we account for him? What can we learn from him? Is there really a physiology of optimism, peace, love and joy?

SELF-INDUCED HEALING

Spontaneous remissions like John's I prefer to call self-induced healings. They make wonderful anecdotes and can also tell us a lot about communication between mind and body. But since most people don't believe in the existence of these remissions—"error in diagnosis" or "well-behaved disease" is the standard explanation for them—there hasn't been much of an attempt to understand them scientifically. The medical profession always gives the credit to the disease rather than the person. We need to start studying the person and success.

The Remission Project of the Institute of Noetic Sciences in Sausalito, California, is now trying to fill the vacuum by analyzing four thousand medical journal articles on the subject of spontaneous remission from all over the world. Since any given article can cover multiple cases, many more than four thousand cases are involved, in addition to which the project is also looking at extraordinary healings such as those that have occurred at Lourdes.

However, of all the thousands of cases cited, virtually none made any comment about the patients' personal circumstances. Brendan O'Regan, the institute's vice president for research, cites one exception, quoting from a paper concerning a woman with metastasized cancer of the cervix, who was considered close to death. Her condition changed dramatically when, in the words of the case report, "her much-hated husband suddenly died, whereupon she completely recovered." (To protect husbands, however, I can tell you that eliminating your husband will not necessarily cure you. We used to have an empty room in the office where I kept twelve husbands so that when a woman would come in and say, "Here's the guy who made me sick," I could tell her to take a new one and leave hers. The women all thought that was a great idea, but everyone ended up bringing the new one back, because the old problems were less troublesome. They all learned that it's yourself you have to change in order to heal.)

It's incredible to think of all these thousands of people who recovered from "incurable" illnesses and were never asked how or why they thought they had gotten well. When you do ask, as I have done and as researchers more receptive to this kind of thinking have also, you find that over 90 percent of the people will tell you about a significant change in their life prior to the healing. An existential shift has occurred in them, and for the first time in their lives they are truly living. They don't see their disease as a sentence but a new beginning.

In an effort to identify any psychological patterns that long-term survivors might have in common, O'Regan has gone to the San Francisco Bay Area Tumor Registry to track down people who are still alive ten years or more after a terminal diagnosis. If he succeeds in getting permission to interview the eighty-nine who have been located for him, they will shed even more light on the nature of the personality factors involved in healing.

Meanwhile, researchers like Dr. George Solomon, Sandra Levy, Joan Borysenko, Nicholas Hall, David McClelland and Candace Pert, at institutions like Harvard, the University of California at Los Angeles and the National Institutes of Health, are clarifying the physiological mysteries of mindbody healing. Gradually they're becoming accepted as "scientific," too, being invited to address major conferences on psychosocial factors in disease, and publishing articles in traditional medical journals as well as more recent ones devoted to the new disciplines of psycho-oncology and psychoneuroimmunology. There is still much to learn about the inner workings of mind-body communication, so we must continue to look at the anecdotal evidence available to us and proceed with the scientific studies that will substantiate it.

Anecdotal material is not statistical, but it is true, and it is evidence that can help us see where to direct our research. I hope that, while this research proceeds, all physicians will give their patients the option to become living anecdotes instead of dead statistics.

Anecdotes that can be used to change belief systems have been walking into my office for years, and I often meet up with people like John who I assumed were dead. Most doctors don't encounter these people, because people who have been told "You'll be dead in six months" don't go back for a checkup. So the doctor never finds out they didn't die.

I believe that studying the lives of these self-induced healers should be an important part of the attempt first to verify, then to identify the ties between mind and body, psyche and soma. Because of their experience, psychologists, neurologists, endocrinologists and immunologists are all much more aware of these connections than clinicians. Veterinarians too: I had a touching letter from one who said that he especially hates to have to put a pet to sleep when it belongs to an elderly person, because he knows that the loss can have a serious impact on that person's health. Clinicians are rarely able to see the connections, however, because unlike the old family doctor, they don't know their patients' lives and don't think it relevant to ask about them. We must get to know the people we're taking care of, as doctors in previous generations did. We should know the person as well as the disease, and take a special interest in those people who have gotten well despite the odds. They are not just lucky. They have worked hard to achieve their healings, and we have much to learn from them. However, this is not to condemn or blame those who don't recover. We are talking about possibilities versus probabilities, not success or failure.

FAITH, HOPE AND PLACEBO

Everyone who has ever experienced the placebo effect also has a role to play in the quest to understand the mindbody connection. These are the people who, for reasons we are now beginning to understand, will show rapid healing and pain-relief after taking a placebo, which is an inert substance or a sham procedure with no properties that would allow it to function as an agent of healing. Sometimes the reverse effect happens, and people suffer serious and unpleasant side effects. When the effects are negative, the substance or procedure that triggers them is not called "placebo," which means "to please," but "nocebo." With both placebos and nocebos, it is the *expectations aroused* by the substance or procedure that are ultimately responsible for the result.

Sometimes the effect can be induced simply by the words or attitude of a doctor or other authority figure. I saw this happen with a patient of mine. One week after major surgery for cancer he was doing very well—no fever, no complications, and a hearty appetite. I was about to send him home when I decided to ask the oncologist and radiologist to see him in the hospital, because he was an elderly man and I wanted to save him trips to their offices. After those two visits his temperature went to 102 and he developed a raging wound infection. The only change in his circumstances had been their visits, which obviously depressed him, suppressed his immune system and led to the infection.

Two other authority figures, however—in this case the parents of a young boy undergoing treatment for a brain tumor—used words to create positive expectations strong enough to diminish the side effects of some very powerful anticancer drugs their son, Kelly, was taking:

The first time he took his CCNV pill we also gave him the recommended anti-emetic to lessen the nausea. He got very sick that night and was on the couch all the next day. The next time we gave it to him we told him that you only get sick the first time. This time we did not give him the anti-emetic and he threw up only once that night. He said he felt much better this time and was up and about all the next day. Hooray!

They also used placebo medications:

We have cut his prednisone dosage in half as he was really getting nasty mood swings. To restore his hair growth we rubbed a "magic mixture" on his head and told him it would make his hair grow. It did! When we stopped using it, it quit growing, and started growing again when we resumed putting it on.

When Kelly is on prednisone he eats like a horse and when he is off he has almost no appetite at all. To help out his suffering appetite I have been giving him folic acid out of the bottle for his prednisone, which he calls his hungry pills. Lo and behold his appetite has returned via the placebo prednisone.

Like the phenomenon of spontaneous remission, the placebo effect has been much maligned by the medical profession, but unlike remissions, placebos have been at least indirectly the subject of scrutiny for years. Researchers have had to study them, because clinical trials done on medications in the developmental stage usually have to show evidence that such drugs are more valuable *than* placebos. Generally speaking, about one-third or more of the people treated with placebos report positive results. So if only about one-third of the test subjects in a drug trial show improvement from the drug, it is generally considered to be no better than a placebo.

In alternative cancer care programs there is something comparable to the placebo effect, which I call the waiting room effect: About 10 percent of the people in these programs get well, and many more improve, for reasons no one in the medical community understands. However, I feel sure that it's because of all the hope expressed in the waiting room. When there's a strong belief in the value of the therapy, the power of suggestion can go to work, causing a fundamental change in the internal environment of the body. Therefore, an alternative therapy with a 10 to 20 percent success rate may have no intrinsic therapeutic value.

Feelings are chemical and can kill or cure. As a doctor I believe it's my responsibility to help my patients use them to cure and heal themselves. While placebos can be useful, because as symbols of hope they activate expectations, my reputation, my training, my belief in my patients and my own hopefulness also have symbolic value, which I can use to guide my patients into health. When some of my patients get better despite the odds against them, you may say that these are people I have deceived into health. But I don't see that as a crime. I will always use all the tools at my command, because all healing is scientific. If I'm accused of offering false hope, my answer is that there is no false hope—only false *no* hope—because we don't know the future for an individual.

Ten years ago a woman with diffuse histiocytic lymphoma and widespread metastases came to see me. Her doctor in North Carolina had told her to go home and die—"Why go three hundred miles to the nearest medical center only to be made sick with chemotherapy?" was his comment. But a nurse friend of hers who was taking care of my father-in-law told her, without my knowledge, "Come to New Haven. Dr. Siegel makes people well all the time." The oncologist I sent her to was not at all encouraging: "As you know," he wrote me, "this is a rapidly progressive illness; survival for more than fifteen months is unusual, the average being six months." He told me he really didn't think he had much to offer her. After she met me at the hospital, however, she told her friend, "I knew I'd get well when he held my hand."

The letters from her oncologist tell the story: July 1979

(just after starting treatment)—"Continues to be weak"; August 1979—"Marked response, weight gain, total regression of lymphadenopathy, and slight regression of lung nodule"; October 1979—"Continues to do well . . . an objective decrease in all disease"; December 1979—"In complete remission." Letters covering the next three years report "Continues to do very well" or "extremely well" or "amazingly well" and, in July 1983, "She came in today looking the best she has in two years. Her physician at home thought the family had switched people (she looked so well)." One day in the corridor of the hospital the oncologist said to me, with a twinkle in his eye, "Isn't chemotherapy wonderful?"

This was a woman who had to travel from North Carolina to New Haven every three months to get chemotherapy. I was concerned about the high hopes she obviously had for her treatment, because I knew her chances were not good. I would have been even more uncomfortable if I'd known what her friend the practical nurse was saying to her: Not only was she going to get well because of me, but when she had side effects from chemotherapy her friend told her, "You don't have to have side effects, Dr. Siegel says so"—and they disappeared. She had been so primed by her friend to believe in me that I think we could have given her plain water and it would have worked. I began by feeling upset that her hopes were so high, and ended by having learned something—about the value of hope.

In the *Journal of the American Medical Association* (henceforth referred to as *JAMA*), a physician writing pseudonymously as Jane A. McAdams told about how a message of hope affected her mother at a time when doctors were expecting her to live only a few weeks more. Her mother had grown up during the Depression and was as a consequence very frugal and opposed to waste of any kind.

I resolved to lift her spirits by buying her the handsomest and most expensive matching nightgown and robe I could find. If I could not hope to cure her disease, at least I could make her feel like the prettiest woman in the entire hospital.

For a long time after she unwrapped her present . . . my

mother said nothing. Finally she spoke. "Would you mind," she said, pointing to the wrapping and gown spread across the bed, "returning it to the store? I don't really want it." Then she picked up the newspaper and turned it to the last page. "This is what I really want, if you could get that," she said. What she pointed to was a display advertisement of expensive designer summer purses.

My reaction was one of disbelief. Why would my mother, so careful about extravagances, want an expensive summer purse in January, one that she could not possibly use until June? She would not even live until spring, let alone summer. Almost immediately, I was ashamed and appalled at my clumsiness, ignorance, insensitivity, call it what you will. With a shock, I realized she was finally asking me how long she would live. She was, in fact, asking me if I thought she would live even six months. And she was telling me that if I showed I believed she would live until then, then she would do it. She would not let that expensive purse go unused. That day, I returned the gown and robe and bought the summer purse.

That was many years ago. The purse is worn out and long gone, as are at least half a dozen others. And next week my mother flies to California to celebrate her eighty-third birthday. My gift to her? The most expensive designer purse I could find. She'll use it well.

Anything that offers hope has the potential to heal, including thoughts, suggestions, symbols and placebos. Many still think that placebos may be fine for "psychosomatic" problems but not for anyone with AIDS, cancer, multiple sclerosis or heart disease. It's interesting that this point of view has been with us for so long, despite innumerable studies showing that placebos can alleviate problems ranging, as psychologist Robert Ornstein and Dr. David Sobel have tallied them, from "post-operative wound pain; seasickness; headaches; coughs; anxiety and other disorders of nervousness [to] high blood pressure; angina; depression; acne; asthma; hay fever; colds; insomnia; arthritis; ulcers; gastric acidity; migraine; constipation; obesity; blood counts; lipoprotein levels; and more." As Ornstein and Sobel put it, "If such a treatment suddenly became available, we would believe that we had discovered a new wonder drug comparable to penicillin. Moreover, no system of the body appears immune to the effect."

So how does the placebo effect work? Since by definition a placebo is a substance or procedure without any actual power to effect a change in a patient's condition, it follows that any change that does result must somehow be mediated through the mind. In other words, the placebo effect can be understood only if we acknowledge the unity of mind and body. We must recognize, as a scientific text explains, that "placebo responses are neither mystical nor inconsequential, and that ultimately psychological and psychophysiological processes operate through common anatomic pathways." The "common anatomic pathways" are the tangible expression of mindbody unity.

A quite dramatic instance of the mindbody connection is that of a Filipino woman who in 1977 was cured of a serious disease by a native healer, after Western medicine had failed her. Suffering from systemic lupus erythematosus, an autoimmune disorder in which the body's immune system attacks its own healthy organs, she rejected her doctor's suggestions for more aggressive treatment as well as his warnings that she might die if she stopped her cortisone, and returned to her native village in the Philippines. Within three weeks she was back in the United States, off cortisone and completely symptom-free, with liver and renal function back to normal, according to the doctor who treated her and who published the facts about her case in *JAMA* some four years later—by which time she had also had a normal pregnancy and delivered a healthy child.

To what did she attribute her miracle cure? A healer back home had removed a curse placed on her! It is interesting to me that one prestigious medical journal chooses to present a case about the healing power of a Filipino witch doctor while another, the *New England Journal of Medicine,* chooses to devote its editorial page to a denial of the healing power of laughter (as you'll be reading shortly)—and both of them, I am told, have refused to publish an article by Dr. Randy Byrd on the efficacy of prayer (which you'll read about in chapter 7). I myself think that we should look at all kinds of healing, for all are scientific.

I have heard of several other miraculous recoveries from lupus, including one reported by Dr. Charles A. Janeway, who described his patient as having "cured herself [by spending a year] unloading all her deep-seated and concealed hostility toward her father"—on him. In fact all the stories I've heard about recoveries from lupus involve confronting authority: Dr. Janeway's patient used him as a way of confronting her father; the Filipino woman confronted her doctor; and another woman, a nurse, was feeling so sick that she confronted God with an ultimatum that He take her that night or make her well (she woke up well the next morning).

The more we learn from stories like these about mind and body as a unity, the more difficult it becomes to consider them separately. What's in your mind is often quite literally, or "anatomically," what is in your body: Peptide messenger molecules manufactured by the brain and the immune system are the link.

There are approximately sixty known peptide molecules in the body, including some with names that may be familiar to you, like endorphins, interleukins and interferon. They make feelings chemical and effect the link between psyche and soma. Endorphins, for example, are now thought to account for the placebo effect. It appears that the pain-relief reported in so many studies can be explained physiologically by the fact that the positive psychological expectations aroused by administration of the placebo lead to an increased production of endorphins, which are painkillers. So the pain relief really is "in the mind"—because that's where the endorphins are.

What interests me most in all of this is the question of how we can eliminate the placebo and go straight to the source of the mind's healing system, as Kelly's parents helped him to do. How can we access it directly? It is possible, as the many exceptional people you'll be meeting in this book will show you.

In an essay entitled "The Mysterious Placebo," Norman Cousins gets to the heart of how it's done, which he knows about from personal experience:

It is doubtful whether the placebo . . . would get very far without a patient's robust will to live. For the will to live . . . enables the human body to make the most of itself. . . . The placebo, then, is an emissary between the will to live and the body. But the emissary is expendable. If we can liberate ourselves from tangibles, we can connect hope and the will to live directly to the ability of the body to meet great threats and challenges.

CHANGING THE BODY
BY CHANGING THE MIND

What the placebo suggests to us is that we may be able to change what takes place in our bodies by changing our state of mind. Therefore, when we experience mind-altering processes—for example, meditation, hypnosis, visualization, psychotherapy, love and peace of mind—we open ourselves to the possibility of change and healing.

A particularly dramatic transformation can occur when a person with multiple personality disorder (MPD, or split personality) switches from one personality to another. Once thought to be extremely rare, MPD is much more commonly reported now, as are the circumstances thought to give rise to it—child abuse. It appears that some victims of abuse learn to switch off their core personality when the suffering they must endure is too great; this enables them to switch into one of what may be as many as dozens of other personalities, which come into being to shield the child. Although no one can say for sure how the switch is accomplished, some sort of dissociation through self-hypnosis seems to be involved.

The first patient I encountered with multiple personalities would go through certain medical tests in one personality, because as that person she would experience no pain, fear or difficulties from the procedures. When the tests were over she would shift back to her dominant personality. Physiologically speaking, however, the differences among the personalities in a multiple can be much more startling than that.

There are certain physiological traits that we assume to be fixed, like diabetes, left- or right-handedness, allergies or color-blindness. It appears, however, that people with MPD may be allergic to cats or orange juice in one personality but not in another, may exhibit burns in one personality but not another, may show drug sensitivities in one personality but not another, may switch from being right-handed to being left-handed. I knew someone who had to keep half a dozen different pairs of glasses in her bedside stand, because she didn't know who she would be when she woke up. I have also heard about a woman with MPD who got drunk at a party, and when her friends told her not to drive home, she said, "Don't worry, the others won't let me. One of them will." Brendan O'Regan, whose *Investigations* newsletter has reported on the current state of research regarding multiples, says he has even heard of a woman whose eyes changed colors when she moved from one personality to another.

What makes the study of multiple personality of general interest is that it reveals the possibility of changing your body by changing your personality. Imagine, for example, having within your conscious power the brain's incredible pharmacy of healers—the neuropeptides.

Biochemist Nick Hall of George Washington University is one of the researchers working on this possibility through research into the effects of meditation and positive visualizations on immunity. In a *Discover* magazine interview with Rob Wechsler, Hall described a lecture he once gave to a group he expected to be resistant to his mindbody marriage of psychology, immunology and neuroendocrinology: "I knew I had to do something to get their attention," he said. "I walked up to the podium, pulled out a book from my back pocket and began to read them an erotic passage from *Lady Chatterley's Lover.* When I was done and they were all convinced I was crazy, I looked up and said, 'If you can arouse the reproductive axis with purely mental processes, why can't you do the same with the immune system?' "

As Hall demonstrated, presumably to his audience's satisfaction, images in the mind can have just as powerful an effect as those in the external world. Blushing is another example of the body's response to what may be purely a mental event. Everybody agrees that these are physical responses mediated by the mind. But what about the immune system? Can you really activate it with the mind? If you change yourself enough, can your disease be rejected as alien to the new you? I believe that you *can* change that dramatically; I have seen it happen many times.

There is beginning to be an impressive amount of research to document the ways in which mind and body, brain and immune system are bound together. Although much more work needs to be done to trace this incredibly intricate network of communications, the most important thing is that we now know such communications do occur.

In 1964 Dr. George Solomon, who is affiliated with the medical schools of the University of California in both San Francisco and Los Angeles, published an article entitled "Emotions, Immunity and Disease: A Speculative Theoretical Integration." When he sent it to me last year, however, next to the word "Speculative" he wrote: "Not any more."

When Solomon wrote that article over two decades ago he started with a single hypothesis—that "stress can be immunosuppressive." Solomon and others have long since proved this to be true. By 1985 he was able to propose and support a total of fourteen hypotheses concerning interactions between the immune system and the central nervous system, and at last count his list numbered thirty-five such hypotheses, for each of which there now exists a varied amount of "hard" evidence.

Dr. Solomon continues to do his pioneering work on the question of how emotions relate to disease, and has extended his work with cancer patients to people with AIDS. In an article on long-surviving people with AIDS, Solomon, Dr. Lydia Temoshok and colleagues list sixteen significant emotional factors and behavior patterns affecting longevity. This list will appear later in the book, as part of the practical advice for dealing with illness. For now, what's important to know is simply that a fairly detailed psychological profile of the survivor personality can be drawn, and that psychological change and healing are possible for all of us. If change weren't possible, there would be no practical point to being able to identify survival characteristics.

OF LOVE, LAUGHTER AND LETTERS
TO THE *NEW ENGLAND JOURNAL OF MEDICINE*

"Psychosocial Correlates of Survival in Advanced Malignant Disease," a study by psychologist Barrie R. Cassileth and colleagues, appeared in the *New England Journal of Medicine* in 1985. In combination with an editorial by *NEJM* deputy editor Dr. Marcia Angell, entitled "Disease as a Reflection of the Psyche," this caused quite an uproar. Though Cassileth's study made relatively modest claims for what it could prove about the lack of any causal connection between psychological and social factors and survival time in cancer patients, Dr. Angell used the occasion to announce that "it is time to acknowledge that our belief in disease as a direct reflection of mental state is largely folklore."

There was an outpouring of letters in response, more than any other article has received in recent years. The respondents did not come to any agreement about *how* mental state affects health, but there was a consensus among them that it did, and that this was a subject worth in-depth investigation, not dismissal.

Cassileth herself had qualified the scope of her conclusions by noting in the article that social and psychological factors "may contribute to the *initiation*" (my italics) of disease. And though she found that "the biology of the disease appears to . . . override the potential influence of life-style and psychosocial variables *once the disease process is established*" (my italics), it must be remembered that the 359 patients in her study did have, as the title indicates, "advanced malignant disease." In other words, the disease process may by then have been so well established that the body's ability to resist it was seriously damaged. In patients that ill, the hope factor may also have been gone. Because of the study's focus, many of the fundamental questions about the mind's impact on our state of health are not addressed.

But with dozens of other studies showing that the connection between body and mind is real and significant, and recent conferences on psycho-oncology at the National Institutes of Health and at New York's Memorial Sloan-Kettering Hospital, it seems clear that the time for dismissing this belief as folklore is long past, and the time for study is here.

Still, Angell is not convinced. "Laughter is a worthy end in itself," she writes, "not as a means or a medicine toward curing disease. That is not science." Dr. Angell may not think so, but as neuropharmacologist Candace Pert of the National Institute of Mental Health has said, we have now come to the point where "the medical establishment is finally going to have to decide what to do about the mind."

SUPERHEALTH

I predict that chemicals we produce in our own brains will become the basis of many therapies of the future. Candace Pert, for example, is already using Peptide T (the laboratory-produced clone of one of these natural chemicals) in AIDS patients, with striking results.

At the vanguard of this new science are the researchers who are studying a group of peptides known as growth factors, which are naturally occurring substances in our bodies now being cloned through the techniques of genetic engineering. In one recent test, described in *Omni* magazine, David Golde, chief of hematology and oncology at UCLA, used a growth factor known as GM-CSF on sixteen AIDS patients with low white blood cell counts, and pronounced the results "a revolution in medicine equal to antibiotics." "Watching the white count come up was the most exciting thing I have ever done in science," he said. "To my knowledge this was the first time it had ever been done in human beings." "Spectacular," commented David Nathan of Harvard Medical School. "A home run," said Jerome Groopman of Deaconess Hospital in Boston.

Neurobiologist Rita Levi-Montalcini won both the Nobel Prize for medicine and the Lasker award for her discovery of nerve growth factor (NGF), which is another of these naturally occurring substances. Levi-Montalcini has shown that NGF affects cells in both the immune and central nervous systems, thus helping to account for the way the psychology of an individual could be related to immune function. "It has always been known that psychological conditions affect the welfare of people through the immune system," she told *Omni,* "but it was never proved structurally that there was any relationship. Now we believe NGF is somewhat of a linking messenger." The hope is that NGF can be synthesized by molecular engineering techniques for use in treating degenerative diseases of the brain, like Alzheimer's, Huntington's and Parkinson's.

Soon physicians may be following in the footsteps of natural healers. Barbara Ann Brennan says in her book, *Hands of Light,* "What the healer really does is to induce the patient to heal himself through natural processes. . . . Your body and your energy system move naturally toward health." This is what the scientists described above are now discovering, as they work with the substances that are the body's own internal healers.

These internal healers have also been stimulated to work in infants in the hospital. When premature newborns are assigned to a section of the nursery where nurses stroke them for fifteen minutes three times a day for ten days, they gain weight 50 percent faster than newborn infants in the same nursery who are not stroked. Why? Remember, our survival mechanisms are rooted in our primitive existence. When the mother lion leaves the den, for example, the lion cub lies quietly, its metabolic processes turned off to help it survive the absence of food and warmth. When momma returns with food, she licks and touches the baby, and the baby responds by producing growth hormones and other neuropeptides so that the food can be utilized appropriately.

Perhaps someday it will be possible to create exactly the right emotional prescription for each person's needs. Until then we will be relying on the work of scientists who are cloning the chemicals that occur naturally within our bodies, as well as trying to get people to live in such a way that they will create more of these life-enhancing substances within themselves. If you will do that, then you can become your own genetic engineer. For it really is true that love, laughter and peace of mind are physiologic.

SURVIVORS: ANGRY, JOYFUL OR LOVING?

Two months before the *New England Journal of Medicine* article appeared, *The Lancet,* a comparable British journal, also came out with an article on mental attitudes and cancer. This study of fifty-seven women diagnosed with early breast cancer ten years before revealed that after the first five years, "recurrence-free survival was significantly commoner among patients who reacted to cancer by denial or 'fighting spirit' than among patients who responded with stoic acceptance or feelings of helplessness or hopelessness."

After ten years, their survival statistics showed that 70 percent of the "fighting spirit" patients were still alive (with or without metastases) versus 50 percent of the deniers, 25 percent of the stoic accepters and 20 percent of the hopeless/helpless group. Though the authors of the article claim only that mental attitude is "associated with" survival time, rather than the cause, these are striking statistics.

However, the paper ends with a very "medical," mechanistic reservation: "Whether mental attitudes can be changed and whether such changes improve survival are questions worthy of further study." What distresses me is the first part of that question: It's one thing to ask whether a change in attitude will improve survival rates, but quite another to ask whether attitudes can be changed. How many years has psychotherapy been around? Have Freud and Jung had nothing to contribute? To think that we can't help people change is absurd. I know from the therapy I have been doing for the last ten years that we can teach people not to be helpless, we can teach them to be fighters, and in even the most desperate of circumstances we can still help them find the will to live.

Sandra Levy, associate professor of psychiatry and medicine at the University of Pittsburgh and director of behavioral medicine in oncology at the Pittsburgh Cancer Institute, has done research on issues similar to those addressed by the British study. In a 1984 article, she too speaks of "associations" between emotions and cancer, not causes, and she too finds that the associations are strong. This she concludes on the basis not only of her own ongoing studies of women with breast cancer, which indicate that survival time is associated with fighting spirit, but also of her review of dozens of other studies published during a thirty-year span. Their consensus is, as Levy summarizes it: "Lower survival rates from cancer are associated with depression or helplessness and higher rates are associated with a sense of coping."

Like the British researchers, Levy asks about the possibility of changing mental attitude—"Can helplessness and the lack of coping among cancer patients be altered?"—but her answer is "undoubtedly yes." Psychological techniques can be used to alter outlook, and other strategies like the relaxation response can work more directly on the damaging hormonal effects of stress while also providing patients with a sense of control over their thoughts and lives.

Levy's latest research has revealed an interesting new finding: While the primary factor that predicted survival was the disease-free interval—the length of time between initial diagnosis and recurrence—to Levy's surprise the second most significant factor was not fighting spirit but a sense of joy. Joy was an even more powerful predictor than the number and location of metastatic sites. Also associated with survival were the woman's relationships with her intimate other and her physician.

While it's helpful to know which feelings are most closely linked with good health, I believe that a healed life need not exclude the so-called negative emotions. Anger, for example, may be a more positive response to a grim diagnosis than passive resignation. Feelings are not to be judged. Anger has its place, so long as it is freely and safely expressed rather than held inside where it can have a destructive effect and lead to resentment and hatred.

A story is told about a snake that terrorized the children

of a village whenever they went out to play. The elders of the village went to talk to the snake and ask it please to stop biting the children. The snake agreed, and for the next few weeks everything went well. The children enjoyed playing outdoors and returned home each day happy and safe. The elders then went to thank the snake, but they discovered it battered, bruised and tied in knots. When they asked it what had happened, the snake said, "Well you told me to stop biting the children." "That's right," they said, "we did tell you to stop biting, but we didn't say to stop hissing."

It's important to express all your feelings, including the unpleasant ones, because once they're out they lose their power over you; they can't tie you up in knots anymore. Letting them out is a call for help and a "live" message to your body. We try to live like this in our own family, and as a result one of our daughter's friends who spent some time with us on Cape Cod said, "Your family doesn't know how to be angry." I said, "What do you mean?" She replied, "When your family is angry you talk to each other after half an hour, but in my family we don't talk to each other for two weeks!" I took that as a great compliment.

Studies are under way to get down to a molecular understanding of how the emotions affect our bodies. Quantum physicists like David Bohm and Stewart Wolf are now saying that we may even be changing ourselves at the atomic level when we experience different emotions. Wolf has talked about fear affecting and perhaps being expressed by electrons, and love by photons.

David C. McClelland, a professor of psychology and social relations at Harvard, is particularly interested in the effects of love: "Right now we are trying to straighten out what the love variable is and what its impact is on the endocrine system," he explains. "We don't have any idea about the hormones that are connected with love and how love aids the lymphocytes and improves immune function. That's what I'm working on now."

While he's working on it, others are putting it to work in their lives. I appeared on television with long-term AIDS survivor Niro Asistent, who had reversed the results of her blood test from HIV-positive to HIV-negative (HIV being the AIDS virus). When asked to summarize what she had done, she said, "When you live in your heart, magic happens." How simple a summary of our total approach, and yet how hard to live in your heart!

The "love variables" that McClelland was discussing were self-love and what he jokingly called "divluv" (for divine love, a phrase he felt would not look good in a psychology journal). "Divluv" refers to the kind of noninvolved striving he sees in many religiously inspired people. It means "that you are not worried about your ego at all. You're not the least bit concerned whether you're succeeding or failing. You might say you're acting from the heart. [Who did we just hear that from?] The state of being egoless comes from recognizing that you're okay within yourself." If you get an F on an exam it is still only an exam; you are not worthless or a failure.

Accepting that she was "okay within herself" became the foremost challenge of an extraordinary young woman named Evy McDonald, who was diagnosed with amyotrophic lateral sclerosis (ALS, or Lou Gehrig's disease) in 1980. She was told by her neurologist, "Evy, you have six to twelve months to live. If you want to do something nice, leave your body to science." That afternoon she was fired from her job as a nurse, because she'd been out sick so much, and that evening she discovered that her apartment had been broken into and all her valuables stolen. At that point she decided that her doctor's advice sounded pretty good.

In a letter to me she wrote, "Death seemed inevitable, and a part of me was truly looking forward to ending this life. Yet I had unfinished business: a strong compulsion to discover what unconditional love was about *before I died*" (my italics). Note that Evy did not deny her mortality. But people like her don't go home to die just because some doctor has sentenced them. They use their diagnosis as the spur to start living, and then feel too good to die.

Evy knew that her journey would have to begin with an acceptance of her own body, which she had always hated, and in an article she wrote she describes how she accomplished that first step toward self-love:

There I sat in front of a mirror in my wheelchair. In the six months since I'd been diagnosed as having ALS, my once firm, strong muscles had wasted away into flaccid, useless ones. I was dying from a particularly rapid form of this incurable disease and had, at best, six more months to live. I looked with disgust at my deteriorating body. I hated it. The mirrored reflection of one spindly, ill-shaped leg (the legacy of a childhood bout with polio) paired with a mammoth, once-muscular one was hideous to me. . . .

As the hours of my day were now relegated to sitting alone in my wheelchair, I began to observe rather than react to my thoughts. I noticed there was one consistent thread throughout the fabric of my life—a relentless obsession with weight. I was sure that if I became "skinny" enough, an admirable body would magically greet me in the mirror. And now I sat in a wheelchair with acutely atrophying muscles. My arms and legs were shrinking.

Was it just coincidence that I'd always wanted a smaller body and that ALS was granting me that very desire? . . .

As I sat in my wheelchair, six months from death, a single, passionate desire pressed to the front of my mind. In my last months of life I wanted to experience unconditional love. I wanted to know that sweetness.

But how could I even hope to realize that goal if I couldn't accept my own body? . . .

The first step was to notice and write down how many negative thoughts I had about my body in the course of each day, and how many positive ones. When I saw the huge preponderance of negative thoughts on the paper, I was forced to confront the degree of hatred I had for my body.

To counter this habitual and ingrained negativity, every day I singled out one aspect of my physical body that was acceptable to me, no matter how small. Next, I'd use that item to begin the rewriting. Every negative thought would be followed by a positive statement like "and my hair is truly pretty," or "I have lovely hands," or "My bright eyes and warm smile light up my face." Each day a different positive item would be added as each day the rewriting continued.

I felt like a jig-saw puzzle being put back together; and when the last bit was in place, my mind shifted and saw the whole perfect picture. I couldn't pinpoint just when the shift occurred, but one day I noticed that I had no negative thoughts about my body. I could look in the mirror at my naked reflection and be honestly awed by its beauty. I was totally at peace, with a complete, unalterable acceptance of the way my body was—a bowl of jello in a wheelchair.

For the first time in my life I knew my body to be esthetically pleasing. A new movie had been written [Evy had earlier referred to the body as "the screen where the movie is shown"], and I experienced a soft, sensuous human being sitting in that wheelchair.

Once the old scripts and demeaning images were finally and totally gone, they were never to emerge again. I accepted my body. It didn't need to be any different; it could be whatever it was and become whatever it was to be. . . .

This was *one* step in a journey that over time brought about unexpected and unsolicited physical improvements. But if the outcome had been different and the deterioration of my body continued, it would not have altered or diminished the inherent beauty I now accepted.

My illness was a challenge and a gift. I was stimulated to examine my deepest thoughts, desires and beliefs. The journey of self-discovery restructured my life and led me into a powerful experience of the mind-body connection.

Her "physical body stopped deteriorating (in other words I didn't die)," she says in her letter, "and began reversing the havoc wreaked by ALS. This reversal was a *by-product* of all the other changes. Physical healing did not occur because I set out to 'cure' myself, but because my job on earth was not complete. . . . Since then, I joyously awake each day, filled with enthusiasm, and continue to play my role in the transformation of medical practice." Notice that her goal was to discover the experience of unconditional love, not to avoid dying. So she was not setting herself up for failure, but for an experience that was within her power to give herself. Love and healing are always possible, even when a cure is not.

Evy has been an incredible teacher. When she heard that I was telling people to live a month at a time, she wrote to me and said I was too lenient—that in order to really think about their lives, people should live ten minutes at a time, as she had

had to do. You will be hearing more from Evy, for she has many practical things to say about her steps toward healing.

PEACE OF MIND: COMMUNICATING WITH THE HEALING SYSTEM

Today many scientists think we should not talk about a central nervous system and an endocrine system and an immune system, but rather one healing system that constitutes a sort of superintelligence within us. Just as that healing system can be set in motion by self-affirming beliefs, self-negating or repressive emotional patterns can do the reverse. As Woody Allen said in one of his movies, "I can't express anger. I internalize it and grow a tumor instead."

Internalizing is exactly what you don't want to do. When someone asks you how you are and you say "Fine" even though you feel terrible, that's internalizing. This kind of behavior disturbs me so much that when I do workshops I ask for volunteers to take an opaque, soundproof bag, pull it down over their heads, tie it at the ankles and go for a walk in the street. Everybody objects: "We could get killed doing that." Right. That's my point, that just as your eyes and your ears and the rest of your five senses are there to protect you from the world, so you have a sixth sense, your healing system, which is meant to repair injuries and protect you from invasion by bacteria, viruses and diseases. But if you deny your needs and don't ask for help, you're pulling a bag over that healing system. The message you give it when you put on a performance is that you don't want to recover, and the result is that your body cooperates by helping you to die.

So don't "try" to be positive—that's just performing, and it's hard work. Our goal is peace of mind, which will give your healing system a true "live" message.

Many techniques for achieving peace of mind are available. These include hypnotic suggestion, biofeedback, relaxation training, visualization, yoga and other consciousness-altering techniques. (Sandra Levy would remind us of joy, David

McClelland of love and egolessness too.) The effectiveness of these techniques can be measured experientially—people feel better if they use them. With the sophisticated new tools of molecular biology, some of the effects can now be measured at the cellular level as well.

Though the precise mechanism of the healing response remains to be elucidated, all these techniques work to create bodymind communication and unity. Thus, what we ordinarily think of as automatic body functions come under the control of our minds. You can use relaxation training, for example, to lower blood pressure, slow your breath and heart rates and reduce muscle tension.

Studies have shown that relaxation training and related techniques can be helpful in combating the negative effects of prolonged stress on the immune system components. A dysregulated immune system can affect everything from your susceptibility to colds to your ability to kill cancer cells or AIDS viruses, and may also be a factor in asthma, allergies, diabetes, multiple sclerosis, rheumatoid arthritis, lupus and other autoimmune diseases in which the body attacks itself.

Joan Borysenko, a cell biologist and psychologist who ran the Mind/Body Clinic at New England Deaconess Hospital, has written about the uses of relaxation in her book *Minding the Body, Mending the Mind.* These include its ability to help diabetics lower their need for insulin. I myself know of one patient who used relaxation to completely eliminate her need for insulin. Relaxation is so commonly acknowledged to be effective that some hospitals now broadcast relaxation programs on closed circuit television in the patients' rooms. The list of diseases altered in a positive way by relaxation would fill this page.

Psychotherapy and other techniques that bring repressed emotional material into consciousness can also heal, both psychologically and physically, by helping us to achieve peace of mind. One interesting series of studies by psychologist James Pennebaker at Southern Methodist University showed that people who confided traumatic experiences to a diary showed better immune function than those who didn't. He and Janice

Kiecolt-Glaser asked twenty-five adults to write down details of disturbing life experiences and describe their feelings about them. A control group of equal size wrote only about superficial topics. Blood tests showed strikingly improved immune function among the emoters, who also made fewer visits to the doctor, but no improvements among the control group. Six months after the experiment was over the emoters still showed positive health effects.

By focusing on events that most people try to forget as quickly as possible, the emoters allowed themselves to express their feelings and hence gave their bodies "live" messages. I also believe that the act of writing these events down allowed the emoters to rethink them. In other words, they engaged in a simple form of cognitive retraining: The events themselves remained the same but lost their destructive power.

What we get back to again and again is that, although there's no question that environment and genes play a significant role in our vulnerability to cancer and other diseases, the emotional environment we create within our bodies can activate mechanisms of destruction or repair. That's why two people who grow up in the same environment, even when they have the same genes, as identical twins do, don't necessarily have the same disease at the same time. A man showed up in my office at age fifty-nine with cancer. Some thirty years before, his identical twin had died of cancer. He told me that until recently he had always been happy and busy, but he had just been through a year of total despair and depression and had wanted to die. His brother, however, had always been unhappy. Sometimes it's not so much a matter of disease grasping us as of our being susceptible to the disease.

The mind-altering techniques mentioned in this section, many of which will be discussed in more detail later in the book, can make us less susceptible to disease, or better able to turn it around if we are already sick. By helping us achieve peace of mind, they give us access to our body's healing system. It takes more distress and poison to kill someone who has peace of mind and loves life.

BODYMIND MESSENGER MOLECULES

Body and mind are different expressions of the same information—the information carried by the chemical transmitters known as peptides. In humans, animals, plants, eggs, seeds and on down to one-celled organisms, the peptides are the messenger molecules that carry the information from state to state. In man they make possible the move from perception or thought or feeling in the mind, to messages transmitted by the brain, to hormonal secretions and on down to cellular action in the body—then back again to the mind and brain, in a never-ending feedback loop.

The key juncture in the loop, the place where body and mind meet and cross over through the action of the peptides, is in the limbic/hypothalamic area of the brain. It is here that scientists have found dense numbers of receptors clustered together in what they call "hotspots." Peptides fit into these receptors, key and lock fashion, to activate the inner workings of the cells on which the receptors are located.

However, it's not just the brain that contains peptide receptor hotspots. Examples of other peptide-rich areas are the linings of the gut and the stomach. This may be why people often say they feel their emotions in those areas. You've heard of "gut reactions"—well, it now appears that there is literal, physiological truth to the expression. In fact, the emotions seem to be everywhere in the body, not just in the brain. "They are expressed in the body and are part of the body," Candace Pert says. "I can no longer make a strong distinction between the brain and the body. . . . Indeed, the more we know about neuropeptides, the harder it is to think in the traditional terms of a mind and a body. It makes more and more sense to speak of a single, integrated entity, a 'bodymind.' "

The research Pert and her immunologist husband, Michael Ruff, have done on peptides may even have given a physiological basis to Freud's and Jung's concept of the unconscious:

For Freud and Jung, the unconscious was still a hypothetical construct. For us, the unconscious more definitely means psychobiological levels of functioning below consciousness. Deep, deep unconscious processes are expressed at all physiological levels, down to individual organs such as the heart, lungs, or pancreas. Our work is demonstrating that all the cells of the nervous system and endocrine system are functionally integrated by networks of peptides and their receptors.

Though it used to be thought that communication between the brain and other bodily systems was mainly one way, brain to body, recent findings, both anatomical and biochemical, make it clear that the conversation is reciprocal. Immunologist J. Edwin Blalock suggests that in the presence of invaders, like viruses and bacteria, for example, peptide transmitters produced by the immune system function as a sort of sixth sense, supplementing the information the brain receives from the other five senses and possibly accounting for the way some people sense that something is wrong before they actually get sick. I see this happening all the time with my patients, especially when we start looking at their dreams and their drawings. Often they can't explain why they think there's something wrong, and they may not show any symptoms, but something in them knows. This is why, when a woman comes into my office and tells me that the lump she's had in her breast for a year needs to come out, even if the exam and the mammogram show no change, you can bet I take it out. I know that just as we were given five senses to protect us and make us aware of what's going on in the external environment, so our Creator also gave us this sixth sense to monitor our internal environment. We are dealing with one unified, comprehensive, self-regulating system, with beautiful intelligence inherent within it. As Albert Szent-Györgyi has said, the brain is not just for thinking; it is a survival organ.

HEEDING THE MESSAGE

For most of us, bodymind unity is of interest mainly because of what it suggests about possible routes to better health. As Candace Pert explains: "We know that the same neuropeptides secreted by the brain can also facilitate the movement of white blood cells of the immune system to a locus of injury. So why could you not direct it consciously? . . . It's a wild idea in that there is no experimental proof for it—yet there is nothing that excludes the possibility either."

Not only is there nothing to exclude the possibility, but there is plenty of evidence that many bodily processes we think of as automatic can be brought under conscious control. For example, yogis trained in Eastern meditative techniques can change their heart rate from thirty to three hundred beats per minute, as Swami Rama demonstrated to the satisfaction of a number of Western scientists at the Menninger Foundation.

Such feats are not confined to Indian mystics, or even to our species. Dolphins who do not want to have blood drawn for experimental purposes can redirect their blood flow so that it is inaccessible to the probing needles of researchers. Studies performed on rats and mice have shown that even the immune response can be "taught," or conditioned, to be either more or less active: When an immune suppressant or enhancer with a specific taste is administered to the animals, that same taste can later cause their immune systems to respond accordingly, even when the drug itself is absent. In fact, the whole principle of vaccination is based on the capacity of the immune system to learn. Think of what this may mean for the future. We have the ability to train our bodies to heal and eliminate illness.

But to me there is something even more interesting than the idea of gaining control of specific body processes. I think we can use the meditative and life-style-altering techniques I've mentioned in this chapter to gain access to the superintelligence I'm convinced resides within each of us. This superintelligence is the message carried by psyche and soma via the peptides—the printout of our DNA, the code to life itself. It makes us who we are and, if we listen to it, will keep us on our path.

The more I see of the workings of our universe, the more mystical I become. I'm not mystical in spite of being a surgeon; I'm mystical because I'm a surgeon. As a surgeon, I watch miracles daily. When I cut the body open I rely on it to heal.

I don't yell into the wound or leave it instructions telling it how to heal. The body knows much more than I do. In fact, every time I perform surgery I rely on its wisdom, because I don't know why a wound heals or how anesthesia works (nor does anyone else—as I had to tell the medical student who made excuses for his failure to explain these phenomena by saying he must have missed that lecture!). Neither do I understand how a fertilized egg grows up to be a human being. But I do know that each cell, organ, system of organs, and person is directed by what I call the loving intelligence of energy.

So the peptides and neuropeptides within each one of us, coursing through our bodies to create an integrated healing network, informed by the superintelligence that is the key to life itself, will help us to achieve our greatest potential—if we heed our body's messages. That doesn't mean some of us won't die at two and others at a hundred and two, but it does mean that our system will function to its greatest capability and provide us with the healthiest, longest life of which we are inherently capable.

Many of us have grown deaf to these inner promptings, though we don't start out that way. As a surgeon who does a great deal of pediatric surgery, I have the chance to observe many children. After I operate on a child, he or she will lie quietly in the crib, healing, and then suddenly one day start pulling out all the intravenous lines and tubes. I know at that moment that the child's body is recovered and healthy and that all these things can be discarded—because the child knows and is telling me so. That self-knowledge is what we must seek to recover.

Quantum physicist David Bohm has suggested replacing the word "psychosomatic"—which he thinks perpetuates the split between soma and psyche, body and mind—with a new word, " 'somasignificance,' to emphasize the unity of soma with significance and ultimately with meaning in all its implications and possibilities." Our bodies mean what they say, and they speak to us in the language of health and disease. Once we learn to take responsibility for our health by listening to our bodies, and talking back to them as well, then we will begin to be able to use our diseases to redirect our lives.

Many people fear that encouraging patients to take responsibility for their own health and emotions will make them feel like failures if they don't cure themselves. That is missing the point. We are asking people to play an active role in their health care, not demanding of them that they get well. Exceptional patients don't try not to die. They try to *live* until they die. Then they are successes, no matter what the outcome of their disease, because they have healed their lives, even if they have not cured their diseases. The next chapter will describe ways of listening to the message that psyche and soma wish to give you about how to find your unique path.

2

*The more I work with the body, keeping my
assumptions in a temporary state of reservation, the
more I appreciate and sympathize with a given
"disease." . . . The body no longer appears as a sick or
irrational demon, but as a process with its own inner
logic and wisdom.*

—Arnold Mindell

*Pathos activates the eyes and ears to see and hear. At
times of pathos illness opens doors to a reality which is
closed to a healthy point of view.*

—Jean Houston

Symptoms and Symbols, Dreams and Drawings: The Self Speaks

One cannot get through life without pain. Carl Jung tells us the reason for therapy is to open the road "to a normally disillusioned life," and Woody Allen said, "Life is full of miserableness, loneliness, unhappiness, and suffering—and it's all over much too quickly." Norman Vincent Peale tells of meeting a friend on the street in New York who bemoaned his terrible life. Norman said, "I know a place in the Bronx where there are twenty-five thousand people with no problems." His friend said, "Norman, take me there," and Norman said, "It's Woodlawn Cemetery."

What we can do is choose how to use the pain life presents to us. I have people sit on my examining table screaming, "Why me? Why did God do this to a wonderful person like me?" In the movie *Harold and Maude* Bud Cort asks Ruth Gordon, "How come you are so good with people?" and she says, "They're my species, you know." If you are alive and a member of the species, you will have problems.

So we move on and say, "Why not me?" But the exceptional patients I know understand life at an even higher level, and therefore understand the second verse of the Twenty-sixth Psalm: "Examine me, O Lord, and try me." They know that our trials have something to teach us, that disease has something to say to us.

The message the inner self is speaking, as manifested through illness, is an expression of what I just called "the loving intelligence of energy." It's the source of our dreams, or, as Jungian psychologist Russell A. Lockhart put it, the "voice and vision of the soul." Jung believed that God speaks to us in dreams and images, and the Bible says so too. So you could also call the message an expression of God—or the life force, the Self, DNA, or the superintelligence residing within.

Psychiatrist Alfred Adler called the message "organ jargon." And psychiatrist Karl Menninger says that we "say it with symptoms." But what exactly are we saying with our symptoms? The message has nothing to do with guilt, sin, failure or a lack of the will to live. Our bodies know better than that, even if our minds do not. Within each of us is the knowledge that we all must die some day. Those people who see dying as their failure to hold death at bay do not know what success is. A successful life is not about not dying. It is about living well. I have known two-year-olds and nine-year-olds who have changed people and even entire communities by their ability to love, and their lives were successful though short. On the other hand, I have known many who lived much longer and left behind nothing but emptiness.

THE DNA OF THE SOUL

Whatever your age, if you learn to listen, your inner voice will speak to you about your path, about what Evy McDonald described as her (and your) "job on earth." In her case, and that of many others I have seen, there was a so-called miraculous recovery from illness, which was, as she said, "a *by-product* of all the other changes" she made once her path became clear to her. When you heal a life, a cured disease may come with the healing. But when you accept your disease as "a challenge and a gift," then the even greater miracle is the inner healing that occurs because you have found your path again.

This wisdom that is directing you from within is your birthright. It's what makes it possible for the fertilized egg to know who to grow up to be, physically, intellectually, psychologically and spiritually, and we can see the signs of that intelligence from the earliest moments of the egg's life. As the cells in the fertilized egg multiply, they reach a stage very much like a ball, called the gastrula, and an indentation occurs at one end of the gastrula, which then defines where the head and the other end are going to be. From that stage on, if you take a cell from the head end and place it at the other end, it will migrate back up to the head end again. It knows what it is, what it is to become and where it belongs. (Now I know all of you have met people who seem to have their head at the other end, but that's an exception to the rule.)

To be serious, I believe that within that fertilized egg is an inner message, an inner awareness that says, "This is your path, this is how you can be the best human being possible." If you follow it, you will achieve your full growth and full potential as a human being before you let go of the Tree of Life—again, whether you die at two or a hundred and two. If you don't, you will become psychologically or spiritually troubled. And if that doesn't call your attention back to your path, your body will become physically ill. The sculptor Louise Nevelson, who loved her work and kept at it right up until her death at the age of eighty-eight, knew that it was what she was put on this earth to do. She once told an interviewer: "I stopped working for a little while and got abscesses and boils. . . . If you're a Rolls Royce, you can't be walking, you've just got to be riding. . . ."

Decades before the discovery of DNA, Carl Jung used a DNA-like metaphor to describe how the master plan for the Self is contained in our unconscious. As explained in an unpublished work by Jungian therapist Tom Laughlin, Jung's concept of the unconscious emphasized its wisdom, not its irrationality:

> The unconscious, far from being merely an empty slate, a cesspool of blind primordial energies, or of repressed contents of the ego, actually has hidden within it an instinctual intelligence that contains in its blueprint a whole series of built-in behavior patterns that when activated will result in our entire future psychological development in the same manner that DNA contains a blueprint of our entire biological development.

For each person, Laughlin continues, the blueprint is different:

> Even though everyone has two eyes, two ears, a nose, and a mouth, there are no two faces exactly alike. Though the DNA is a common denominator to us all, to billions of us, it still manages to create each single human being as a unique . . . individual.
>
> So too, the psychic DNA, the Self, though common to the human species, contains a blueprint for each personality that is unique and special to that individual. Though behavior patterns may be similar, no two individual personality blueprints, [like] no two faces, are exactly the same.

We all need to be reminded when we deviate from our personal blueprint—that fullest expression of the Self—and, as Laughlin points out, illness is one of the ways by which we may be recalled:

> Every illness, no matter how slight, should cause us to ask the question "What am I doing in my life that Nature's design in the unconscious wants me to get out of doing because I really . . . should be doing something else instead—something that is good for me because it is more consistent with my true nature—with Nature's own individual blueprint for me hidden in my Unconscious?"
>
> The more serious the illness, the more we have overloaded ourselves, and usually not even for our own sake, but because of pressure or for the sake of a parent, a peer group, or some other loved one. . . .

Again and again we come up against the fact that there is a hidden force within us that constantly exerts a stronger control over us than our Ego's control. This inner force does not let us rest until we develop ourselves to our fullest potential, just as it would not let us rest with a three-year-old's vocabulary when it first taught us to speak.

Jung liked to refer to a person's blueprint as his or her individual myth. I think all of us need to discover our own myth. Often our diseases can help us to do that, for each person's experience of illness has a unique meaning, expressing something of the individuality of the person who is having the experience. One disease is not more symbolically significant than another; for that matter, one disease is not necessarily more threatening than another. I don't find patients willing to switch diseases when asked if they would trade their blindness for cancer, or diabetes for heart disease, or AIDS for quadriplegia—or vice versa. Each of us must learn to deal with the experience of our own disease and its symbolic message for us.

"The key question in . . . all diseases," Tom Laughlin says, "is 'What is the Self trying to get me as a patient to learn about myself?' " That is the question I try to help each of my patients answer, which is why I think of myself as a Jungian surgeon. To move toward an answer, we start with more questions. These questions will help us get into the private world of the patient, not just the mechanistic world of the patient's disease.

THE FIVE QUESTIONS

In my first book I suggested that readers ask themselves four questions about their illness. The list is now expanded to five, and because of what I have heard from participants in the workshops I've been giving around the country, I have also gotten additional insights into what can be learned from the first four. So read through them again, even if you've seen them before. By putting you in touch with what is happening at deep levels of consciousness, these questions can help direct you toward healing.

1. *Do you want to live to be a hundred?*

When I first asked this, I was trying to find out whether people felt enough in control of their lives to be able to look forward to the future without fear. How much ability did they have to confront pain and loss and use them as redirections? Only 15 to 20 percent said yes. Most just weren't willing to live that long unless they could get some guarantees—good health, enough money to live on and so forth. I started to realize how much difficulty and pain there is in living to be a hundred.

What about all the phone calls you'll get telling you friends and loved ones have died? What can you do with all this suffering? I talked this problem over with God (we speak frequently—surgeons don't need an appointment), and now when I ask the question I tell people I have a bunch of cards in God's favorite colors, purple and gold, to give out to whoever wants them. They read "The bearer of this card is guaranteed a life of one hundred years, with all the resources necessary." But God also said to me, "Bernie, don't forget to tell them to turn the card over and read the back before they take one, because on the back of the card it says, 'If not used properly you may outlive everyone you love.' " Think about what it's like to live to be a hundred, watching a child die, a spouse die, friends die. Probably you're thinking you don't want to do that, that it would be less painful to be the first to go. But I know how to avoid the fate of outliving everyone you love.

Find some ninety-five-year-olds. They know all the answers, because they've lived through everything that can happen. Whenever I have somebody who's ninety or ninety-five in my office I introduce her (or him) to whichever medical student is being my shadow that month. I walk in and say, for the student's benefit, "I guess you've had a tough life." And the answer is always, "No, I haven't had a tough life. That's why I'm ninety-five." "But," I say, "didn't your house burn down?" Yes. "Business go bankrupt?" Yes. "Child run away from home?" Yes. "Youngest son die?" Yes. "Husband die?" Yes. "Second husband die?" Yes. And then she'll say, "Gee, I guess I have had a tough life." But people like this have learned that the only way to make sure you never outlive all the people you love is to find new people to love. This is always possible, because God has given us a never-ending source of people to love. Through our pain we can find others to love and to heal. That's what groups like Alcoholics Anonymous and Exceptional Cancer Patients (ECaP) are all about. In fact, I always say that if you're fortunate enough to be an alcoholic or drug addict or have a disease, you can find a group to be part of, and you'll have lots of people to love and be loved by. We need to start groups for people who just enjoy living.

2. *What happened in the year or two before your illness?*

Originally this question was intended to get people to think about what traumatic events might have occurred in the years leading up to their illness that could have made them susceptible to it. In other words, if your organs are speaking to you, what events in your life might they be talking about? But many people criticized me for making them feel guilty over having caused their own illnesses, which was not at all the point. What I'm trying to do is to empower people, to give them ways to help them get well, not make them feel guilty for getting sick. I want people to realize that, although they may not be able to control all the events in their lives, they can control their response to those events. When people sit in my examining room and say things like "I'll make this marriage work if it kills me," I want them to hear what they're saying, and see what kind of damage they are doing to themselves with these messages. The mind and body are a unit; they can't be separated. Look at what's happening in your life. Stop killing yourself.

3. *Why do you need your illness and what benefits do you derive from it?*

If I could change anything in my first book, it might be the wording of this question, which got so many people upset. It needs to be looked at together with the preceding question. Given what happened to you in the years leading up to your illness, what wishes do you think are being met by the illness, what benefits are you deriving from it? Freud long ago showed us the benefits of mental illnesses. The psychiatric literature is filled with case histories illustrating the erotic, self-punitive and aggressive needs that illness can meet. The problem is that those of us in the body specialities have not been taught this and are not aware that physical diseases can meet similar needs. In looking at physical disease we tend to concentrate on the body and act as though a person and a mind do not come with it. But they cannot be separated, and in order to understand a patient's illness we must always consider the possibility that it meets certain psychological needs that might not be met without it.

Our daughter Carolyn handed me a cartoon one day that showed a gentleman waking up and saying, "I feel great, what a beautiful day, I'll call in sick." Of course, we often think we have to get sick literally in order to get the rest or pleasure we need in our lives. Bobbie and I therefore taught our children when they were younger that if they needed a day off from school, they should just say that and take a health day, not a sick day. That made them look at life differently. I think all of us need to rethink our attitudes toward health and sickness.

Once you start looking at these issues, you see that there's often a reason why illnesses attack specific body parts or occur at particular times. The body can be very ingenious in getting what it needs. If you're an overworked television reporter and you want a day off, a broken ankle won't keep you off the set, so you get laryngitis. Sometimes the illness is so effective at getting the sick person the care and attention he needs that everyone around him is exhausted by the effort of meeting those needs. In physical diagnosis there is something I call "Siegel's Sign." When a family comes into my office with everybody looking sick except for one individual, I know that the one who looks well is the one with the illness. That one person is manipulating and controlling everybody else.

A lady who lived in housing for the elderly came into my office one day complaining about how sick she was and how many troubles she was having. I told her that if she wanted to feel better she should go back to her housing project, find someone sicker and with more troubles than she, make that person feel better, and watch what that did for her. When she came back to the office two weeks later I asked her, "Well, what happened?" She said, "I went through the whole project, there's nobody sicker, with more troubles than me." People like her need their illness to relate to the world. It is too frightening for them to try connecting to others without it.

I'm not blaming anyone for using illness. Rather, I want you to look at how you might be benefiting from illness and then figure out how you can meet those same needs in a healthier way. Stop punishing yourself in order to get what you need. Take your health days, tell your family what you need from them, get out of that job that you hate—then maybe you won't need an illness. You are mortal. Think of the value of your time.

4. *What does the illness mean to you?*

People who think their disease represents a failure were generally made to feel like failures by parents or other authority figures. But that doesn't mean that they are failures. One woman who described her disease as a failure was the daughter of parents who had both committed suicide. It's not hard to see where she got her feelings about herself.

Another answer that people often give is that they see the disease as a punishment or crucifixion. One woman wrote me that she thought her disease was tied to her guilt at not being able to be with her mother when *she* was sick. Her mother used to say to her "that she hoped I would suffer everything that she suffered." Parents can have this effect on us—but we can also escape their legacy by becoming aware of it, as this lady was in the process of doing. She knew that she was entitled to resurrection and not continued persecution.

Of course, some parents give their kids a great legacy. People whose parents gave them the message that "F" is for feedback, not failure, understand that they can make use of the setbacks that occur in their lives to help them grow and be redirected. (Five "F"s, for example, while a bit heavy, will certainly serve to "redirect" a child toward another, more suitable course of study.) They understand the Book of Job's message that afflictions heal and adversity opens you to a new reality. If you can see your illness in that light, you and your family can grow from the experience and be healed by it. As you'll see when we get to chapters 6 and 7, the person with the illness can be the great healer in the family, by showing everybody how to live and love despite an affliction. From that example, they can learn that life is full of challenges—challenges that represent an opportunity for heroism. When the individual is gone, the family will not forget those lessons.

However, for those of you who cannot forgive yourselves for the failure you think your disease represents, who feel that you shouldn't have been vulnerable to it in the first place or should have been able to defeat it if only you'd fought harder, visualized better or prayed longer, there can be no such healing. Instead the burden on everyone will be greater. The message you give your family is that anything short of a cure is a failure. When you do that, you leave behind a terrible emptiness—not just the sense of loss that we all feel when someone we love dies, but a feeling of hopelessness and meaninglessness. Don't pass on to your children the legacy of hopelessness that you received. Now is the time to say no to those feelings in your own life and to the people who created them in you, so that your life and the lives of those around you will be different, no matter how short or long the span of time remaining to you.

Later in this chapter you'll read that an illness may be your greatest dream trying to come true. I know this may be hard to believe when you are dealing with a serious illness, but when you hear one person after another say that their illness is the best thing that ever happened to them, you may start to believe. It's up to you, however, to decide how to interpret your illness—as a failure or as an opportunity for new direction.

5. *Describe your disease* and *what you are experiencing.*

Contrary to what Susan Sontag has written in her book *Illness as Metaphor,* there is always more to disease than the mere physical diagnosis. When you ask people to describe their disease, fewer than 5 percent say things like "I have far-advanced ovarian cancer" or "carcinoma of the colon." Yes, a few intellectuals and physicians do respond that way, but those are the people it's hardest to help. I have to say to them that I know how to treat their diseases, but I don't know how to help them with what they are experiencing.

The people it is easier to help are the ones who describe their experience of the disease, because as they talk about their illness, the words always apply to the life that gave rise to it. One friend of mine told me that she had a bad pain in her neck for several days, until she started talking to it and asking it why it was there. Then she remembered that she had always called her brother a pain in the neck, but he had died quite suddenly a year before and she had been missing him terribly. Once she realized that she had brought him back to her in this form, she decided she could hold on to her memories of him without the pain—and it went away.

A couple came in to talk to me because the wife said she was having trouble communicating with her husband. When I asked the husband to describe his disease, he told me, "I'm in remission." But when I asked the wife to describe her experience of his disease she said, "I'm in hell." When one person is in hell and the other is in remission, you start to see why they can't communicate.

I talked to a woman who said, "My cancer is invisible, they can't even find the primary site." Her response made her realize that she was putting too much of her energy into hiding something. Then I asked her if she came from a home where she was taught never to reveal her feelings. My questions started her on a process of inner exploration that helped her heal her life.

When a lady hospitalized for abdominal pain described the pain as being like a basketball inside, I told the medical student who was with me to ask her what pressures existed in her life. It turned out that she was chauffeuring all three of her daughters to basketball practice every day and she was worn out. I told her that if she found another ride for the kids, I thought the basketball would be removed from her abdomen.

A gentleman and his daughter came in to see me and she

told me that he just wasn't living. "What's going on inside you?" I asked him. "Oh, I've got something wild and uncontrollable inside of me," he answered. Sometimes people who live very quiet, controlled lives have their bodies rebel against them in order to create some excitement, so I suggested to him that if he made a little more noise in his life, maybe he wouldn't need something wild inside of him. A few weeks later I got a wonderful call from his family: "Our father's alive again! He's speaking up and asserting himself and doing things he enjoys."

Thinking about what the disease metaphor means in your life can be very empowering. Jungian psychotherapist and author Arnold Mindell often shares a little myth in which a child is walking through the woods and in the roots of a tree sees a bottle with a cork in it. When he picks up the bottle and yanks the cork out, a genie appears. It says to him, "Aha, I've got you in my power now." But the boy is no dummy, and he looks at the genie and says, "Well, if you're so powerful and smart, let's see you get back in the bottle." The genie goes back in, and the boy slaps the cork in, so that the genie is now rebottled. When we turn toward our disease and ask, "Why are you threatening me, what do you want from me, why are you here?" even "Why do you want to kill me?" we can rebottle the symptoms and obtain their potential gifts. When we do that we also begin to see the positive side of our disease.

"I don't believe that a person actually creates disease, but that his soul is expressing an important message to him through the disease," says Mindell. This was common knowledge in other times and other cultures, but our own focus is so exclusively on the mechanics of disease that we ignore the message. When you start looking for the message, however, you realize that there always is one.

I was in the hospital one night when I was stopped by a gentleman who wanted me to visit his wife in her room. Rachel had been an exceptional patient, he said, but now she was lying in a coma, close to death, and she was in the hospital to die. I walked in to see her, leaned down and whispered into her ear—because I know people can hear you in coma (as well as when they're asleep or under anesthesia)—"Your husband tells me you have been an exceptional lady. But if you're tired and sore and need to go, it's all right. Your love will remain with your family."

The next day when I walked into the room she was awake, and she said, "I don't want to die." So I asked her to describe her illness. "It's an obstruction," she told me, and I suggested to her that she needed to deal with all the obstructions in her life. It was five days before I had a chance to visit her again, but when I walked into her room there was no one in the bed. Instead there was an attractive lady sitting in the windowseat. I asked her if she knew where Rachel was. "I'm Rachel," she said, "and I'm going home today." At least nine months later she was still at home, and although I've lost track of her since, I feel sure that she did indeed deal with the obstructions in her life. Her story is just one of the many I've witnessed that show the truth of my belief that illness is symbolic of life's dilemmas. "The physical disorder," as Jung says of such cases, "appears as a direct mimetic expression of the psychic situation."

A recent letter that moved me very deeply described another of these cases in which the disease was a direct expression of an inner dilemma. "Love and happiness surrounded Peter" during his life, his widow wrote, "but not a single day passed that he did not feel the pain endured by his people during the Holocaust." She went on to describe his experience:

In June of 1985, Peter underwent a fourteen-hour operation which not one of his many physicians expected him to survive. They were further astounded by the diagnosis—a large malignant tumor of the heart. What followed were twenty months of unbearable suffering for Peter and for us a frantic search for treatment, help and answers. The first question we asked ourselves was how a man who led such a healthy life could be afflicted with cancer. But in this respect we were not unique, as many other cancer victims are puzzled by the same question. What made Peter's case so unusual was the site of his lesion. Our search led us to doctors researching psychological aspects of illness. . . .

Tragically it all became very clear; Peter's condition was the physical manifestation of the Holocaust. The cancer in his heart was the internal expression of the ugliness he witnessed and carried with him in that heart. Peter was just not able or willing to confront and "release" the past, although he was urged by therapists to do so. He was unable to translate his subconscious rage and pain into verbal expression. Although Peter was, by nature, a tolerant and nonjudgmental man, he vehemently opposed the suggestion that he "forgive the world" for allowing the Holocaust to happen.

There is such love, understanding and wisdom in this letter that I am reminded once again not just of the meaningfulness of illness, but of the solace to be gained from acknowledging that meaning, rather than seeing our afflictions as random. If we see disease as an opportunity for the revelation and unfolding of our individual blueprint, we heal, inwardly and sometimes outwardly as well. As one workshop member said, "We need to heal from the inside out."

One of the most vivid and revealing disease descriptions I've ever seen came from a woman who wrote me about her experience of multiple sclerosis:

This disease could be described [as] an inactive volcano that suddenly goes crazy. At first it sits there blowing just enough smoke to be irritating. And I feel safe during these times. When the main eruption begins, I want to flee and get off the island. There is no place to escape to. I have to watch while the hot lava flows wherever it wants to in my body. I never know how high it is going to blow or what damage it will do. I never know if flowers will be able to grow again in those damaged spots or if the trees will grow again to protect me from the painful burn of the sun. Will fruit trees grow on this barren land so that I can pass something on to others? The lava that flows scares me. I don't know what areas to protect and I don't know when to protect them. The burns caused are so painful, and the healing is very slow. The losses caused by the burns may never be replaced. But when the healing comes, it feels good. At first, I was very disappointed that the burns weren't healed in a way that returned me to me. I have been very angry over having no control over the lava flow. This volcano even causes some of my friends to flee the island when it becomes active. But for the friends who stay we share the burn and soothe each other. It is when we feel the pain and the healing together that it is really all right inside.

Writing that description was part of a journey of self-discovery that transformed the life of a woman who had been ill for many years. "When I stop to consider the inner healing that has taken place over the last eight years," she wrote in a recent letter to me, "I can truly say that this disease has been a blessing that has allowed and is allowing me to make the inner changes that are necessary for me to become a healed person." Does that sound like guilt, fault or blame?

Another description of a disease, perhaps less vivid but no less revealing in its way, came from a critically ill gentleman who was in my office one day. When I asked him to tell me about his disease, he said, "It's an inconvenience." I told him, "You could die of an inconvenience, you know." He was putting on an incredible performance for his neighbors and co-workers so that he could convince them that that's all it was. Every day he would leave the house, go to work, come home and collapse the second he got there. Then his family would feed him and put him to bed, and the next day he would start the whole grueling act again. He was determined not to deal with the reality of his illness but to perform, and there was no time for sharing or communication with his family. The effort to deny his illness was draining them all. I worked with him and got him to take some time off to be with his family and to share love with them. This was a healing experience and a relief for everyone.

Some people think of their illness as a blockage or as something trying to manage their lives, and I ask them what might be stopping the flow or taking over their life's energy. One woman said, "My tumors are barnacles." Her mother is hanging on to her. A man described his disease as an incredibly beautiful white light, and I said, "It sounds as if your disease is too beautiful to give up," which forced him to see how dependent he was on it. The man who described his disease as "proliferating" felt that he was being crowded out by his family. The woman who described her disease as a prison resisted all the treatment options I offered: "Surgery hurts, radiation burns, chemotherapy makes your hair fall out," she said. When I finally asked her "Why don't you just eat vegetables," her answer was, "I don't like them." She couldn't see that she had any choices, hence her prison.

Once you start to use the questions to redirect your life, however, your experience of illness changes. You may have started out thinking of it as a volcano, a barnacle or an obstruction, but you may move on to thinking of it as a gift, a challenge, a wake-up call or a beauty mark, as you'll hear people characterizing their afflictions in chapter 6.

By calling your attention to feelings and problems you may not have been aware of, the disease may be the first step in overcoming them. That's one of the reasons why I think the five questions are so important and why I hope more doctors will use them in addition to the traditional review of systems. But doctors tend to be mechanics who focus only on defects in the physical mechanism, because that's what their inadequate training has taught them to do.

In a study done at Ben-Gurion University in Israel by psychologist Dan Bar-On, eighty-nine male heart-attack patients and their doctors were interviewed about why they thought the attack had occurred. The physician was much more likely than the patient to put the blame on strictly physiological factors like obesity or smoking, while many of the men tended to blame psychosocial circumstances like a bad work situation. Men who saw their own role in bringing on their heart attacks—for example, those who considered themselves "angry people" under a lot of pressure at work—planned to do something to change their circumstances, and these men made the best recoveries. But regardless of how much progress the patients made, they were better at predicting their degree of recovery than their doctors were, which Bar-On attributes to their greater understanding of what caused the attack in the first place. I agree with Bar-On and see this as yet another instance of the necessity for the doctor to understand the patient's disease as the patient does. Asking for a description of the illness is one step in that direction.

THE LANGUAGE OF SYMBOLS

Symptoms as Symbols

I wish that somebody had told me when I was in medical school that over fifty years ago Carl Jung had interpreted a dream and made a physical diagnosis. It might have changed the way I practiced and saved me from lots of pain as a mechanistic physician. It never occurred to me that disease is symbolic or that its meaning or diagnosis might be found in dreams.

But why, you may wonder, do we have to get to the meaning through symbols? I too wondered about this. Why couldn't we just go to sleep at night and have a flash card appear telling us what to do and how to live? So in one of my conversations with our Creator, I asked. The Creator responded: "Bernie, I tried the cards, but there were so many languages that if I'd had to make flash cards for every single one, Creation would have taken an extra day. So I decided on universal symbols." Please pay attention to these symbols. They speak from the soul. You can go anywhere on this planet with a box of crayons and communicate with people via their symbols.

What was news to me has been known for thousands of years. The ancient Greeks built temples to the god of healing, Asclepius, where the sick would go to spend the night and wait for a diagnosis or even a cure to come to them in their dreams. Hippocrates, whom we call the father of medicine, Aristotle, the great rationalist philosopher, and even Galen, the last of the great Greek physicians, who was born in the Christian era—all believed in dreams for both their diagnostic and their healing powers. And all valued dreams as messages from the gods.

Russell A. Lockhart contrasts the ancient Greek attitude toward dreams and illness with our modern, mechanistic approach and shows what we have lost along the way:

The purpose of sickness, the meaning of affliction, was to force the individual to confront his disconnection from the Gods, to sacrifice his hubristic acquisitions, and to re-place himself in the proper spirit of relationship by binding himself *(re-ligio)* through suffering in service to the Gods.

Modern man and his medicine have lost touch with the special sense of the importance and value of sickness, and the central role that dreams play in connecting his soul to the powers beyond himself. We are indebted to Jung because he rediscovered this religious attitude not only toward the dream but toward man's ills as well. "Man needs his difficulties," he said, "they are necessary for health." Unfortunately, this attitude has not permeated medical practice and the dream is rarely heard in the current medical shrines. The dream is no longer consulted for diagnosis, no longer recruited in treatment, no longer sought for in healing or cure. We may ask the question: Is there a place in modern culture for a revival of the ancient theurgic attitude toward sickness, suffering, healing, and the central role of the dream?

I would of course answer yes to that question, using the words of Meredith Sabini and Valerie Maffly, who like Lockhart are Jungian analysts who have worked extensively with dreams:

Not only patients but doctors also have to find a . . . way to provide a . . . new attitude which recognizes the paradox that illness may contain the seeds of a healing process. Those who work with cancer patients have found that this new way involves turning to the inner doctor, or archetypal healer, via dreams and active imagination in order to see what course lies open for each patient. This approach obviously may create conflicts with traditional medical approaches, but nevertheless it seems to be one way by which the isolated ego may hope to find its "Foundation," and the lonely man his self.

I would simply add that I think this approach is potentially as valid for AIDS, neurological disease, arthritis, multiple sclerosis, lupus, amyotrophic lateral sclerosis, heart disease—in fact, all significant disease—as it is for cancer. As Jung states: "One cannot say that every symptom is a challenge and that every cure takes place in the intermediate realm between psyche and physis. One can only say that it is advisable to approach every illness from the psychological side as well, because this may be extraordinarily important for the healing process." This is why, whenever people have to make decisions about their medical care (or anything else important in their lives, for that matter), I ask them to describe their illness, draw pictures of their situation and tell me their dreams.

Marrow Christmas

I have in front of me a card that says: "Have yourself a marrow Christmas. Thank you a million, trillion, zillion for helping make the decision to have this bone marrow transplant." But I didn't make the decision; this woman's unconscious did. The story of how this came about is told in her letters, the first of which was written in September of 1986: "I need to know whether I should undergo a bone marrow transplant which offers a 50 to 65 percent cure rate of my nodular histiocytic lymphoma but could also kill me due to an infection, *or* should I try for a 'spontaneous' remission which I'm willing to work hard for. My third option is to postpone this bone marrow transplant until or if I should relapse again."

The medical history behind this woman's dilemma began with a lymphoma, which had been diagnosed in 1983, about the same time that she became pregnant with her third child. Although the initial diagnosis was that of a slow-growing tumor, when her baby was delivered by cesarean section, a one-and-a-half-pound diffuse histiocytic lymphoma was discovered on her ovary. Her oncologist termed it highly malignant and recommended aggressive chemotherapy, which offered a "40 to 50 percent chance of cure." She read the Simontons' book *Getting Well Again,* did visualization and worked hard at accepting her chemotherapy and changing the problem areas in her life. The results were promising: Although a CAT scan performed after she was through with chemotherapy didn't look normal, exploratory surgery showed no disease present.

This apparent remission lasted almost two years, during which time, as she tells the story, she ignored her own needs in favor of the demands of her three young children and lost a number of people close to her (all to cancer). Then, in July of 1986, a new node was discovered on her neck and diagnosed as lymphoma, at which time she was found to be an excellent candidate for an experimental but highly risky bone marrow transplant procedure that was being performed at the Dana-Farber Cancer Institute. The procedure involved harvesting the patient's own bone marrow, cleansing it with monoclonal antibodies and infusing it back into the patient by dripping it in intravenously. "And the body is so smart," as she explained in her letter, "it knows right where to send the cells." Still, as a nurse it frightened her to contemplate the procedure and its risks.

In making her decision, she had to take into account not just the risks to herself but the demands that were going to be made on her family. After the transplant there would be a five- to six-week period of isolation in the hospital:

. . . and I'll be getting multiple blood transfusions because the doctor said I'd be literally bloodless and vulnerable to any infection known to mankind. . . . After the six weeks of isolation I'll have to stay in the Boston area for up to six more weeks getting blood as an outpatient.

When I'll need only one transfusion a week I can come home but I'll have to leave the house if any of my children get sick. I can't be their primary caretaker.

I love my kids, Dr. Siegel, and I want to be here to see them through college, and live to see my grandchildren. The doctors told me that since this disease came back after all the chemo that means there is no other treatment that will cure me besides this bone marrow thing.

I'll do the transplant if I have to but what I feel bad about is all those healthy cells they'll destroy including the lens in my eyes. I really don't feel a bit sick, no night sweats, no fevers.

What I'm scared of is getting an infection up there in Boston and dying in a room all by myself in November 1986. . . . Part of me however (my scientific mind) says maybe it is a gift from God that I am the right B-cell type that can undergo this transplant and these doctors have a solution that can offer a good chance at cure.

My other side doesn't really believe that I am sick and I feel as if they are going after an ant with a cannon. I wonder if I exercise, increase my Vitamin C intake, meditate, clean up my diet and do as much as possible to decrease my stress, could that be as curative? I'd still have my daily hugs and kisses from the kids and my husband.

The most important thing is I feel healthy, well and whole right now and I intend to stay that way by one path or another. . . .

I wrote back and asked her to tell me any dreams she was having. When she sent me a dream, we went through it and discussed its symbolism, which resulted in her being able to make a conflict-free decision. Here is her description of her dream:

I was in a high-rise hotel in San Antonio, and I wanted to stay with my husband and kids as we were apparently vacationing. So rather than fly back home for my chemotherapy, I inquired by knocking on doors in the high-rise and three people all said, "Go see Dr. Oslund." Two were gay and one was a lady. . . . The other part I didn't tell you [she wrote later] was, in the dream my neighbor was staying in a room next to mine, and she has a daughter named Dana.

As we analyzed her dream, we took it step by step. First I asked her why she thought she was in San Antonio. The city itself had no meaning for her, but Saint Anthony did, as the patron saint of lost objects, and she is searching for an answer. Next we looked at the doctor who was recommended to her, Dr. Oslund. If you know Latin, *os* is bone and *lund* is earth or marrow. I believe the two gay people were associated in her mind (because of AIDS) with the immune system, the lady was herself, and all three of them favored Dr. Oslund. "So now you know you are to have a bone marrow transplant," I told her. But where? The friend who was staying down the hall has a daughter named Dana. Down the Massachusetts Turnpike from her home in Hartford, Connecticut, is Boston and the Dana-Farber Cancer Institute. So her dream was telling her to go to Boston and have the transplant at Dana-Farber. At the time she told me the dream we were both puzzled by why it took place in a high-rise hotel, but once she got to the hospital she called to tell me she understood—she'd arrived and been taken to the twelfth floor.

The symbolism and coincidences don't stop there. In fact, this woman's story gives new meaning to my belief that coincidence is God's way of remaining anonymous.

One day a couple of months after these dream analysis discussions, my wife, Bobbie, and I flew home after doing a workshop in another city, and we went to the airport parking lot to pick up our car, which has a license plate reading ECAPMD (a reference to our exceptional patients groups). There we found a note on the windshield, which read: "Is this Bernie's car? I hope so. Just wanted to tell you how much peace you and your program have brought to our lives. My sister is going to undergo a bone marrow transplant at Dana-Farber and your tapes and meditation and self-healing are preparing her and all of us in the family. We love you. P.S. Just happened to be at the airport giving a ride to someone."

Our car was in the right place at the right moment, so that we could be given this message about what was happening. Once you start to become receptive to these messages, you get more and more of them. I can't tell you how many times Bobbie and I, as we travel around the country, jump into a taxicab at an airport and find a penny on the carpet, letting us know we're in the right cab in the right city. Recently I ran the New York Marathon. I wasn't sure if I'd make it to the end, but I figured I'd be given a sign, though even I wasn't crazy enough to think I was going to find twenty-six pennies. However, as I was standing at the starting line on the Verrazano Narrows Bridge, along with 23,000 other people, I looked down and there at my feet was a quarter. So all I needed to find was a penny. About ten miles farther I looked down and there was a shiny penny, but if I stopped I'd be trampled. So I ran to the side and eased out into the street. People could see I wasn't running. As I bent to pick up the penny, one runner said to another, "What's wrong with that guy?" And the other one said, "He must be really poor."

Brand-new pennies in unexpected places, elevators that open without a button being pushed, even a flat tire—they can all be messages. In fact I now call them "spiritual flat tires." Why flat tires? Let me tell you about something that happened to Bobbie and me one time. We were in Keystone, Colorado, trying to make a plane out of Denver and get back home to Connecticut. Everything went wrong: The bellboy was late in getting us the car, I took a wrong turn and we got lost in the mountains, I had to pull somebody over by forcing his car off the road to get directions—and then, after I finally got back on the highway, I developed a flat.

I changed the tire, threw it in the trunk and headed off to the airport again. By now I was not only late but dirty and upset. When we got to the airport building (I never use the word terminal), we ran down to the gate just in time to see them shut the door. We had missed our plane. But as we walked dejectedly out of the airport we heard people talking: The plane that we missed had just crashed. Bobbie and I went back out to the car, raised the trunk, embraced the tire and now have it bronzed and hanging over our mantelpiece. (Only the first part of this story is true but the rest held your attention and, I hope, made the point.)

That is what I call a spiritual flat tire. When you are open and aware, you will have them in your life. They help you get in touch with the schedule of the universe, as opposed to your own personal schedule, which relates only to questions like "Am I late? How do I look? What do other people think?" They get you to look at the *real* questions: "How can I live and understand the moment?" Diseases can be our spiritual flat tires—disruptions in our lives that seem to be disasters at the time but end by redirecting our lives in a meaningful way. These will occur more often when you are in touch with your intuitive, unconscious awareness.

Soon after the message on my windshield, I received another update, this time from my original correspondent, and it seemed as though the coincidences confirming the rightness of her decision just wouldn't stop:

Well, I'm now nine days post bone marrow transfusion, and doing very well. I'm writing to you just after one unit of red blood cells and six units of platelets that I don't think I even needed, but people like to stay busy around here. My spirits are up. My room is friendly and nowhere near as isolated as I expected. I'm even making friends with Pedro and Blanca, my cleaning people. At first I thought Pedro was a doctor cause he came in all gowned, masked and gloved. Before I exposed whatever orifice I thought he was interested in, he reached for the mop, so it was a great clue to what he was after.

Again, I can't thank you enough. The fear has left me and I'm sailing through, much to my and my doctor's delight. . . .

Here's another ditty you'll love. The doctor referred to my bone marrow infusion as my new birthday or re-birth. It happened six o'clock, December 11th. It was myself, the doctor monitoring my umbilical cord of marrow and a nurse, Maura, whom I've never seen before or since. *My mother's name is Maura!* And I thought how ironic that it was a doctor, my nurse mother-Maura and me again, as in 1953 when I was born. After the doctor disconnected my bone marrow infusion, I started a typical post marrow shaking chill, which Maura soothed by swaddling me in blankets. I know I'm doing the right thing.

And with so many wonderful signs, how could she not know? Recently I got to meet this woman when I was telling her story at a workshop I was giving and she stood up and said, "That's me!" She's doing beautifully—another proof that at a deep level we each know our path and our way of healing, if we can just get to that level.

Dreams as Symbols

Dreams can sometimes announce to people that they are sick long before they have any symptoms. Marc Barasch, a journalist and editor whose account of his experience with cancer of the thyroid is to appear in *Esquire* magazine, had a terrifying dream one morning in which torturers placed hot coals beneath his chin. "I distinctly felt the heat start to sear my throat and I screamed, the sound becoming hoarser, a raw, animal desperation, as the coals gnawed my larynx." While lying in bed trying to shake free of the horror of the dream, he received a long-distance phone call from his girlfriend in Colorado, where it was 5:00 A.M. She'd just had an awful dream, she told him, in which they were together in a bed that was filling with blood. "What does it mean, do you think?" she asked. "It means I have cancer," he told her, "I have cancer growing in my throat"—a diagnosis that would be confirmed months later, when Barasch finally went to a doctor because he was starting to have symptoms.

The doctor was skeptical when Barasch announced that he thought he was seriously ill. "You don't even have swollen glands, let alone cancer," the doctor said, "and all your blood tests are normal." Barasch then told him about another dream he'd had in which medicine men formed a circle around him and stuck hypodermic needles into something called "the neck brain." Could that refer to a real organ, he wanted to know, but the doctor obviously thought he had a bizarre hypochondriac on his hands and only reluctantly scheduled him for a thorough checkup. During the checkup several weeks afterward, he found a lump and told Barasch they'd have to do a scan. Of what, Barasch wanted to know. "Your thyroid gland," the doctor said, then smiled grudgingly: "The neck brain."

Barasch also had dreams in which alternative methods of healing were suggested to him, but with great ambivalence he went ahead with the operation his doctor recommended, about which he still has serious doubts. I know many other people, however, who have followed the medical path set out for them in their dreams.

A couple of years ago I met a gentleman who had just discovered that he had leukemia, and I asked him about his dreams. Three dreams in particular were most meaningful. In one he was in the water when a crane dropped a large truck on him, but he was able to dive down and get out from under it—which said to me that he was going to survive, and I shared that with him. He also said he had had two dreams about his brother, who pulled him out of a volcano in one dream and reached out of a window in a high-rise building in time to catch him as he fell in the other. I told him I thought his dreams meant that his brother would be the best match for a bone marrow transplant, which would save his life. Later he was at a major cancer center where they were considering using his sister for the bone marrow, but he told them his brother would be the better match, and that indeed turned out to be true. In October he was admitted to the hospital to receive the transplant from his brother, and I feel certain that it will all turn out well.

Dream interpretation can reveal much about not only the physical dimension of disease but the emotional factors too. Psychologist Meredith Sabini studied sixty dreams about illness, gathered from her colleagues, her patients and published cases, and said in the conclusion to one of her articles about the project:

When I began studying dreams of illness, I was astonished at what they revealed, for illness was shown, more often than not, as belonging to a larger process involving central issues in an individual's life. Even an illness thought to be organic—multiple sclerosis—was associated with repression; cancer was said to be an "invention," a projection onto the body of certain long-neglected problems; heart attack was likened (in a dream not cited here) to suicide by gunfire. Simple, ordinary symptoms such as nasal congestion and lower back pain turned out to be merely the tip of an iceberg, the visible surface of tremendously complex internal issues.

Sabini and other analysts who have focused on dream interpretation agree that dreams, like physical symptoms, are often direct mimetic commentaries on the psychological wound afflicting the dreamer. I see this as a way of giving the dreamer multiple opportunities for understanding the message. If the physical symptom doesn't call attention to the psychological problem, then perhaps the dream will. As Jung said, "Not infrequently the dream shows [the] remarkable inner symbolic connection between an undoubted physical illness and a definite psychic problem"—if only we will make use of the dream to illuminate that connection.

Dream interpretation can sometimes be an enormously complex business. If you were to read Jung's description of the mental process he followed half a century ago to make that diagnosis I mentioned earlier, you might throw up your hands and decide that God had better use flash cards after all. But many dreams don't require the skill of a Jung, and most dreamers don't find their dreams so impenetrable that they require professional assistance to interpret the symbols. As psychologist and dream expert Ann Faraday says in her very helpful book on dream interpretation, *The Dream Game:*

> It seems that symbolic language is quite the most efficient way of articulating a whole constellation of feelings. . . . Poets, playwrights, movie makers, and artists have always used this language. In many ways a dream is very like a movie that flashes a series of pictures across the mind's eye during sleep, conveying its message by means of visual imagery and association of ideas. . . .
>
> Thinking by means of pictures and pictorial idea association is probably the most primitive of all modes of thought, going right back to the dawn of the human race when the power of speech was only just beginning to develop, and abstract thinking had not yet been born. The caveman glancing across the cave at his woman probably actually *saw* her as a she-wolf or a deer long before he was able to articulate the concept that she was *like* an animal—a form of thought that may lack scientific accuracy but has great emotional immediacy. In fact, we still rely on it for expressing feelings . . . for the bulk of our speech consists of pictures translated into verbal metaphors—"wolf in sheep's clothing," "ships that pass in the night," "bridge over troubled waters," "missing the bus," "getting into hot water," "going through the roof" and countless comparable turns of phrase. . . . So when the dreaming mind expresses itself in movie terms, cutting out all the "as ifs" and showing us literally crossing roads and bridges when we are facing major life decisions, or literally being devoured when we feel "eaten up" by something, it is using the most fundamental of all languages, shared by men and women of every age and race.

This is the language which, in Aldous Huxley's words, shows us "for a few timeless hours the outer and the inner worlds, not as they appear to an animal obsessed with words and notions, but as they are apprehended directly and unconditionally, by Mind at Large." Accessible to us in childhood, it eludes us later, as our obsession "with words and notions" causes the language of symbols to fade. But like any language, it can be relearned with practice. Keeping a dream diary in which you record every night's dreams is an excellent way of getting back in touch with the unconscious. I recommend to all of you that you keep a journal right next to the bed so that when you dream and wake up, you can make notes immediately, before you lose the dream. This technique may also convince those of you who think you don't have dreams that you do.

Everybody dreams. As soon as you start recording your dreams regularly, you give a signal to the dreaming part of you that what Huxley called "the doors of perception" are open, and your dreams will probably start surfacing into consciousness more and more often. When I started to meditate and in a sense to take the lid off my inner symbols, one of the first dreams I had was of a young man walking up to me, smiling, looking me in the eye and saying "Thanks for letting us out," then turning and walking away. And I knew he was saying thank you for allowing this material to come to the surface at this time. I had opened the door to the dark closet of my unconscious mind.

Now I look to my dreams for help with all kinds of issues, from the practical to the philosophical. When I was having some trouble with my neck, I had a dream that said to read Carlos Castaneda's *Journey to Ixtlan.* In the book, Don Juan tells Carlos to get a backpack and stop carrying things in his hands, and I realized the message applied to me, too, because I was always carrying an attaché case filled with heavy books and papers and tapes to play in the operating room, which was starting to affect my neck and back.

In another dream I was in California, carrying an enormous but very lightweight fir tree under my arm. I thought this meant we were supposed to move to California. But Tom Laughlin pointed out that the tree was uprooted, and that made sense in the context of all the traveling Bobbie and I were doing. The fact that the tree was uprooted but was very light to carry told me both that this traveling was what I was supposed to be doing at this stage of my life, as opposed to sending down new roots, and also that it would not be a burden.

My recent dreams have been related to how busy my life has gotten since *Love, Medicine and Miracles* was published—speaking all over the country, running workshops and answering the thousands of letters I receive, on top of continuing to be a surgeon. In one dream there was only one parking space left, where a tractor trailer was to be backed in, and no driver wanted to undertake the job because so little space was left. But I jumped into the truck, said, "Oh, I'll take care of it," backed it in and dented the other trucks. That made me realize that sometimes you just can't fit everything in. In another dream I was driving on some slippery roads trying to find a safe place to get away from all the people who were following me. They weren't threatening people or dangerous in any way, but they wouldn't stop following me. When I woke up I thought about how everyone seems to be after me these days, so many people wanting something of me.

The last dream I want to share with you was one in which I was told to read "The Rime of the Ancient Mariner." When I went to a bookstore to find it, a beautiful copy was sitting right on the front counter. I opened the book directly to the words "He prayeth best, who loveth best/All things both great and small;/For the dear God who loveth us,/He made and loveth all." I realized I was being told that there are no exceptions—if you're going to love, you have to love everyone.

Faraday's book, *The Dream Game,* is one I would refer you to if you are interested in interpreting dreams. There is a wealth of practical information in it, including an inventory of frequent dream themes and images, and a no-nonsense approach that everyone can utilize.

Patricia Garfield's *Creative Dreaming* is also an excellent resource. There the emphasis is not so much on interpretation as on playing an active, shaping role in one's own dream life. Garfield shows us how to use the wisdom of cultures more steeped in dream lore than ours to enhance our creative and problem-solving abilities. Stephen LaBerge's *Lucid Dreaming* is another book that helps you participate actively and constructively—"lucidly"—in your own dream processes. I also recommend Gail Delaney's *Living Your Dreams,* and I urge everyone to read a book by Marie-Louise Von Franz and

Fraser Boa entitled *The Way of the Dream,* a very worthwhile introduction to the Jungian approach.

The title of Eugene Gendlin's *Let Your Body Interpret Your Dreams* aptly describes his technique. "The basic touchstone of the method," Gendlin writes, "is your own bodily experience of something opening up in you . . . a physical felt shift." This "felt shift" he compares to the feeling you get when you want to remember something: You try out a bunch of alternatives in your head until suddenly the thing you are trying to remember comes back to you, and you experience a sense of relief or release that is actually physical. His book presents a series of questions and exercises to be used in conjunction with this somatic touchstone.

What I like about Gendlin's technique is that it enables you to use both psyche and soma in your search for meaning. Since the sense of confirmation you wait for is something internal to your own body, it protects you from well-intentioned but misguided individuals (including your conscious self) who would attempt to impose their interpretations on your dreams. Gendlin warns therapists and other would-be dream counselors against mixing their own "stuff" into someone else's dream. Individuals must always be the final authority on their own symbols, whether in dreams or drawings.

I would only add that you should be gentle with yourself as you face the inner world of your dreams. Dreams do not speak in a punitive, moralistic voice; they are sent to help you. If what you hear when you interpret them is judgmental, then perhaps you need to quiet your external everyday voice in order to hear your inner voice. The same caution applies to frightening dreams, particularly dreams of death or uncontrollable threats to your life. Don't be too quick to leap to a dire conclusion about the meaning of such dreams. Although I believe that some people do have precognitions of death in their dreams, and I have even delayed surgery in response to a dream of impending death, I think that often we interpret dreams in which death appears too literally. Death can stand for many things besides our own (or our loved ones') actual death. As Ann Faraday explains:

Normally the dreaming mind uses death as a metaphor to express the fact that our feeling for someone, or someone's feeling for us, is dead, or that we have allowed something in our inner life to die. . . . The most interesting dream death is our own, for this indicates the death of some obsolete self-image, from which comes rebirth into a higher state of consciousness and authentic self-being.

You may be particularly likely to have such dreams if, as a result of illness, you have embarked on the path of inner exploration that we've been discussing. In my experience, however, this inner place you are exploring is not hostile or threatening. Story after story from my patients and other people who have corresponded with me indicate that the "loving intelligence of energy" that guides us from within is exactly what the words say it is—"loving."

A psychologist has written me about a client of his whose loving inner guides have helped her deal with cancer of the colon and leukemia:

[My patient] and I have explored an inner-communication process with her diseases. Her diseases have communicated back to us giving certain instructions for us to follow. At first, the communication from the "inner sources" was in the form of kinesthetic signals, as answers to questions we asked. Then communication began to occur in more direct language through what we at first thought were dreams. Now she can make a momentary shift in consciousness and receive the messages or instructions directly from a kind of "Guide" or "Energy Source." And, to the best of our ability to understand the "messages," we comply.

Tracing the history of the communication, he explains:

Three months ago we communicated an agreement with a certain "internal structure" to remove the tumors. "It" said they would be gone in five days. She was examined at the hospital and it was confirmed that the tumors were gone. Then, last month, we worked out an arrangement with the "immune system" for the colon to be recognized. We also made another arrangement with the "leukemia system" to stop producing cancerous white blood cells. With both of these "inner systems" coordinated, the "immune system" reported that the infection in the colon would be cleaned in thirty days and the blood normal in thirty days. We made an appointment for her to be "scoped" at the hospital on the thirty-first day. . . . Her colon is now CLEAN; and she has had the colon infection since 1979. Then she was given a blood test. It was NORMAL—for the first time in her life, NORMAL, as in no presence of leukemia.

Next she had a bone marrow extraction. Her marrow sample reveals that she *has* leukemia. Her blood, on the other hand, does not. Our next move of course is to go to the bone marrow system and ask for a change there. . . .

Four months later I received this update on their progress:

One recent "instruction" required that [my patient] be examined by her physician—including the bone marrow test, blood work, colon scope, etc. Her physician was disturbed by the results:
1. She showed no signs of disease—neither cancer, nor leukemia, anywhere in her physical body. 2. Her body carried no evidence that she had ever had any such disease. This second one I believe bothered her doctor most.

So, Bernie, now her doctor is very uncomfortable about this. He cares very much about her and he fears that she is messing around in the "twilight zone" territory and is being placed in danger by whatever is causing this to happen. He doesn't want to meet me. I think he is scared and angry.

I, too, have been afraid to talk to him (or anybody for that matter) about what we are doing. . . . It seems obvious to me that these "Guides" are not only some kind of energy system within the individual, but also beyond the individual . . . way beyond, as in perhaps spiritual beings.

I know these things happen, though unfortunately physicians often withdraw or become angry about such successes. Recently, a physician wrote to me about his success eliminating his extensive cancer. He said his associates were confused and thought it was all "bunk." So he now tells everyone he got well eating celery tops. It creates less trouble. I know that our diseases can speak to us. If we open the doors of perception, we will be amazed at what comes in. But I do not think we need to be afraid.

Drawings as Symbols

Drawings can serve as yet another door to our inner selves. In addition to asking patients the five questions discussed earlier, I also ask them to do some drawings for me. I give all new patients the following instructions:

1. On a white sheet of paper, held vertically, draw a picture of yourself, your treatment, your disease, and your white blood cells eliminating the disease. Be sure to have all the colors of the rainbow, plus brown, black and white, available to you, and use crayons.
2. On another sheet of white paper, this one held horizontally, draw a picture or scene in color, using crayons.
3. You may also choose to draw an additional picture of your home and family, along with any other images that are interesting or important to you. If you are facing important conflicts or choices—for example, in connection with your illness or some other aspect of your life—you may want to depict them. Use this picture as an opportunity to explore any unconscious material that might be helpful to you in dealing with current problems you are confronting.

In view of my own limitations as a dream analyst, I have found it easier to work with drawings than with dreams, and the results seem to be much the same: At the very least, both patient and doctor are put in touch with the patient's deepest feelings about the disease and its treatment. For example, if chemotherapy is depicted as a beautiful bottle of sunshine and energy, that is a good sign that the patient will find healing in it, often with a minimum of side effects. Conversely, if the doctor is drawn as the devil giving poison, it's no surprise to learn that the patient is not doing well under that treatment regimen.

Recently, a physician who was just about to start practicing developed cancer of the larynx. A laryngectomy would have meant his having to learn esophageal speech and would have severely affected his ability to communicate. When radiation was offered to him as an alternative and I asked him to draw it, he depicted the x-ray machine as God and the radiation as coming from God (the drawing is shown on page 75). For him, radiation was an incredible gift, because it would save his voice.

Sometimes drawings reveal that patients' feelings are at odds with what they say they feel, as was the case with a young man who professed to believe that radiation would be good for him, but then drew it as a death ray being zapped at him by a mechanistic monster. This was someone whose family had insisted on his having the radiation. His side effects were so terrible that he was even throwing up at stop lights, because the red light reminded him of the red light that goes on when the x-ray machine is in use. The underlying issue here was control. By taking the decision about his treatment away from him, the family had deprived him of control over his own life. Once he did the drawings and his real feelings about the treatment were revealed, they realized the importance of allowing him to make his own decisions. He decided not to have further radiation therapy, but he did accept surgery in its place. The drawings he did were important tools for exploring the psychological issues at stake.

Of course, the reverse can occur too—sometimes the drawings will reveal unconscious positive feelings toward a treatment that the patient fears at the conscious level, and that can be very encouraging to the patient when it is pointed out. Since I feel strongly that treatment works best when there is no conflict between conscious and unconscious feelings, I use drawings to bring any ambivalence to the surface, where it can be discussed and resolved. Often this results in patients' being willing to accept therapy they had previously rejected.

For example, a woman came to my office with a very difficult decision to make about her treatment. She had breast

cancer, which had been diagnosed at an early stage, and she needed to decide whether to have a lumpectomy, which would ordinarily have been adequate treatment, or a mastectomy. The mastectomy had been suggested to her because both her mother and sister had had breast cancer, and the family history seemed therefore to call for a more extensive procedure than would otherwise have been the case at her stage.

When I asked her to draw a picture for me, she drew a tree with every branch pruned at a 90-degree angle (see the drawing on page 77). Her unconscious was telling her that to keep the Tree of Life healthy, it sometimes needs to be pruned, and a mastectomy would be the appropriate treatment for her. Once this message came to consciousness, through this and other drawings she and her family did, it enabled her to see the mastectomy as healing rather than mutilating. After the operation, she reached up and hugged me in the recovery room, saying, "I love you, thank you for healing me"—which was a wonderful healing for me, too, and helped me to feel that the surgery I had performed was not being received as a mutilation but a gift.

Drawings can also be useful for both diagnostic and prognostic work. Dr. Caroline Bedell Thomas, whose research (which you'll be reading more about in chapter 5) has focused on personality and disease, did studies showing that figure drawings her subjects did of themselves when they were in young adulthood proved to be predictive of various physical and mental illnesses later in life, including heart disease, suicide and—to her surprise—malignancies. In my own practice I've often been able to make use of patients' drawings to help with diagnoses.

One day a little girl was brought into my office with enlarged lymph nodes in her neck and jaw. Her parents were alarmed because lymphoma ran in both their families. I asked the child to do some drawings for me because I wanted to help her deal with any fears she might be experiencing about going to the hospital for the necessary diagnostic tests. One of her drawings was of herself and another was of the family pet, a cat, which she depicted with exaggerated claws (the drawings

appear below and on the next page). As I stared at her drawings, wondering why this cat was such a vivid presence to her at a time when she was so sick, it suddenly dawned on me that she had cat scratch fever. Tests confirmed this diagnosis, and the diagnosis itself confirmed, yet again, the bodily wisdom we all possess.

I've seen many cases in which drawings revealed the general prognosis for a patient, even the time and cause of death. A four-year-old with an extensive sarcoma of the head and neck drew a purple balloon floating up in the sky with her name on it and multicolored decorations around it, plus what resembled a cake. I felt this meant that she would die soon, as a gift to release her mother from a long, difficult time, and in fact she died on her mother's birthday.

I would not as a physician ever suggest when someone is going to die—that is their choice—but I do use what I see in patients' drawings to help them (and their families) come to an awareness and acceptance of death when they seem ready for it, or to help them turn things around if they still want to try.

Drawings are wonderful tools for bringing to consciousness material that the patient wants to deal with but needs to approach indirectly.

You don't need to be physically ill to use drawings in this way. I have a wonderful letter from a woman who attended one of my workshops for medical professionals. She was there to accompany her husband, a dentist, and had no interest in the subject matter. But as a "confirmed doodler" she decided to stay for the lecture when she saw the crayons being set out for the drawing exercise.

The drawing she did of herself was all in blue and black and showed an empty cavity in her chest with her heart on the floor beside her. It happened that that day I had told a story of someone who developed a sarcoma of the heart out of grief over lost family members. That story plus the drawing she did of herself suddenly brought home to this woman what was happening in her own life: She was making herself ill with grief over her father, who had been facing a life-threatening degenerative disease for two years. Somehow the simple experience of seeing her situation clearly for the first time put it into perspective. "The tragedy of my father is still there, but . . . the joy came back to my life and I did not see the whole world as tainted with tragedy," she wrote to me later. The even more remarkable inner healing that occurred was her five-year-old daughter's. "She is sensitive and perceptive and had been in a state of disharmony for about nine or ten months—moody, stubborn, narrow, inflexible, crying in class and sad." One week after her mother confronted her own grief through the drawing, she was transformed:

Her teachers said she was like a new child—happy, spontaneous, giving, sharing and concerned. They couldn't account for the change, but I could. I realized then how much our children pick up from us, especially nonverbally. She had picked up on my change and my awakening and it is nothing short of wonderful. We still go to see my dad regularly. He is still getting worse, but we are still not crying on the way home.

I learned the basics of what I know about the interpretation of drawings from workshops given by Elisabeth Kübler-

Ross and from articles by Jungian therapist Susan Bach, who has done this work for decades, as well as from the thousands of people I have worked with. Psychologist Joan Kellogg does similar interpretive work with mandalas, circular images used originally in the sacred art of Oriental and Indian cultures. The subject is too vast for me to go into in more detail here, but if you wish to explore it further there is now a book on the symbolism of drawings—*The Secret World of Drawings: Healing Through Art,* by Gregg Furth—published in 1988 by Sigo Press in Boston. If it is not in your bookstore and you want further information about ordering it, call 1-800-338-0446, or call ECaP at 203-865-8392.

Drawings can be powerful tools for helping us deal with the important issues in our lives. Like dreams, they speak in the language of symbols, of metaphors. If we are willing to listen to that language and allow it to help us confront our fears, revelation will occur. We will be directed with all the energy and knowledge needed, and love and peace of mind will enter our lives. I wish all physicians would add a box of crayons to their diagnostic and therapeutic tools.

MOVIE SCREENS AND METAPHORS

Dreams, drawings, metaphorical language and the experience of illness—they are all an expression of Self. Arnold Mindell would say that they are all aspects of what he calls the dreambody, "our total real personality," manifesting in different *channels.* Tracing his discovery of the dreambody concept, he recalls work that he did with a patient of his who was dying of stomach cancer, which resulted in the patient's realization that he wanted to "explode," to express himself as he had never done in all his life. Just before going into the hospital, the man had dreamed he had an incurable disease, which could be treated by a medicine that was like a bomb. Suddenly Mindell saw the underlying unity in the man's symptoms, his dream, and his need to release his pent-up feelings by shouting:

At that moment I knew that his cancer was the bomb in the dream. It was his lost expression trying to come out, and finding no way out, it came out in his body as the cancer, and in his dream as the bomb. . . . His body was literally exploding with pent-up expression. In this way, his pain became his own medicine, just like the dream stated, curing his one-sided lack of expression.

The dreambody appeared visually as the firecracker in his dream. It was felt by him proprioceptively as his pain, pressing him to explode. It appeared afterwards as his shouting, in a verbal or auditory channel. The dreambody, then, is a multi-channelled information sender asking you to receive its message in many ways and noticing how its information appears over and over again in dreams and body symptoms.

Though the patient had been on the verge of death when he started his work with Mindell, he recovered enough to leave the hospital and put his new self-knowledge to work. He lived several years longer and during this time he changed his life through his new-found ability to express himself. Hearing a story like this one, you begin to understand how Mindell can say, "A terrifying symptom is usually your greatest dream trying to come true."

Evy McDonald, whom you read about in the preceding chapter, has a similar view of the relationship between symptom and psyche, which she expresses in her article "The Body Is Like a Movie Screen." Having quoted Dr. Irving Oyle's saying that your state of health mirrors your state of mind, she takes that metaphor one step further to analyze her own case:

My body seemed like more than a simple mirror, however; it was a movie screen where my real attitudes and feelings, acknowledged or withheld, were actively portrayed. . . . If we don't like what is being shown on the movie screen . . . the only real solution is to change the reel in the projector. And so it is with our bodies. They are powerful senders of messages and can alert us to our real thoughts about ourselves. In the theater of my own mind and body the choices I had were: to leave (die); to work solely on my body (the screen) through physical therapy, special diets, medical treatments, or alternative therapies; and/or to put a new reel in the projector—i.e. to transform my thoughts about my body. As long as the beliefs of unattractiveness and undesirability were the support pilings for the stage of my life, there was no possibility for any experiential and/or physical shift to occur. My thoughts were both the judge and the jailer which kept my experience of my body imprisoned. Most of us have heard the phrase, "You are what you eat." In my view, it is more accurate to say, "You become what you think."

Most of the time illness is not a premeditated act; *all* of the time there is some relationship between an illness and our thoughts. Nothing happens onto us; *we* are the happeners. The mind and body work together, with the body being the screen where the movie is shown.

You have already heard how Evy wrote a new script for her life by sitting before a mirror every day, learning to love herself. You too can put a new reel in the projector by communicating with your inner self. Meditation, relaxation, visualization, direct verbalizations and feelings are just some of the ways to initiate the communication, as you will discover in the next chapter.

It is this intangible thing, love, love in many forms, which enters into every therapeutic relationship. It is an element of which the physician may be the carrier, the vessel. And it is an element which binds and heals, which comforts and restores, which works what we have to call—for now—miracles.

—KARL MENNINGER, *The Vital Balance*

Communicating with Your Body

Having talked about how to receive messages from the inner self, I now want to explain how to send messages back to it. From the responses to *Love, Medicine and Miracles,* I have learned a great deal of practical information about how to direct symbolic messages and suggestions to the unconscious, and how meaningful they can be. The fact is, for better and often unfortunately for worse, we communicate with our inner selves all the time. And so do those around us—especially people in positions of trust, power or authority, like parents, teachers and doctors. We need to make sure that the message that gets through is a healing one.

Communications to the inner self take many forms. Our feelings are our primary means of communication with the inner self. Feelings aroused by the touch of someone's hand, the sound of music, the smell of a flower, a beautiful sunset, a work of art, love, laughter, hope and faith—all work on both the unconscious and the conscious aspects of the self, and they have physiological consequences as well. Even the animals we take into our homes can play a role in our physical well-being. A recent report by the National Institutes of Health summarized findings from a number of researchers showing that pets can influence heart rate and blood pressure.

Probably the most direct and volitional of the communications that affect us are the words we say to ourselves. But how do they get through, how does verbal language get translated into physiological events? According to psychologist Jeanne Achterberg in her book *Imagery in Healing,* images are the bridge. Achterberg feels that messages in the form of words "have to undergo translation by the right hemisphere into nonverbal, or imagerial, terminology before they can be understood by the involuntary, or autonomic nervous system."

Once we have formed a mental image of whatever the words we say to ourselves are naming or describing, these words can become meaningful messages to the internal environment of our bodies. Given that we have a lot of control over the word-inspired images we create, we should make sure that we always use them to paint affirming, life-enhancing pictures. The self-fulfilling prophecy is a reality that we might as well turn to our advantage. Sometimes we can make it a physiological reality.

In support of her ideas, Achterberg cites studies showing the impact of the imagination on physiological processes as varied as salivation, heart rate, muscle tension, skin resistance, blood glucose, gastrointestinal activity, blister formation, blood pressure and respiration. This catalog of effects includes both autonomic nervous system changes, which we normally think of as being outside conscious control, and musculoskeletal system changes. A comparable list of healing processes, expanding on the work of hypnotherapist T. X. Barber, appears in Ernest Rossi's book *The Psychobiology of Mind-Body Healing.* All the changes listed can occur in response to the kind of imaging that takes place in the mind when it is asked to mentally picture (or hear, smell, touch or taste) some event or object. How suggestion puts these changes into motion remains unclear—perhaps by alterations in blood flow, as Barber suggests, or neuropeptide levels. But that they do occur is indisputable.

However, because most of us don't really take the power of word images seriously, we often cripple ourselves with negative messages, from ourselves or our authority figures, instead of empowering ourselves with positive ones. Words can kill as well as heal, a fact more physicians need to be aware of. Cardiologist Bernard Lown tells two stories that illustrate this point in his introduction to Norman Cousins's book *The Healing Heart*. They illustrate why communication is so vital and why it should be taught in medical school.

In one instance a doctor was making hospital rounds with his students and referred to a patient's condition, tricuspid stenosis, by its initials. He announced, "Here is a classic case of TS," for the benefit of Lown and the other residents in the room, and then exited. As soon as he left, Lown noticed that the woman was in great distress, her pulse elevated, her previously clear lungs filling up with fluid. When he asked her why she was so upset, she told him it was because the distinguished doctor had declared her a "Terminal Situation." All reassurances to the contrary proved useless—the great doctor had spoken after all—and she could not be persuaded that her problem was relatively minor. By nightfall the woman had gone into acute heart failure and died.

In later years Lown was on rounds with his students when he pointed out a critically ill patient who had what he called a "wholesome, very loud third-sound gallop" to his heart. In medical terminology a gallop rhythm means that the heart is failing because the cardiac muscle is badly damaged and dilated. There was nothing further to be done for this man, and little hope for his recovery. Nonetheless he did make an amazing return to health, and explained why some months later: As soon as he heard Dr. Lown describe his heart as having a "wholesome gallop," he said, he figured that meant it had a strong kick to it, like a horse, and he then became optimistic about his condition and knew that he would recover—which he did.

Perhaps most dramatic of all is the story a woman told me in a letter about her aunt. The aunt was diagnosed with a malignant brain tumor and given three months to live. In desperation she went to Mexico for laetrile, returned home and was doing beautifully a year later, having gone back to work and started driving a car again. She felt great. Then one day she ran into her original doctor, who expressed shock and surprise that she was still alive. When she told him what she had done, he indignantly proclaimed laetrile quackery and berated her for wasting her time and money and said he could show her proof. She died that night. What did he have against success and her being alive?

Obviously there is a moral here for doctors and all other people in the healing professions, and it certainly has nothing to do with the relative merits of laetrile. If the power of belief has enabled something to work for someone, I'm not about to use the authority of my profession to destroy its benefits. I know that hope and faith can sometimes provide patients with options that extend their lives when conventional medicine can do nothing. The quacks of the world are well aware of this, too, and have stepped into the vacuum that doctors, with their exclusive reliance on the mechanics of disease, have allowed to exist. Doctors need to learn the vacuum can be filled by them with a hope and a prayer.

Actually, doctors like the one described above do worse than leave a vacuum—they fill it with negative messages. When their medicines are ineffective and they can't cure, they become frustrated and destructive. What do we as physicians have against success, and why must we kill anecdotes? I ask of every physician, please, when an anecdote walks into your office, don't kill it. If people are successful doing things outside your belief system, accept them and love them, even if you don't agree with their choices. In that way patients will feel comfortable and cared for by the medical profession and be able to make use all of the options available to them. They can tolerate disagreement, but not destructiveness.

It can take a very strong, self-reliant patient to reject the words of a destructive physician, and many people, like the woman you just read about, are unable to do so. But recently I heard from someone who had devised his own way of dealing with the negatives that the doctors and nurses kept sending his way. Diagnosed with a rare form of cancer and told he would be dead in three months to a year, he qualified for an experimental chemotherapy program. Instead of encouraging him, however, medical personnel seem to have gone out of their way to stress that his chances were small, the radiation he was undergoing useless, and he was sure to have terrible side effects from the chemo (this last at a time when he still hadn't shown any, so a nurse went to the trouble to point out that "sometimes it takes longer for symptoms to show in some people"). In self-defense, he taped to his wall "Edwards' Credo," addressed to "any new physician on my case":

WHAT I KNOW:

1. I have a bad cancer. I read my protocol and know it may kill me.
2. I know how bad this cancer is—I used to be in hospital management.
3. I know all treatments involve risk, including death.
4. Many people die from what I have. I know the statistics.

THEREFORE:

1. There is no need to repeat the above. I have heard it many times from well-meaning people who feel it is the physician's duty to level with the patient on the dark side, particularly when I have appeared too hopeful at times.
2. Good thoughts, friendship, advice, encouragement, hope, love, energy, smiles are all gratefully accepted. Please leave pessimism, downers, bitterness, pity and negative preachiness at the door, without of course being dishonest.

PLEASE KNOW:

1. I know you can help me in a positive way if you want to. But please remember that my life belongs to me, those I love and those who love me.
2. My wife and I are convinced that good medicine is more than highly important knowledge and skills, chemicals and protoplasm. We also believe in the body's mental powers and immunological abilities as well as the spiritual. We need all the help we can get to bring all of these resources to bear on my problem and to help you help me.
3. I have much to live for and I am trying very hard to do whatever I can mentally and physically to make whatever you prescribe or do as effective as possible.
4. I personally know of people with what I have who have done well despite the poor odds. I intend to also, by buying as

much good time as I can for me and those I love. Perhaps we can do even more. That is why I am here. Otherwise I would not be.

5. There is hope in my heart. Do not do anything to encourage its replacement with pessimism or bitterness, for it will inevitably lessen my comfort level and worsen my condition.

I wish both doctors and patients would read "Edwards' Credo"—doctors so they'll stop undoing the potential benefits of their medicines with the destructiveness of their words, and patients so they'll be inspired to defy those doctors who persist in sentencing their patients to death.

DIAGNOSES, PROGNOSES AND PROTOCOLS

In case the spoken word isn't destructive enough, the written word, as it appears in medical texts, statistical analyses and treatment protocols, might be enough to finish you off. A recent letter did a good job of describing the devastation that can be wrought when the medical profession launches this triple assault against a patient.

First there was the terror this man felt as he listened "to the sometimes hourly voluntary reports of the younger doctors" who insisted on trying to interpret his test results for him, and then his despair when he was given a diagnosis of metastatic oat-cell cancer of the lung, which would leave him with somewhere between ten and thirty days to live. To this he had a pretty normal reaction:

My main objective was to get home, straighten out my financial affairs, see to it that my will, insurances etc. were in order and properly organized so that my lawyer could see that everything was taken care of for my family. . . . I intended to spend those last few days with my family and friends, and then take a hunting trip to the woods, with my favorite 12 gauge and one Heublein's Manhattan so I could depart this vale of tears without messing up the house.

Another case of a man sentenced to death by his doctors, until he was given a new lease on life by the good efforts of a friend and a concerned oncologist, who sent him to one of my workshops. And what was it he got there? "A purpose, a goal, self-participation, a chance . . . inspiration to control my destiny, perhaps to go on to help others, undoubtedly to gain more time."

Now I'm no magician, and there are no mysterious ceremonies performed at these workshops; nor do I know what became of this man, because he wrote to me only one month after the events he described, so I certainly can't claim a miracle cure or even, without knowing more facts, an impressive remission, though he says in his letter that he is doing well on his combined program of chemotherapy, guided imagery and meditation, diet and exercise.

The only thing I would lay claim to on my behalf is the ability to inspire hope in people. I gave the gentleman who wrote the letter a chance to be heroic and he accepted it. He decided not to give up, and he felt good about his decision. To me that's miracle enough—especially now that we're beginning to discover something about the physiological consequences of optimism. When you think of the fate to which this man had consigned himself after he was given his diagnosis, you have to wonder about doctors who worry about giving their patients "false hope." This is another of those cases in which "false no hope"—the kind that makes you want to blow your brains out—is the real problem. I believe in using hope to facilitate change in the healing of lives. Years ago I felt like other physicians about "deceiving" people into getting well, and I almost canceled my first ECaP group. I told them to go home—they were getting well for illegitimate reasons. Now it's ten years later and I have no difficulty using all the tools at my command, including hope, to help people live.

The negative messages in this man's experience did not end with his prognosis. Like so many critically ill people, he was put on a treatment protocol that was described exclusively in destructive terms. The document in this case was a U.S. Department of Health and Human Services pamphlet entitled *Chemotherapy and You.* "That's great reading to be handed to you when you have been told you have cancer; if that don't send you over the edge, nothing will," as this patient put it.

You might just try reading a chemotherapy protocol. There is not a single word on it suggesting that it will help— only destructive information. About the only thing on it that is even neutral is the physical description of the medication. It's no wonder so many people feel they'd rather die a quick death than submit to the tortures described in these documents, and no wonder that those brave souls who do submit so often proceed to suffer from virtually every one of the possible side effects that have been so vividly described for them.

Any good psychotherapist knows how destructive such negativity can be. If the people who write these protocols were exposed to the works of psychiatrist and hypnotherapist Milton Erickson, they would know how to get across the same information while putting it in a context of positive affirmations and suggestions, so that not only the medicine, but the protocol

---

ADRIAMYCIN®
(doxorubicin)

What It Looks Like:
Red fluid after dissolved.

How It Is Given:
Injection into vein.

Common Side Effects:
Nausea and vomiting may occur 1 to 3 hours after the drug is given and may last up to 24 hours.

Complete hair loss generally occurs 2 or more weeks after treatment begins and is not permanent.

Discolored urine (pink to red) may occur up to 48 hours after the drug is given.

Reduced blood counts occur 1 to 2 weeks after treatment.

Less Common Side Effects:
Heart muscle damage may occur so studies are done before the drug is given and at certain times throughout treatment to assess heart function. Report any shortness of breath or ankle swelling.

Fatigue, weakness, the "blahs."

Mouth sores may occur.

The drug can be irritating to tissue if it leaks out of the vein. Tell the person giving the drug if you feel any burning, pain or stinging while the drug is being given. If the area of injection becomes red and swollen after the injection, notify your doctor.

itself, would be converted into an instrument of hope, therefore of healing.

SUBLIMINAL LISTENING

Suggestion acts on the unconscious as well as the conscious mind. From my experiences with unconscious patients, I have long been a believer in the ability of people in coma, asleep or under anesthesia to hear meaningful words, and I always go on the assumption that anything said in their presence has the potential to affect them. Since hearing is probably the last of the senses to go as we lose consciousness, there is nothing farfetched about the idea that many seemingly insensate people do hear.

As explained by Henry L. Bennett, a psychologist in the Department of Anesthesiology at the University of California who has done much of the research in this area, "Even under adequate anesthesia, the auditory pathways in the brain may not be touched, up to and including the auditory cortex, where meaning registers." Once they regain consciousness, people may not be aware of remembering what was said when they were under anesthesia, but that doesn't mean that they didn't hear it or that they aren't affected by what they heard.

The same holds true for patients in coma. The information operates at an unconscious level and can affect subsequent behavior, attitudes and health. An interesting comparison of thirty patients that appeared in *The Lancet* indicated that talking to and otherwise stimulating people in coma may even make a life and death difference. All sixteen of the comatose patients who were spoken to and touched as part of an "environmental enrichment program" recovered, whereas eleven out of fourteen comparable patients who did not receive such stimulation died.

Studies like this reveal that there are a variety of ways of communicating with people who are not conscious, including touch. Talking and touching are both forms of "environmental enrichment" that we can use to change the internal chemical and neurological environment in ways that are conducive to healing and growth.

I know this not just from studies I've read but from many firsthand accounts. One recent letter from a Methodist minister I found particularly touching. He writes about an eighty-year-old member of his church who had barely survived a house fire and was not expected to recover because of the damage done to her lungs.

> Perhaps a week after the fire I found her in a coma, totally unresponsive. . . . I had a strong feeling she was dying and that I would not see her alive again.
>
> Ruby was a grandmotherly type person who always baked cookies for the church to use with the children in Sunday School. . . . I suddenly got an inspiration. I took her hand in mine and in rather a loud and firm voice said, "Ruby, I think you've given up and you're ready to die. You can't do that! If you die, who is going to bake all those cookies at Christmastime for the children at Sunday School, and who is going to bake cookies for my children? We need you to get well and bake cookies."
>
> The next day she was more responsive and a little stronger. Soon she was eating. Eventually she got back home in time to bake cookies for that next Christmas. Several years later . . . my wife and I decided to call on Ruby. . . . She got to talking about the fire and how sick she had been afterwards. She said, "You know, I was so sick that I know I had given up and was ready to die. But I suddenly had the feeling, no I can't die. I must get well and come back to bake more cookies."

Though he never told her what he had said to her in the hospital room and was self-conscious about the episode for a long time, he now follows his instincts and talks to (as well as prays with) unconscious patients whenever he ministers to them.

Surgeon David Cheek has been studying the phenomenon of awareness under anesthesia ("unconscious perception") for several decades. In a review of the professional literature on the subject, he cites such studies as the one in which an anesthetist delivered a customized message something like the following to each of 1500 patients as they neared the end of their operations: "Mr. Smith, your gallbladder has now been successfully removed. No serious disease was found. You will have no pain in the area of your operation. The tube in your nose is there so that you will not be sick. Therefore you will not be sick, and the tube in your nose will not bother you."

Fully half the patients who received these messages required no postoperative medication for pain. Similar studies on smaller groups of people showed even better results. Other studies have shown the effectiveness of suggesting to anesthetized patients that they will not bleed during surgery, or that they will relax their pelvic muscles after surgery and have no difficulty voiding. A recent article in *The Lancet* shows that positive suggestions in the operating room lead not only to less discomfort after surgery but to earlier discharge as well. Anesthetists have begun to observe the value of making similar suggestions to patients in a preoperative visit, too, preferably the day before the procedure, then reinforcing them during the operation.

According to Cheek, for healing messages to be heeded by the patient under anesthesia, they must come from a meaningful source—that is, from the surgeon or the anesthetist—and must be delivered at the right moment, which would be as the surgery is coming to a close. I think that that is too limited. My common practice is to make use of what is known about patient suggestibility from the moment I enter the operating room. I talk to patients while they are still conscious. As the anesthetist puts the mask on the patient, I explain how we all wear masks in the operating room and that they are nothing to be afraid of. I heard about one woman who sat up on the operating table and asked everyone to remove their masks and introduce themselves to her. This was very effective in allaying her fear. Other patients may respond to a paradoxical approach: I had a woman in the operating room who kept saying how wonderful everybody was and how she was being taken care of by such nice people, until finally I leaned over and whispered in her ear, "I know them, and they're not nice people." At that moment she broke out into a big grin and her fear disappeared.

After my patients are relaxed, I instruct them to divert the blood away from the operative site so that they won't bleed; I tell them that when they awaken they will feel comfortable, thirsty and hungry and will have no difficulty voiding; and I give them whatever other messages might be appropriate to their particular situation. When the anesthesiologist says, "You'll be going out," I may talk about going out on a date, so that the image becomes something positive. I stand by, holding my patients' hands and gently guiding them into the anesthesia with soothing words and healing music. Afterward, some of my patients have even asked if I operated with one hand, because they had the impression I continued to hold their hands after they fell asleep.

I keep talking to patients throughout the operation, telling them how things are progressing and enlisting their cooperation if I need it. For example, I may suggest that they stop bleeding, or lower their blood pressure or pulse. People who have worked with me in the operating room know how effective these suggestions can be. One day, as I was preparing to leave after finishing an operation, the anesthesiologist tore off a foot or two of electrocardiogram and said to me, "Here, you fix it." I looked and saw that the patient, who was still anesthetized, was having an arrhythmia, so I whispered in his ear, "You are on a swing. It's going up and back, in a nice and steady, even rhythm. Up and back, slow and steady." And his cardiogram reverted to a normal rhythm.

Often when a patient's pulse rate is too high during an operation I'll simply say, "We'd like your pulse to be 86." I always pick a specific number because I want everyone to see the pulse go down to that exact number. How does it do that? Again, we don't yet understand how the body converts healing suggestions to reality. But something in the body hears these messages and knows how to respond to them—if only we will give them to our patients (and ourselves).

It was ten years ago that I began using these techniques in the operating room to show how effective they could be. The first reactions of my colleagues were negative, because people don't like change. They respond like addicts being asked to give up their addiction. But the nurses began to notice the difference in the patients, and they began supporting me and my work. Recently I had a great compliment from one of these nurses. When I walked into the operating room Kathy saw me and said, "Oh, I'm glad it's you and not one of the other lunatics."

If I had had any doubts about patients' ability to register events when they are unconscious, they would have been dispelled by the experience I had with Bobbie when she was being operated on. I stayed with her while the anesthesia was being administered, and of course held her hand until it took effect. But when I wanted to leave so that I wouldn't make the anesthesiologist and the surgeon uncomfortable with my presence, I discovered that I could not get my hand out of Bobbie's because she was holding on so tightly. She has no memory of this because of the medication she received, but even in her unconscious state, our love for each other and the fact that we are meant to be a team was being expressed.

A recent experience we had during a plane trip shows how much awareness people have when they are asleep, too. It is our habit always to hold hands during takeoff, but on this occasion our plane was delayed on the ground a long while, and Bobbie had fallen asleep by the time it was finally ready to leave. I felt deprived that I was not going to have her hand in mine as we took off, but I didn't want to wake her, so I didn't reach for her. However, just as the plane started out on the runway, her hand came out from under the blanket and grasped mine. I thought to myself how nice it was that she had awakened in time for us to hold hands as usual. About an hour later she turned to me and said, "I feel sad. I was asleep and didn't hold your hand when we took off." I realized then that she had been fast asleep, but that her unconscious had directed her hand to do the appropriate thing, and I told her what had happened. And was she surprised.

SELECTIVE (AND UNSELECTIVE) PERCEPTION

A recent study on how the mind and body react to unconsciously processed words supports what I've been saying—that what we know beneath the level of consciousness can have an effect on our lives. Yale psychiatrist Dr. Bruce Wexler and his collaborator Dr. Gary Schwartz used a special computer to enable their subjects to hear two paired words simultaneously, one emotionally neutral, the other positive or negative. The subjects did not know they were hearing two words, and half the time reported having heard the emotional word, half the time the neutral word. But often the words they were not consciously aware of having heard continued to live on in the unconscious. For example, one person reported hearing the word "door" when both "gore" and "door" were spoken. However, when asked to allow his mind to wander afterward, he described someone walking through a door with blood on him.

Brain waves and electrical activity in muscles that control smiling and frowning were also measured after the pairings, and according to Wexler the results showed that the "response to unconsciously processed negative words was just as great as to consciously processed negative words."

Another finding in this study was that people classified as high anxious, low anxious or repressors (on the basis of personality tests) had different physical responses to the unconsciously processed negative words. Both low-anxious subjects and repressors reported feeling little anxiety after the negative words that they were not aware of hearing. This was in fact borne out by measurements of tension in the muscles of the low-anxious group, but not by muscle tension measurements of the repressor group. Repressors, like the high-anxious group, measured even higher in muscular tension when they did not consciously register the negative word than when they did. Wexler thinks that this evidence of physical tension may suggest ways in which repressed, unconsciously experienced emotions live on in the body and can lead to psychosomatic illness.

Some intriguing research conducted at Cambridge University may have a bearing on how certain experiences that don't reach conscious awareness can nonetheless be a part of us. Psychologist Anthony Marcel studied people who were blind due to a stroke or brain damage rather than damage to their eye. When asked to point to an object placed in front of them, they would, of course, say that they could not see it, but once they were talked into trying, they could do it with amazing accuracy. This ability in certain blind people to locate objects is called "blindsight." Marcel's explanation, based on extensive research, is that their vision is in fact unimpaired, but their awareness of vision has been damaged. Somehow they don't know that they can see, because the area of the mind that controls awareness is not getting the message. People with this condition, which relates to occipital lobe damage, can be retrained to see. The brain can relearn. New parts can be taught to assume the function of damaged areas. I know of one young lady who was blind and is now in college, seeing normally.

The phenomenon of partial awareness was noted in a completely different context by hypnosis researcher Ernest Hilgard. He observed a classroom demonstration of hypnosis in which a student who'd been told he would be temporarily deaf showed no signs of a reaction to a gunshot and other loud sounds. But when the instructor whispered to the student that perhaps "some part" of him might be able to hear and that if this was the case he could indicate it by raising one of his fingers, the student did so, much to his own surprise, as he had no idea why his finger had suddenly risen.

I myself witnessed a quite startling example of selective perception in my office one day. I was performing minor surgery on a man with whom I was having a very intense discussion on a subject of great interest to us both. After I was well into the surgery, I noticed that in the corner of the room the nurse was frantically waving her arms and pointing to the syringe with the anesthetic, which I had never used. When I asked the patient if he was comfortable, he said yes, so we kept on with our discussion and I completed the procedure without his ever feeling any pain, despite the lack of anesthetic. He had a 2-inch incision in his back but was so distracted by our conversation that the pain that would ordinarily accompany such a procedure never entered his awareness. I told him afterward that we both had been hypnotized during the procedure. We both laughed.

I've had a personal experience with this phenomenon too. There was a time when my back was giving me a great deal of pain because of an injury. On days when I had to be in the operating room, I would be terribly uncomfortable—until I started performing surgery. Once the surgery got under way, I became so absorbed in what I was doing that I forgot all about the pain, even during operations that lasted for many hours. As soon as my part in the operation was completed, however, my back would start to hurt again, and sometimes I even had to lie down awhile before leaving the operating room.

Unfortunately, the ability of the mind to block out certain phenomena may not work when we are under anesthesia, which can result in great psychological distress to patients when the surgical team refuses to acknowledge that it is possible to hear and process information while unconscious. It's not just a matter of their failing to give the patient healing messages during and after the operation. They may do the opposite, wisecracking and even making abusive remarks about the patient who lies unconscious on the operating table, or offering their opinions about the patient's dismal prognosis. In our conscious lives, selective perception often allows us to deal with material that is painful for us to hear. But under anesthesia, these protective mechanisms may cease to work, leaving us defenseless. Although most patients never consciously remember the destructive remarks that enter the unconscious at such times, a number of psychological studies have shown that they may suffer ill effects from them nonetheless, with results ranging from postoperative pain and slow healing to prolonged depression.

But change is in the air. Many times I'm asked how other doctors accept what I've been doing. One answer is that that doesn't concern me; it's how my parents accept it that concerns me. The other answer is that while there is still a lot of resistance in the medical profession to things not taught in medical school, the fact that I've frequently been asked to speak at anesthesia and general surgery grand rounds within the past year indicates to me that the resistance is dying down.

What I've learned over the years is that acceptance comes with success. You can't convert addictive behavior or beliefs with statistics. So I don't confront people, but in the course of my working day I show them techniques that are successful.

One recent convert to these ideas, a cardiac surgeon, was introduced to them by his wife, who had attended one of my workshops. He called home one night to say that he wouldn't be able to get back in time for dinner because the patient he had just operated on couldn't be taken off the heart-lung machine. His wife said, "That's probably because for hours she's been listening to you worrying about whether she'll make it. You go back and do what Bernie would do and tell her she'll be fine." She then went out shopping, and when she returned her husband was sitting in the living room with his feet up, talking to the children. "What happened?" she asked. "Well," he said, "I took your advice and gave her positive messages, and she got better." At a recent meeting I attended, an operating room nurse told me about when she was participating in an emergency replacement of a ruptured aortic aneurysm and the patient continued to bleed. She asked the surgeons if they had ever heard of Dr. Bernie Siegel and they said yes. "Then why don't you talk to the patient and ask him to help you?" They responded, "*You* do it." So she went to the head of the o.r. table, told the patient the situation and asked for help in stopping the bleeding. "Within three to five minutes it stopped and he did beautifully post-op."

WHAT YOU CAN DO FOR YOURSELF IN THE OPERATING ROOM

If neither your surgeon nor your anesthetist is willing to talk you through your operation, I can only suggest that you take a tape recorder into the operating room with you. You could bring in one of my tapes to play, or a tape with specific messages appropriate for your particular circumstances. You can do the taping yourself or ask someone close to you to do it—any friend or family member whose voice would be meaningful and carry the weight of authority. Use music too, preferably soothing classical music, perhaps Pachelbel's Canon (especially the version played by Daniel Kobialka, which you can find out about through ECaP) or something that has helped you feel peaceful in the past. Some patients have reported that when their music was played in the operating room, the medical personnel who thought it was nonsense changed their minds and said they would use it in the future because it made them feel less fatigued. At the hospitals in New Haven, every operating room has a tape recorder, and the atmosphere is improved.

Do not be afraid to assert yourself about something you feel will be good for you. A letter came the other day from a woman who said that when she was on her way into the operating room a nurse saw her tape recorder and told her it would have to go. "If it goes, so do I!" the lady told her, so she got past the first obstacle. But the nurse warned her to just wait until the surgeon arrived. When the surgeon came in he said, "What the hell is that paraphernalia!" When she told him it was her Bernie Siegel meditation tape, he ordered the nurse to get rid of it. The patient told him it was important to her to be able to keep it, but surgeons are used to getting their way, and he announced, "This is my operation and the tape goes!" The patient declared that it was her operation, too, and if the tape didn't go in the o.r. she wouldn't either—to which he replied, "Okay, but keep the volume down."

If patients keep insisting on their rights, more and more health care professionals will come around, especially when they see the positive results. I love hearing from patients who say they went into the operating room and told the surgeon they were not going to bleed and were pooh-poohed—until they proved themselves under the knife. One woman said that her surgeon came in to see her afterward to tell her that he had been so impressed by her lack of bleeding that he brought six other surgeons in to watch the operation. "I'm going to tell my other patients to do that, too," he said. "Well it isn't that easy," she replied. But many people find that if they take the trouble to prepare themselves mentally before surgery, visualizing a bloodless procedure, it is *just* that easy. Many surgeons I know have also used this technique when they themselves were undergoing surgery, and now they really believe. An example of this I met recently was a woman who had extensive transplant surgery and received three units of blood when someone else received two hundred after similar surgery.

ALTERED STATES

Though we are still only beginning to understand the mechanisms by which mental suggestion is translated into physiological reality, the evidence is strong that there is some supervising intelligence within that presides over such changes. It tells the blood where to flow, directs the lymphocytes and phagocytes and gives whatever directions are necessary to get the job done.

We were built for survival, if we will just give and receive love messages. How did we lose the ability to do that? How did we lose our feelings of self-love? I think we lost them by listening to false messages from authorities. But our lovable nature is still there, buried deep within us. It is this perfect core self that presides over our healing processes. In Joan Borysenko's eloquent words (from *Minding the Body, Mending the Mind*), this core self contains "an essential humanity whose nature is peace and whose expression is thought and whose action is unconditional love. When we identify with that inner core, respecting and honoring it in others as well as ourselves, we experience healing in every area of our lives."

However, most of us are in touch with the inner self only intermittently, if at all. It's not located in the conscious mind; in fact, it may be obscured by the fears and concerns of consciousness. For me, this superintelligence, this perfect core self, seems to fit in with the neuropeptide theories advanced by Candace Pert and other like-minded researchers. Neuropeptides as the locus where mind and body meet and cross over, the expression of the self's DNA, the carrier of the loving superintelligence of energy—this map of reality satisfies both the scientist and the mystic in me.

I first got to know this perfect core self through meditation. But however you get there, you'll know when you've arrived at that still quiet place at the center of your being where mind and body are unified. "It's like coming home," Larry LeShan quoted one man as saying in his book *How to Meditate*. And home is where the healing can begin—within your true, unique and authentic self.

I believe there are many ways of communicating with the inner self. Words, music, feelings, progressive relaxation, yoga, meditation, hypnotic trance, visualization and prayer can all help you find your way home. You can put some of these into action with little preparation beyond a basic commitment to do the work. Others, obviously, do require some special training, because they depend for their effectiveness on your reaching a particular kind of altered state—a state in which the unconscious can be accessed directly.

Some researchers believe that these states are "altered" in the sense that they reverse our usual reliance on left-brain logical thought in favor of right-brain imagery and immediacy of experience. They theorize that this switch facilitates the communication of healing messages from our conscious selves to the internal environment of our bodies. As Jeanne Achterberg explains, "The specific functions that have been attributed to the right hemisphere, and the connections between it and other brain and body components, support the premise that images can and do carry information from the conscious fore to the far reaches of the cells."

Questions of left- and right-brain dominance aside, we *feel* altered in these states because in all of them, whatever their differences from one another, our everyday mode of thinking is abandoned. The ceaselessly busy conscious mind, which we normally identify as the "I," is stilled, and in the resulting quiet we attend to inner rather than outer events. As we stop letting the external environment control us, we experience a trance-like absorption in the moment. Perhaps as a result of this change, we enjoy an access to the inner, unconscious self that routine daily life does not allow.

Methods for achieving altered states are described in the literature of most of the great religions and cultures throughout history. Dr. Herbert Benson of Harvard Medical School says he has found them in sources as varied as Chuang Tzu's rendering of Taoist philosophy in the fourth century B.C., Mahayana Buddhist texts from the first century A.D., the writings of early Christian and Jewish mystics and, more recently, the poems and prose of the English romantic poets who aspired to what Wordsworth called "a happy stillness of the mind." Sufis, yogis and shamans have their own versions.

But where the mystics and meditators of the world sought unity with God or a sense of oneness with the universe, the Harvard research project headed up by Benson in the late sixties was seeking only to lower blood pressure. Eventually, thanks to practitioners of Transcendental Meditation who were eager to submit themselves to scientific study in order to demonstrate the benefits of TM, the Harvard group discovered what Benson in his ground-breaking work of the same title called the "relaxation response." This book captured the interest of a secular, scientific age by showing that the practice of certain spiritual disciplines that elicited the relaxation response resulted in a constellation of quite specific physiological effects.

RELAXATION RESPONSE TECHNIQUES FOR PHYSICAL AND SPIRITUAL HEALING

The physiology of the relaxation response is what distinguishes it from what we usually mean when we talk about relaxing. The body both feels and is in better balance when the relaxation response is evoked, because: Heart rate, metabolism, oxygen consumption and respiration slow down, blood pressure and muscle tension are lowered, and brain activity is characterized by alpha waves, which are slower in frequency than what is usual in a waking state.

Whether your motivation is partly spiritual or strictly physiological, relaxation techniques can be a great boost to your health, as well as your peace of mind, so I recommend them as preventive medicine. Don't wait until you're sick to enjoy the benefits of a stronger immune system and lower blood pressure. But if you are sick, you should know that there is an ever-expanding list of medical conditions in which relaxation techniques, with or without accompanying visualizations, have proved helpful.

Relaxation has been helpful for cardiac patients. Dr. Dean Ornish, a cardiologist who is director of the Preventive Medicine Research Institute in San Francisco, is conducting a study on the impact of life-style changes on heart disease. He has shown that relaxation training as one part of a program of overall life-style change is able to lower cholesterol levels and improve the flow of blood to the heart. This has been demonstrated by angiographic studies comparing a control group with a group that received the training. Relaxation heals from within; bypass operations may merely bypass the real problems in your life.

Joan Borysenko's Body/Mind groups have shown that many diabetics are able to use relaxation to reduce their need for insulin. Relaxation training has also helped asthma sufferers, according to Dr. George Fuller-von Bozzay of the Biofeedback Institute of San Francisco and Dr. Paul Lehrer of Rutgers Medical School, and people with chronic as well as acute pain, according to more people than I can list here. You probably already know about the successes oncologist O. Carl Simonton and psychologist Stephanie Matthews-Simonton have had with cancer patients who used visualization to enhance immune function. This very brief listing doesn't begin to exhaust the possible medical benefits of relaxation and visualization techniques, but it does give an idea of their range.

You can read about how to elicit the relaxation response in Herbert Benson's book by that name or in his latest, *Your Maximum Mind,* both of which are excellent resources. Benson writes not only about transcendental meditation, which can create the specific mental and physiological state he calls relaxation, but about certain types of prayer, abdominal breathing and a number of other forms of passive mental concentration that focus the mind completely in the present. Other books on meditation and relaxation include Lawrence LeShan's *How to Meditate* and Joan Borysenko's *Minding the Body, Mending the Mind.* I have also provided some sample meditations at the back of this book, which you might want to record for yourself. Or you can write or call ECaP (at 1302 Chapel Street, New Haven, Connecticut 06511; 203-865-8392) for further information on audio and video tapes.

Many meditations begin with a progressive relaxation exercise in order to free the body of any physical tensions that might distract the mind. Progressive relaxation was first described in the 1930s by Dr. Edmond Jacobson, who based it on a yoga technique. It usually involves sitting or lying down and taking a five- to ten-minute tour of all the muscle groups in your body, during which you tighten and relax each one, beginning at the feet and ending with the face and neck (or vice versa). The idea is that, by consciously creating tension, then letting it go, you learn what both tense and relaxed states feel like, and can then use this sense memory to achieve simple muscle relaxation at will. Many people practiced in this technique can use it to achieve a relaxed state almost immediately. Progressive relaxation may be done whenever you feel a mounting sense of tension. It provides a wonderful respite from the pressures of the day. Instructions for this kind of relaxation were included in the appendix of *Love, Medicine and Miracles,* so I won't repeat them here.

I suggest you have four to six healing intervals in your day to destress yourself, using either progressive relaxation alone or relaxation combined with meditation, prayer or music. Keep in mind that whatever technique you use should above all be a way of alleviating the pressures of the day, not adding to them. Performance anxiety has no place in meditation and relaxation; they are not something to grade yourself on. If you find that they are becoming just one more thing to fail or succeed at, then you should use other techniques to create a relaxed state.

It's better not to do your meditations right after meals or before bed, as those are times when you are likely to slip from a meditative state directly into sleep. Ideally, meditation relaxes you but does not put you to sleep; in fact it leaves you much more alert and focused. The lulling of the conscious mind that you do in meditation is only for the purpose of awakening the unconscious. This "allows the science of being naturally right to occur," as my friend chiropractor Jim Parker says. However, I know that many people go to sleep with my tapes, and that practice is not to be discouraged if it is difficult for you to relax enough to get to sleep without it. You will hear the tapes even in your sleep. I would only suggest that you use the tapes at other times, too, in order to get the full benefits of meditation.

For those nurses and doctors who are working in the hospital, I suggest going down to the chapel and sitting there quietly, several times during the day. This accomplishes many things. Among others, it changes the way you relate to the people you meet there as you deal with them later on: If you meditate or pray together with an x-ray technician, it is highly unlikely that you will berate that technician when you work together. So you change and relationships change.

The spiritual healing that occurs with meditation is at least as important as the physiological benefits, though more difficult to describe. Everybody's experience of it is different, ranging from general feelings of peacefulness to very specific insights into the dilemmas of individual lives. One woman wrote me a moving letter thanking me for the healing that occurred in her family life after she and her husband participated in a guided meditation at one of my workshops. When she asked her husband afterward why he had been crying, he explained that, as he got to that part of the meditation where one visualizes opening a chest to find a message, their daughter, who had died twenty-four hours after birth nearly three decades before, had appeared to him as a young woman. Her appearance signaled the beginning of a process of reconciliation with their daughter-in-law, whom he had not spoken to in the months since a bad family scene the preceding Christmas. He called her and ended up telling her that he loved her as the daughter he had lost, which was the beginning of their healing. A woman who had been abused during her childhood visualized her mother about to strike her again. She reached up, took her mother's hand and kissed it. They sat together and she learned why her mother had acted as she did, and healing occurred at that moment.

Ainslie Meares, an Australian doctor who specialized in a kind of intensive meditation work done with groups of cancer patients, described what he saw as the ultimate aim of meditation:

Not only is there a reduction in level of anxiety, and in some cases a regression of the cancer, but patients take away from these sessions a nonverbal understanding of many things, including, most importantly, life and death.

It is a genuine understanding, but is quite different in quality from any intellectual examination of such matters. It is a philosophical understanding, but at the same time beyond the logical meaning of words. . . . In general terms, there comes a sense that life and death are simply different facets of an underlying process.

Although Meares attributed this understanding of the "mysteries of life" to the particular kind of meditation he had his patients do, I quote his words because I think they are such a good description of what any of us can hope for as the end result of our meditative practice, whatever it may be.

When Meares talked about the spiritual growth he had witnessed in his patients, he was talking about what he called the "onflow," that is, the way in which the results of meditation spill over into one's life. Though this is a natural process, I know many people find it a struggle to carry over into their workday lives the centered awareness that they achieve while doing their meditation. An article I came across recently by one of the directors of the Stress Reduction and Relaxation Program at the University of Massachusetts Medical Center, Saki F. Santorelli, gives twenty-one tips on how to achieve this integration. I'll mention a few of them, each aimed at returning us for a brief moment or two to the kind of focused peacefulness attained in the meditative state:

1. Take a few minutes in the morning to be quiet and meditate—sit or lie down and be with yourself. . . . Gaze out the window, listen to the sounds of nature or take a slow, quiet walk.
2. Use your breaks to truly relax rather than simply "pause." Take a two to five minute walk, or sit at your desk and recoup.
3. Decide to "stop" for one to three minutes every hour during the workday. Become aware of your breathing and bodily sensations. Use it as a time to regroup and recoup.

4. Pay attention to the short walk to your car [at the end of the workday], breathing the crisp air. The feeling of the cold or warmth of your body, try to accept it rather than resist it. Listen to the sounds outside the office.
5. While your car is warming up, sit quietly, and consciously make the transition from work to home. Take a moment to simply be; enjoy it for a moment. Like most of us, you're heading into your next full-time job: home!
6. Change out of work clothes when you get home; it helps you to make a transition into your next "role." You can spare the five minutes to do this. Say hello to each of the family members; center yourself at home. If possible, make the time to take five to ten minutes to be quiet and still.

In general, even if you're in the best of health (especially if you want to stay that way), it's a good idea to call a time out for yourself whenever you're getting overwhelmed by the events of the day. A few minutes of quiet several times a day during which you relax and center yourself, focusing on the sensations you are experiencing in the present and the pleasures you don't usually take the time to enjoy, is all that's required.

From personal experience I know that these healing intervals can take many forms. They don't have to be formal meditations; sometimes running, for example, can accomplish the same thing. When I am outside on my early morning run and it is totally quiet, the only things I hear are my own inner voices and the sounds of the trees and the winds and the birds, all of us talking to each other. At times like that it is easy to understand why the Indians, in their closeness to nature, were so spiritual.

VISUALIZATION—AN IMAGING MEDITATION

Visualizations are particular kinds of meditations, which make use of imagery. You put your imagination to work to create images of what you are trying to achieve. These visualizations have been effective preparations for goals ranging from improved sports performance to natural childbirth, but readers of this book will probably be more interested in their application to health care, most specifically their potential for improving immune system function. Although relaxation alone has been shown to be effective in enhancing the body's defenses, Harvard psychologist Mary Jasnoski has done research demonstrating that when students trained in muscle relaxation were also given instruction in guided imagery, their defenses were even stronger.

Dr. Michael Samuels and Dr. Irving Oyle have written books that also contain persuasive evidence of immune system enhancement through visualization. Dr. O. Carl Simonton and Stephanie Matthews-Simonton popularized the use of visualization techniques for cancer patients in the book they wrote with James L. Creighton, *Getting Well Again,* which has inspired many doctors and other health care professionals as well as patients in the more than ten years since its publication. My own work with imagery began after attending a workshop they gave in 1978. These ideas are becoming so popular now that there are even special interactive video game tapes that put the visualization on screen, where young patients can play at conquering their diseases.

Many hypnotherapists consider mental imagery to be just another version of hypnosis—self- or autohypnosis. In an interview with Ernest Rossi, psychiatrist Milton Erickson talked about the early experiences that led him to his lifelong interest—both personal and professional—in the uses of autohypnosis. After nearly dying of polio when he was seventeen, he spent the next two years training himself in what he later came to realize was autohypnosis, so that he could learn to move and walk again. In his self-induced trance state, he would delve into his sense memories in order to re-experience mentally what movement had been like when he had full use of his muscles. The imagined movement taught his muscles how to move again.

Erickson used autohypnosis for pain control as well. Once he realized that the fatigue he felt after walking would get rid of his pain, he discovered that if he just imagined himself walking and then feeling fatigued, he could reduce his pain. In later years he used visions of scenes from his childhood, the period when his body was still sound and he was beginning to enjoy the beauties of nature, to rid himself of pain. He also used images from married life for this purpose. When troubled by arthritis, for example, he would go into an autohypnotic state in which he imagined the warm pressure of his wife's body against him replacing the pain. If you want to learn more about his philosophy and techniques, you might want to read *My Voice Will Go With You: The Teaching Tales of Milton Erickson,* by Dr. Sidney Rosen.

Few adults have Erickson's immense capacity for imaginative work, but most children do, because they haven't yet made the black and white distinction between "real" and "imaginary" that makes visualization so hard for many adults. At a conference sponsored by the Institute of Noetic Sciences, Dr. Karen Olness of the Children's Hospital in Cleveland described some of the work they've done with children who have chronic problems such as cancer, asthma, rheumatoid arthritis and hemophilia.

One young boy with hemophilia so severe that he was wheelchair-bound was instructed in the use of imagery to control his pain and, as he said, "stop my bleeds." He created a visualization in which he saw himself flying a plane through his blood vessels and dropping off loads of Factor 8, the blood-clotting factor that he was missing, wherever it was needed to control bleeding. Another child, a little boy who had to endure multiple operations, learned to use a biofeedback fingertip temperature monitor to help with pain control. Once he saw on the monitor that he could make his temperature go up by imagining himself sitting in the sun, he was on the way to understanding that he could control other body functions too. Besides pain and temperature control, the children have learned to control numerous autonomic processes, including galvanic skin resistance, blood pressure, transcutaneous tissue oxygen saturation and salivary immunoglobulin production.

Visualization can be hypnotically induced, under the guidance of a doctor, psychotherapist or hypnotherapist, or it can be self-induced. People with vivid imaginations who are familiar with meditative techniques will find that visualization comes very naturally to them. They may wish to purchase a tape with a guided imagery exercise suited to their needs, or to prepare such a tape themselves, perhaps using the sample visualization scripts provided in the back of this book. Information about where to order prerecorded tapes is also provided. If self-hypnosis seems daunting to you, even with the help of a prerecorded tape, you can check with the Milton H. Erickson Institute of Hypnosis for a referral to a qualified therapist who can help you find and evaluate the imagery that will work best for you.

Any visualization script or tape must leave room for you to supply your own personal imagery. As I mentioned in my first book, the warlike imagery of attack and assault against disease that the Simontons encouraged won't suit most of us. Many people aren't comfortable killing anything, even if it's their cancer cells. One teenager was so distressed that she had her cancer cells saying "Help me!" On the other hand Garrett Porter, who was nine years old when he was found to have an inoperable and supposedly incurable brain tumor, used visualization skills he learned at the Menninger Foundation's Voluntary Controls Program to create a Star Wars scenario for himself. He visualized his brain as the solar system, his tumor as an evil invading planet and himself as the leader of a space squadron fighting a successful battle against the tumor. The imagery of warfare worked fine for him—within five months the tumor had disappeared, without benefit of any other therapy. He's now a young man in fine health. With his therapist Pat Norris he has written a book sharing his experiences, entitled *Why Me?* He also appears on the videotape *Fight for Your Life,* available from ECaP.

Approximately 80 percent of us are lovers, not killers, however. I base this figure on a study that was done on young men who had been inducted into the army and were asked if they could kill on the battlefield. More than three-quarters of them said they could not. For people who are not comfortable with the imagery of battle, I might suggest visualizations in which the disease cells are ingested as a source of growth and nourishment. A lady with oat cell cancer had mares and does eating her oats. Many people have enjoyed using this kind of imagery. Here's one such account, from a woman whose mammogram indicated a recurrence of the breast cancer she had been treated for two years before.

> I imagined small, delicate birds searching my breast for crumbs. To my surprise my imagery took the form of the cancer being golden crumbs, filling in their richness. Each day the birds would eat the golden crumbs. It was amazing to me that I visualized the cancer in this form, as being crumbs too golden rich for my body. After the birds had eaten their fill, I would then imagine a pure beam of intense spiritual white light entering my body. I would then pray to God for guidance, renewal and protection.
>
> One morning after a particularly exhilarating bike ride, I sat down for my meditation and visualization. The white light suddenly appeared, immediately, and coursed down through my head, spreading like white heat through my breast and limbs. I felt the power take hold of me and I let go of it while my heart raced and pounded. After a short intense interval I slumped sidewise in exhaustion. I knew something extraordinary had happened.
>
> The next morning, when I sat down to visualize, I could no longer find any golden crumbs. An inner voice whispered, "There isn't anything there." And each morning I had the same experience. I told my husband, "I wish they'd take another mammogram. I bet they wouldn't find anything."

And a week later, when she went in at her surgeon's request for a second mammogram, they didn't. Whatever had shown up in that earlier mammogram, noted as a "spiculated area, suspicious for malignancy," had disappeared.

People's imagery is as varied as their fingerprints. One woman saw her cancer cells as garbage, and since she didn't want to burden her white cells with anything nasty, she used pigs to eat up the garbage. Another woman turned her household chores into healing meditations by imagining, for example, that her dishwashing suds were washing away her disease. Jim Wood, one of our ECaP members, imagined a great ocean wave, with foamy whitecaps, continually sloshing over his cancer. After he got about halfway through his chemotherapy, he went through a ten-day period in which he felt a tremendous internal itching in the area where most of his cancer was located. He feels certain that this was when his healing occurred. In any event, exploratory surgery several months later revealed that a quite extraordinary healing had taken place, for there was no longer any evidence of his mesothelioma. A year later he still showed no signs of recurrence.

If you have a disease like multiple sclerosis or lupus, in which your immune system is attacking your own body, you might want to imagine your white cells as being like the seven dwarfs, who can be used to stop the self-destruction, go out on repair missions at locations throughout the body, or just suppress the attacking white cells.

Another thing to keep in mind when selecting your personal imagery is that it should appeal to your dominant sense faculty, whether it's visual, auditory, tactile or olfactory. Everyone tends to rely more heavily on certain senses than on others. To figure out which sense is dominant in you, pay attention to the language you use. For instance, if you were buying a car what would attract you, its sleek looks, the hum of the engine or how smoothly the door shuts? This kind of analysis may help you to understand your own nature and patterns. I read about someone who needed to "hear" her immune system; she imagined it as the hero of an opera in which it and her cancer cells sang arias at each other until the hero prevailed. Another woman "felt" her immune system as a rushing stream washing over her.

Some experts who do visualization work think that the images you use should be anatomically correct. That is, you should learn as much as you can about what is taking place in your body and the healing processes and then visualize them in detail, complete with the different kinds of immune system cells performing their specialized functions, or whatever else needs to take place. I myself believe that the superintelligence residing within us knows more than we do about self-healing, and that we do not need to know anatomy to heal. This is the Milton Erickson philosophy, too: You give the unconscious the problem and then trust that the unconscious will take over and solve it in its own way.

Intuitively and instinctively, the unconscious knows what is needed. Our job as individuals confronting disease is to set it free to do its best for us by giving it "live" messages. What confuses it is "performing." "How are you?" I ask. "Fine," you say. "What's wrong in your life?" "Nothing." It's the repressors, the people who won't admit either to themselves or to anyone else that something is wrong, who give their body "die" messages. If you refuse help, you are telling your body you really want to die. Please don't do that. Share your needs. Reach out for help. Express yourself. If you love yourself, you will give your body all the help it needs, but that can only happen if you accept yourself and your needs. Let out the pain and love will fill the space.

THE POWER OF HOPE

Perhaps more powerful than any visualization or other specific technique you can use to alter the inner environment of your body are feelings of hope and love. I consider it my job as a doctor to give my patients both, because that's what they need to be able to live. Since I don't know what the outcome will be for any individual, no matter what the pathology report says, I can in all honesty give everyone hope.

I offer the doctors in my audiences a standing bet of a year's salary. I will read a pathology report, and if they can guess the date of that person's death within six months they get my salary, but if not I get theirs. Even though they have a total of twelve months leeway, I've yet to find anyone willing to take me up on my offer. When I challenge them, they say they can't tell from a pathology report when a person will die. Then how can they use path reports to sentence people, as so many of them regularly do? You can't tell the future from a pathology report, and anyone who says otherwise is wrong. There are differences between probabilities and possibilities.

I used to sit in my office wondering why I was spending

all those hours with people who had diseases they couldn't get over. But some of them did get over their diseases, and wrote me letters years later saying "Thank you for giving me the option to survive. I did." So now it's easy for me to pass that option on to others, people with AIDS, cancer, diabetes, heart disease, lupus, multiple sclerosis and amyotrophic lateral sclerosis. It doesn't matter what the disease is. There's always room for hope. I'm not going to die because of statistics. I hope you won't either.

*It is our duty as physicians to estimate probabilities
and to discipline expectations; but leading away from
probabilities there are paths of possibility, towards
which it is also our duty to hold aloft the light, and the
name of that light is hope.*

—KARL MENNINGER, *The Vital Balance*

*Statistics are the triumph of the quantitative method,
and the quantitative method is the victory of sterility
and death.*

—HILAIRE BELLOC

Who Is the Healer, Who Is the Healed? The Doctor-Patient Relationship

I have always made a distinction between healing and curing. To me "healed" represents a condition of one's life; "cured" relates strictly to one's physical condition. In other words, there may be healed quadriplegics and AIDS patients, and cured cancer patients who are leading unhealthy lives. What this means to me is that neither my patients nor I need ever face the inevitability of failure, for no matter how life-threatening their disease or how unlikely a cure, healing is always possible.

Even the most mechanistic of today's doctors may become interested in healing once they understand that a healed life may include as a by-product a physical cure—this was the

• 117

original impetus for my own interest in healing lives. I find, however, that the healing has increasingly come to seem the most important aspect of my practice, which is why Bobbie describes it as a clergical practice. Recently a woman wrote and asked me to find her a clergiologist for her heart problems. Patients want to be seen as people. For me the person's life comes first; the disease is simply one aspect of it, which I can guide my patients to use as a redirection in their lives.

When doctors look at their patients, however, they are trained to see only the disease. That is why so many of us need to be reminded that there is a human being in the room with us. One woman did this by placing a sign on her sick husband's hospital room door saying "Danger, human being inside." This sign (and the wife's climbing into bed with her husband to rest with and comfort him) caused quite a disturbance at the major medical center where he was hospitalized. When they later had to go to a smaller local hospital in an acute emergency, the man's wife again hung the sign on his door. This time a nurse noticed it and asked her where she had gotten it. Expecting the worst, the woman explained that she'd found it at a nearby store—to which the nurse replied, "Will you get me a dozen more?" Then there was my patient who wore an Egyptian belly dancer outfit to the oncology clinic one day. You can be sure the doctors didn't treat her as just another case of breast cancer ever again.

A man who came to one of my workshops had his own methods of reminding everyone (including himself) that he was not just a disease. While hospitalized during diagnostic tests for what turned out to be a brain tumor, Jake wore his own clothes instead of hospital gowns, decorated his room with pictures of all his favorite sports figures, moved his bed next to a window so that he could see the sky, and in general just refused to act like a patient. These activities create a more active immune system—and a stir among the hospital staff!

During this same hospitalization Jake, who is a very powerful-looking man at six foot three, was on his way to the operating room prior to brain surgery. When the surgeon came down the hall Jake reached out to shake his hand but the surgeon pulled his hand back. Jake thought that the surgeon might be trying to protect his hands, so he then asked for a pat on the head instead. But the doctor again pulled back, saying that they were running late and needed to get into the o.r. At that point Jake roared, "I refuse to have this man work on me! If he won't shake my hand or pat my head, I'm not letting him go into my brain."

I have to admit that behavior like that can make a mess out of the operating room schedule. But it's survival behavior. Jake knew intuitively that a man is not separate from his disease, and it was important to him to have a doctor who knew it too. Doctors who persist in thinking they can cure the disease without caring for the person may be excellent technicians, but they are incomplete doctors, because they have an incomplete understanding of illness.

The doctor I would want for myself or for anyone else I cared about would be one who understands that disease is more than just a clinical entity; it is an experience and a metaphor, with a message that must be listened to. Often the message will speak to us of our path and how we have strayed from it, so that our life is no longer a true expression of the inner self, or, as Larry LeShan would say, we are no longer singing our own song. Only by listening to that message can we mobilize all the healing powers that lie within, and that is what the doctor must help each patient to do. Psychiatrist Milton Erickson told a story he thought would shed light on how his own profession could assist patients in self-healing:

I was returning from high school one day and a runaway horse with a bridle on sped past a group of us into a farmer's yard . . . looking for a drink of water. The horse was perspiring heavily. And the farmer didn't recognize it, so we cornered it. I hopped on the horse's back . . . [and] since it had a bridle on, I took hold of the reins and said, "Giddy-up" . . . [and] headed for the highway. I knew the horse would turn in the right direction . . . [but] I didn't know what the right direction was. And the horse trotted and galloped along. Now and then he would forget he was on the highway and start into a field. So I would pull on him a bit and call his attention to the fact that the highway was where he was supposed to be. And finally about four miles from where I had boarded him, he turned into a farmyard, and the farmer said, "So, that's how that critter came back, where'd you find him?"

I said, "About four miles from here."

"How did you know he should come here?"

I said, "I didn't know . . . the horse knew. All I did was keep his attention on the road."

. . . I think that's the way you do psychotherapy.

What I like about Erickson's concept of therapy is that he knows that the doctor does not prescribe the patient's path. The path is prescribed by the intrinsic awareness of the DNA in the fertilized egg that becomes you, and if you follow it you will become the best you possible. This approach to healing is as relevant to the body doctor as it is to the psyche doctor.

The physician is in a unique position, however, quite different from the psychotherapist's, because people who come to our offices aren't coming to change their lives. They're coming because of physical problems. Some may even want to die. But if we are willing to treat more than their diseases, by being there for them, supporting them and loving them, in addition to caring for their physical problems, we may be able to redirect lives, not just treat illnesses.

THE WAY OF THE SHAMAN

Most of today's doctors shun the informal psychotherapy that family doctors practiced routinely in the past. They take down the facts of the patient's medical history, without paying much attention to the patient. But we must never forget that the look on the patient's face, the tremble in his hand, the falter in his speech, the lowering of his eyes, the dreams he has, the drawings he makes, are all potential signs of what really troubles him, and at least as important as anything he may say about his symptoms. In fact, so much of the important communication that takes place between doctor and patient is non-verbal that I've even had the experience of being able to treat a man from Greece who spoke no English. When this man was brought to my office I spoke to him as if he could understand me, and the effect of my hope and my concern got through to him without words. When he needed surgery, I played Greek music for him—another nonverbal form of communication.

It was common knowledge among doctors from Hippocrates on that we need to tend to the patient as well as the disease, "for some patients," as Hippocrates said, "though conscious that their condition is perilous, recover their health simply through their contentment with the goodness of the physician." In the last hundred years, however, the role of the physician has changed drastically, for both better and worse. It used to be that doctors were ill equipped even to diagnose, much less to cure, most ailments. Practically all they had going for them besides the occasional herbal remedy and painkiller was their understanding of human nature.

During the final decades of the nineteenth century, however, the practice of medicine was changed dramatically by advances in the doctor's ability both to diagnose and treat disease. Then, in the first half of the twentieth century, the introduction of the sulfa drugs in the thirties and antibiotics in the forties made this the age of the medical miracle. The doctor-mediated placebo effect no longer seemed needed.

There is no question at all that the curative powers of the physician are vastly greater today than ever before. And I certainly wouldn't give up any of the medical miracles that we twentieth-century doctors have available to us. That's why I've remained a surgeon. But I can't help noticing that our power to heal people and their lives seems to have diminished as dramatically as our power to cure diseases has increased. This is because the knowledge of human nature that used to be the doctor's principal resource has been abandoned as irrelevant in an age of science. Science has become God, and separated itself from the patient. Recently I visited a woman who had undergone a heart-lung transplant. Think of the enormity of it: Her blue fingers were now pink; she was alive. She told me that she had asked for psychiatric help because of the many issues she was having to deal with, including whether to thank the family of the individual whose death had made it possible for her to receive these organs. When she brought the subject up, the basic advice she received from her surgeon was to get on her exercise bike and work it off.

What has been lost is the human dimension. To recover a sense of what medicine used to be, when doctors relied on their inspirational powers because these were the only real powers they had, we must look to cultures where traditional medicine still plays a role. Ernie Benedict, a Mohawk Indian elder, is quoted in Jeanne Achterberg's *Imagery in Healing* as saying that the difference between the white doctor and the shaman is that "the White doctor's medicines tend to be very mechanical. The patient is repaired, but he is not a better person than he was before. It is possible in the Indian way to be a better person after going through a sickness followed by the proper medicine." I think this is what the shaman knows and the Western doctor, alas, has forgotten.

But what do I mean by trying to reclaim the shamanistic role for the doctor? Those of you who are already suspicious of the medical establishment's authoritarian impulses may be justifiably wary of a doctor trying to reclaim the moral and even spiritual authority that his profession has lost (some would say abandoned). However, I believe there is no disease whose treatment cannot be enhanced by a doctor who knows how to inspire and guide patients and so to bring into play the body's internal healers. It is when I can help my patients find what Schweitzer called the doctor within—when I play coach, as one of my patients put it—that I am most fulfilled in my role as doctor and I serve my patients best. We become a team with joint participation and responsibility.

In a wonderful letter that a couple wrote to their doctor after he diagnosed the wife's recurrence of cancer, they ask him to play this role with her and to support them in their struggle:

> We need your skills as an oncologist, but we also need your faith as a human being that exceptional people can do exceptional things, and that Isabel is one such exceptional person. . . . It's important for you to know that neither of us believes that cancer can be stopped by using medical techniques alone. It also involves keeping joy in your daily life, exuberance in your outlook,

determination in your soul and unbridled faith in your heart.
These things are not possible if your doctor adopts an attitude
that you are "incurable." We need you to treat Isabel medically,
but we also need you to root for her and believe in her. We ask
you to be patient and loving.

The doctor who truly believes in the uniqueness and spe-
cialness of each patient can have an effect that transcends the
mechanical. I read a story recently that *New Frontier Magazine* columnist Alan Cohen told about a chiropractor who had
an opportunity to change a patient's life. One day a man who
was an utter mess came into his office. The chiropractor was
repelled by the man, but since he had been taught (by Indian
healers, in fact) to find something lovable in each of his patients, he looked him over, searching for something he could
appreciate. He saw that the man had new and very neatly tied
shoelaces, so he got himself to relate to the man through his
shoelaces and treated him in a loving way.

A few days later the man came back to his office, clean,
well dressed, and looking much better, and he explained that
on the day of his previous visit he had been headed to a nearby
bridge to commit suicide when he decided he would give one
more person a chance to change his mind. "The first place I
saw was your office, and so I came to you. I must thank you for
being so kind to me. I felt your acceptance and your love. You
encouraged me to continue living, doctor, and I want you to
know what a difference your kindness made."

We as physicians have the opportunity to do this with
every patient we see. Some come to us so filled with pain and
self-loathing because of the negative voices in their past that
they expect and even want to be abused and punished. But we
have the ability, through loving our patients, to help them to
love themselves. My painful lesson was learning how difficult
my patients' lives are. Not all of them want to live. Some of
them will find the will to live only if their doctors do as the one
in Alan Cohen's story did.

There are also patients who do want to live but don't know
how. I think that's who is referred to in Ecclesiastes where it
says, "He who sins before his maker, may he fall into the care

of a physician." The issue here is not sin as we usually interpret it, but living an unhealed life. Only if we help to heal lives can we develop the kind of patient who is more likely to be cured of diseases.

As part of my clergical practice, one day I walked into my examining room and asked a lady sitting there with a staph abscess, "Why do you have difficulty saying no without guilt?" When she responded, "Who called you from my family before I got here?" I could honestly say, "No one, I'm reading your body." Because I have learned that diseases are often signs, and that if I can read the message the disease is communicating, I may be able to help patients change not just their physical condition, but their lives. When one does that, one can indeed have patients come up and say, "The disease was the best thing that ever happened to me. Thank you for being on my path and guiding me."

On my desk is a letter from a patient who had come to me for counseling as well as medical care. At the time she wrote, her ovarian cancer had disappeared, in response to her program of hope, meditation, visualization, autohypnosis, chemotherapy, psychotherapy and inspirational self-healing exercises. She says, "You have saved my life, enriched it and taught me to love." What she is talking about is not the recovery she made from her disease, but the change that came about in her *because* of the disease, a change I was able to help her to make.

I have a dream, and the dream is to help my patients find their dream. Often the factor that motivates them to live and to find their dream is their disease. (Again we remember Arnold Mindell's words: "A terrifying symptom is usually your greatest dream trying to come true.") One woman whom I had operated on a number of years before wrote me a letter about the effect I had on her life:

During the first years after surgery, I kept a journal detailing my thoughts and feelings—it was a journal—ultimately—of growth and renewal. I have turned it into a book entitled *The Uses of Adversity*. Of course, you figure quite definitely in the book—from first considering you my savior, to blaming and hating you, to finally making peace with you in my mind. You didn't know you had so many "uses," did you!

No I didn't, but I'm grateful to her for telling me I did. When we can help people transform affliction into a challenge and a gift, then we have reclaimed everyone's dream.

THE COMPULSIVE HEALER

Like most doctors, I have to try to remember that I am merely a facilitator of healing, not the healer himself—a frequent source of confusion for doctors! That's why I've asked my patients to call me by my first name. As Bernie, I'm a human being whom my patients and the people I work with can relate to; they will accept my being perfectly imperfect. When no one expects the impossible of me, including me, that's an immense burden off my shoulders. But "Dr. Siegel" is a label that assigns me a fixed role and means I'm supposed to be perfect. I will inevitably be a failure at being perfect.

Because there is always the danger that I will revert to the old doctor roles, Gwen, one of the nurses in the o.r., often greets me by asking "Who's here today, Bernie or Dr. Siegel?" One day when I was Bernie, a nurse who was changing shifts in the middle of a long, arduous operation leaned over and kissed me on the back of the neck as she was leaving. That was an incredible gift to me. It gave me strength to go on, because it said so much about the pain and the love we had shared in that operating room. M.edical D.eities don't get gifts like that, because they're so aloof from everyone around them that they don't share anything. So now I try always to be Bernie.

Being human means you get to share a lot of laughter as well as hugs and kisses. One of my partners, Bill McCullough, who is a human being as well as a surgeon, was doing some rectal surgery and asked Maureen, the nurse, to shine the light on the asshole. She replied, "Which one?" Nurses like that are really an enormous help to us. They help us to deal with our pain as surgeons, they let us know they care, and, in case we forget, they remind us that we're human. I heard a story about a nurse who discovered that a patient had died and called a young resident into the room to pronounce him dead. He went through his various procedures, postures and pontifications, and finally with great ceremony pronounced, "The patient is dead." "No shit," was her reply! The physician later described that experience as a turning point for him, which helped him to change and grow up. It's the physicians whom the nurses say they can't hug or laugh with (and sometimes at) who are the problems, both to themselves and to others.

What is it about us physicians that makes us want to play God? Woody Allen says it's because we have to model ourselves after someone. Studies that have been done on the psychology of doctors suggest that we're trying to deny our mortality, for people who choose medicine as a career are often motivated by a fear of death. Every victory over death confirms such doctors in their feeling of power, and conversely, every patient they lose represents a profound failure, a dread reminder of personal inadequacy. Curing becomes an addiction for them—one that is just as destructive as any other addiction. Since all doctors are bound to lose some of their patients, you can imagine how their sense of failure grows as every year adds to the tally of losses.

That's why I call medicine a failure-oriented profession, with its emphasis on disease rather than people. Attend any medical convention and take a look at the doctors to see what I mean: Gone is the glowing optimism of the medical school student, and with it that aura of healing, of healers being sent into the world, that is palpable to everyone in the audience on graduation day. When you see them gathered together not so many years later at one of their professional meetings, worn out by their collective feelings of failure, you can sense the change they've made from a life-oriented to a death-oriented profession. This is not an inevitable result of dealing on a daily basis with serious diseases, as is evident when you attend a convention of other types of health care providers. No less concerned about their patients, they tend to talk about quality-of-life issues rather than disease, defeat and death. When they treat patients, they often have their families and office staff present so that they function as a healing team.

If doctors would do the same, they would not feel so isolated, and they would find they could succeed even when they are unable to cure. That's why I sometimes receive beautiful letters of thanks from the families of patients who died, or am asked to deliver a eulogy at the funeral or attend weddings. These people know I did my best, and they know that death does not mean that either my patient or I was a failure. A letter that came recently said:

We can never thank you sufficiently for the wonderful care you gave my mother. Her name was Hope, and that was the precious gift which you alone among the many medical people involved in her case gave her.

My mother was truly an "exceptional patient," to use your phrase. Such was her faith and fighting spirit that she refused to consider herself a statistic, insisting never to be told her prognosis, even during her final illness. Instead, her great trust in God, positive attitude, and involvement in her own healing, through the various techniques you suggested, allowed her to do marvelously well, living considerably longer [and] more actively than she should have, from a strict medical perspective. In our greed and deep sorrow we long to have had a complete miracle, however recognize with thanks the limited miracle we truly received.

We are indebted to you for providing my mother with the most effective medicine she received: vigorous encouragement, sincere care, and love.

God bless you and thank you for your kindness, concern, and above all, for being my mother's friend.

And indeed I feel blessed, and healed, when I read such a letter, or am invited to the funeral of someone I cared for.

In years past I would feel the weight of loss and failure in the face of death, but then I would receive a message to remind me that none of us down here is capable of filling God's shoes. A number of years ago a patient of mine died on the operating table. Although he had been critically ill and the family and I knew even before I started to operate that his chances of survival were small, nonetheless I was much affected by the loss. After he died, I phoned the family from the operating room and shared with them that I had tried to keep the death as spiritual as possible under the circumstances, which I think was some comfort to them. But they found a way to comfort me too. I received a poem in the mail from a member of the gentleman's family, which restored me. When I read parts of it at the medical conference that always follows a patient's death, there was total silence, as every physician in the room recalled his own pain and his own losses. The poem begins by saying:

> This man the surgeon who with his hands
> Works hard to mend where he can
> Works hard he does this man the healer
> Works hard yet at times he'll fail.

and ends this way:

> Carry on physician, do what you can,
> Your common sense surely does the job
> No one expects any miracles from you,
> No one expects the impossible.

No one, that is, except everyone at medical school and in house staff training, as well as the individual physician. I know what those expectations are, and I too have been a victim of them. But I say we only fail if we are trying to keep people from being dead. Then we will inevitably fail, since life has a 100 percent mortality rate. I've done the research, and I hate to tell you, but everybody dies—lovers, joggers, vegetarians and nonsmokers. I'm telling you this so that some of you who jog at 5:00 A.M. and eat vegetables will occasionally sleep late and have an ice cream cone.

If we doctors would admit our mortality, then we would find a way to succeed with even the sickest of our patients, sometimes simply holding their hands when they are frightened and in pain, other times helping them understand the meaning of their illness and how they can use it to experience life and love. It is my patients, out of their kindness and their wisdom, who have taught me this, and it seems to me that whenever I am in danger of forgetting it, another patient helps me return to that knowledge.

One evening as I made rounds I came into the room of a woman with diabetes. She had lost her sight, her kidney function, her leg and several fingers. A patient like this can destroy a doctor in "cure mode," and I felt the pain and weight in my stomach that I always get when I'm walking around trying to cure everyone. Not knowing what else to do, I simply went up to her and held her hand and spoke from my heart: "I wish I could help you." And she said: "You are helping me."

She didn't ask me to cure her. She didn't ask me to take away her diabetes or give her back her sight. She only asked me to hold her hand. And then I kept her company as she wrestled with the issue of stopping her dialysis and whether that meant she was committing suicide and would therefore go to hell, which was a concern of hers because of her religious beliefs. We talked a long time that night about her options and choices, until she seemed to me to be more at peace. I hope that I in some way helped to heal her, for I know that she helped heal me. She reminded me that I can never know all the answers, but I can help all my patients if I can just know their pain.

As is so often the case, it's a psychotherapist, talking about his own profession, who has come up with the metaphor that best describes what doctors can do for their patients at times like the one just described. Comparing Virgil and Dante in *The Divine Comedy* to therapist and patient, Rollo May quotes Dante's cry as he wanders through hell:

> O my beloved Master, my Guide in peril, . . .
> . . . stand by me now . . . in my heart's fright.

"I hear in those words the cry of the patient who asks the physician to stand by and care," says May. "Virgil responds as we should":

> Take heart . . . I will not leave you
> to wander in the underworld alone.

Like Dante, patients must ultimately take responsibility for their own journeys, but like Virgil, the physician must not desert the patient, even the patient for whom it might at first appear that "nothing can be done." Every patient can use what May describes as a "guide, friend and interpreter" through the private hells and purgatories of illness, and every doctor has the opportunity to play that role, to lead the way from the crucifixion to the resurrection.

THE DETACHED HEALER

Franz Kafka said, "To write a prescription is easy, but to come to an understanding with people is hard." Medical school teaches everything we need to know about writing prescriptions, but nothing about understanding people. In fact, it teaches students to keep their distance so as not to be overwhelmed by the suffering of their patients. Better not to know them too well. The prescribed attitude is called "detached concern."

What is detached concern? Do you think you could use detached concern with your family? What you would do is destroy them—and yourself, because estrangement from your own feelings is ultimately deadly. We need to show rational concern, not detached concern. With rational concern I've even been able to operate on people in my own family. And it was not an inappropriate act, but a caring act, a loving act.

As doctors, many of us have cultivated our detachment so effectively that our patients find us completely inhuman. The truth without compassion is hostility. I had a patient come to my office the other day who had had a mammogram in Spain, and she told me that when the time came for her to get the results, both the technician and the physician walked out and embraced her before telling her the news that she would need surgery. When she came to this country for treatment, she was shocked by the difference in physicians. The first surgeon she was referred to talked to her with his back toward her as he completed a chart, and got angry at her for asking how her breast would look after surgery. She found a similar coldness in the radiology suite she visited. She felt so uncared for that she left and ultimately found her way to my office.

Some have criticized me for being too tough on the medical profession. But since I am a physician, I feel I have the right to be tough—more right than those who have not felt the pain of the physician. For I do know our pain, I do know our burdens, and certainly I also know that many doctors feel more than they reveal. (You try being an oncologist or a surgeon for a week!) A recent "Piece of My Mind" column in *JAMA* reminded me that the apparent indifference of such doctors may be a mask for their pain, and may also simply be a result of poor training for dealing with that pain. "Jailhouse Blues" recounts the anguished feelings of a prison doctor who must inform yet another prisoner that he has AIDS. "I can't afford to get involved," he writes, for "there is too much to be done," too many patients requiring his care. He obviously fears that he will be overwhelmed and immobilized if he allows himself to feel his patients' pain: "To be able to care for this man I must withdraw, to protect myself and my own drained emotions. I rise quickly and summon the security officer: 'Next patient, please.'" Instead he could reach out to his patient and say "I need to hug you." I did that for years, thinking I was helping the person with the disease. Eventually I realized that the need really was mine and that the hug restored me as much as it did the patient.

I used to go through the same pain whenever I had to tell a patient there was nothing that could be done. Once I realized there is *always* something *I* can do, however, I discovered the antidote to that pain. At a workshop we were both attending, a woman patient of mine with breast cancer who turned to me and said "Office visits are okay but I need to know how to live between office visits" gave me the clue I needed to create a success-oriented practice. No longer would I just keep people from dying. That was over ten years ago, and that remark was my inspiration for forming the first ECaP group. Now I understand that everyone, be they prison inmates or people of wealth and privilege, is looking for a way to live between office visits. That is the one thing I can always help my patients with, regardless of their physical condition.

Several years ago I was asked to visit a young nurse who was on a respirator, dying of pulmonary metastases. The family was hoping I could help her. I went into the intensive care unit with fear in my heart, not knowing what I was going to say or how I could possibly help. When I reached her cubicle, she saw me, sat up, respirator and all, and opened her arms to embrace me. There was no problem with visiting her. She healed me, by teaching me once again how beautiful and courageous people are, how basic their needs, how simple their demands.

The morning I was going to speak at the Cornell University Medical School commencement, I asked two critically ill patients what they wanted me to tell one hundred new doctors on their graduation day. Both patients were young, one with metastatic breast cancer, the other with liver failure secondary to cystic fibrosis, and both died within several months of the request. What message did they wish to give to these future caretakers? Did they want me to ask them to find a cure for cancer or cystic fibrosis? No. They had five simple requests. One patient said, "Tell them to let me talk first," and the other, "Tell them to knock on my door, say hello and goodbye, and look me in the eye when they talk to me." These simple lessons are never taught in medical school.

THE UNTRAINED HEALER

We doctors are totally unprepared by our education for what we are going to meet in our practice. While I don't think most physicians are villains, I do think the training process of physicians is villainous. Students have their natural desire to help people drummed out of them by medical school training that, on the one hand, has warned them about maintaining a professional distance from their patients and, on the other, has not helped them with such difficult problems as how to tell someone they have AIDS or cancer or how to deal with the fears that arise within themselves as they treat the critically ill.

I have known people whose doctors have given them a life-threatening diagnosis over the telephone, in the most abrupt, thoughtless way, and then ordered them to appear at the hospital the next day to have some part of their body removed.

A group of oncologists, psychiatrists and medical school workers at the University of California at Los Angeles have for this reason spent four years making a film called *Cancer Disclosure: Communicating the Diagnosis.* Using physicians in combination with actors coached by cancer patients, they are trying to help medical students and doctors avoid the kind of disastrous scenario described above.

Another training program I've read about was started over ten years ago by Professor Sandra L. Bertman at the University of Massachusetts. Her medical humanities program makes use of literature, art and pop culture to teach compassion and caring to medical students. For example, the students in her "Death, Dying and Dissection" course are helped to explore rather than ignore what they feel as they make their way through such rites of passage as the encounter with their first "patients"—the cadavers they will dissect in anatomy lab. Bertman has them read excerpts from Irving Stone's book *The Agony and the Ecstasy,* a fictionalized biography of Michelangelo, which portrays the feelings of the young artist as he secretly dissects his own first cadaver as part of his anatomy studies. She also has them study Rembrandt's painting *The Anatomy Lesson,* because the faces of the people standing around the body reveal so much about their reactions. Rather than stifling their inevitable feelings of pity, fear and excitement in the face of death, the students learn from Rembrandt and Michelangelo that these feelings are universal; they're part of what makes us human, and must not be denied.

At the conclusion of the anatomy course, students in Bertman's class hold a memorial service for the human beings who donated their bodies to the cause of medical education. Thus they come full circle, purging themselves of the desensitization they had to undergo in order to sink their knives into a human body. Other schools are starting similar courses in which it is safe and desirable to discuss feelings.

Recently I read about a hospital in California where first-year medical residents are admitted incognito as patients for a day so that they learn about hospitalization from the patient's point of view. I myself fantasize starting every medical student's training with a physical. The student would show up for a routine blood test, and I would call a few hours later to say, "I think there's something a little peculiar about the results of your test. You'd better come in tomorrow." The experience of sleeping on that uncertainty would be quite an education for most students. Then I'd hospitalize the student for a few days of tests so that the fear experienced by every patient in the hospital, the discomfort and depersonalization, the loss of control, would become part of the student's experience too. After a few days I'd announce, "Sorry, we made a mistake. Your blood test got mixed up with someone else's and you're fine." They would learn from this what it's like to experience illness, and I hope would see that diseases cannot be treated separately from the people who have them.

I'd like to see medical school curricula with courses taught by patients, nurses and doctors who have been seriously ill, because that too would be a new experience for students. I'd like to see some teaching time devoted to the healing power of touch—a subject that only 12 out of 169 medical schools in the English-speaking world deal with at all, according to a survey reported a few years ago in *JAMA*, despite the fact that touch is one of the most basic forms of communication between people. I work with osteopathic students as well as medical students. The osteopathic students have been taught about touching and manipulating the body, and when they're in my office and a patient who has some pain comes in, they know how to use manipulation and massage to help relieve that pain. The medical student is more prone to prescribe a pill. We need to teach medical students how to touch people. Perhaps this training could be part of a whole course on communication, which is almost completely neglected in medical school.

The course in communication would teach students how to tell patients their diagnoses, how to write a chemotherapy protocol, how to answer the questions of those dealing with life-threatening diseases—and would also help students understand what they themselves will be feeling during these communications, because doctors have feelings that must be dealt with.

I would have a course called "Why You Became a Doctor," so that students can understand what motivated them at both a conscious and an unconscious level to choose the medical profession. This course would help students deal with their feelings as they face up to the fact that some of their patients are going to die, and that they themselves are mortal—which doctors don't like to admit.

During the first year of medical school I would like to see every student assigned to a patient with a chronic illness. The students would remain involved with their assigned patients for the entire four years of medical school. They would be required to show up every time that patient came into the hospital and would visit the patient at home as well, so that they could see how the lives of both patient and family are affected over time by the experience of chronic illness.

Students would also be expected to attend a healing service at a shrine and told to go out and help one of the thousands of incurable people who show up for these events. "But how can I possibly help someone who is incurable?" they would ask. I know, because I too have gone to these services, and I remember my feelings of helplessness and frantic attempts to think of some medical solution that hadn't yet been considered, even though many of these people had already had the best that the medical profession had to offer. But then one day I was at one of those services when a woman with a congenitally deformed grandchild in her lap reached out to me and said, "Please pray with us." She taught me the one thing I *could* do, and reminded me that doctors are health care providers, not health cure providers. That saved me, and now I can be comfortable using what I learned from that grandmother.

In the absence of the kind of training I'm describing, however, it is not hard to understand why today's young doctors, many of whom have never had to confront death or serious illness in their own lives, have no idea how to help their patients. Overwhelmed by the magnitude of what they must tell patients and families facing serious disease, they withdraw. The patient, however, sees only the detachment, not the concern. Too often, the result of maintaining our "professional distance" is that we build a wall around ourselves. When we do this, our patients are not the only ones who suffer. We hurt ourselves as well. (Look at the high suicide rate of physicians.)

THE WOUNDED HEALER

The pain of the medical student and the doctor is very real. If you doubt it you have only to read more "Piece of My Mind" columns in *JAMA*. A recent contributor, a seventeen-year-old girl who intends to be a doctor, expresses her dismay at the despair she sees in most of the columns written by doctors. "Sad, heartwrenching or simply depressing" she calls them, as she wonders whether in twenty years she too will be speaking only of "frustration, anger, and a sense of defeat." But if Joy Matthews can just keep wanting to "heal lives," as she puts it, she may remain true to her name long after colleagues who seek only to cure disease have lost their own sense of joyfulness in the practice of medicine.

I receive hundreds of letters testifying to the pain of doctors who feel defeated by the demands of their profession because they have focused on diseases and not on the people who have them. One such letter was deeply gratifying to me because it described how *Love, Medicine and Miracles* was able to play a role in healing that pain. The woman who wrote it was just starting her fourth year of medical school, after three years of what she had found to be dehumanizing, soulless work.

My third year of medical school, although better than the first two years of sitting in class, was still about 80 percent drudgery. Rushing through admissions and orders, chasing down labs, endlessly arranging and rearranging x-rays, CTs etc. and laboring over progress notes. Some patients I connected with and enjoyed, but most of my energy was spent in anxiety about presenting cases, knowing dosages, finding vacutainers, missing veins, and the day to day management of patients on almost a purely secretarial level.

Reading your book reminded me of why I was going to medical school in the first place. I'm thirty-six years old and switched from a career teaching literature to medicine after I had my first child. I switched because I liked taking care of people, I liked being around when they were in trouble and I liked being able to help them. . . .

I finished your book in July and started a rotation I was truly dreading in August—my subinternship in medicine. I was dreading the long hours and the complicated patients with multiple chronic diseases and mainly the feeling of being overwhelmed by all I didn't know about diseases. . . . About halfway through the rotation I began to notice the curious sensation, heretofore not associated by me with ward medicine—I was enjoying myself. By the end of the rotation I was telling people I loved it.

What made the difference was the amount of time I spent with my patients. I ate lunch with them, arranged for their children to get HIV testing, listened to their family problems, compared prices of nursing homes with their wives. I realized I didn't have to know a lot of medicine to help them out. I relaxed and learned as much as I could about the diseases as I went along. . . . I was thoroughly enjoying myself, simply because I was listening to my patients and getting to know them. I was helping them enormously by just being there.

This woman knows the secret I would have every medical student learn: If you withdraw you die; if you share your patients' pain, you begin to live. Let your patients heal and teach you.

Once the shared humanity of doctor and patient is acknowledged, doctors can be relieved of the burden of thinking that the responsibility for life and death lies with them alone. I like George Bernard Shaw's advice in *The Doctor's Dilemma*. He thinks it should be compulsory for all doctors to have inscribed on their brass plates, in addition to the letters indicating their qualifications, the words "Remember that I too am mortal." My version of this advice is to recommend that all doctors hang their own x-rays in their offices as reminders of their mortality, and move their desks against the wall so that they meet their patients face to face with nothing between them, as vulnerable mortals. I know what a shock it was the first time I looked at my x-rays and realized they looked like everyone else's. That meant I could die too—no matter which side of the desk I was on.

Too often physicians learn the pain of their patients only by going through pain themselves. In another "Piece of My Mind" column, Dr. Marian Block described what she felt when she had to submit to procedures she'd been prescribing for years for her patients:

"I guess I have to say this, but you're going to be all right. If this is breast cancer, it's the earliest kind we know."

His words are meant to reassure, but I almost burst into tears. I am a thirty-nine-year-old physician who has just had a screening mammogram, having waited to engage in the procedure about as long as a physician who recommends it to her patients can wait.

. . . Two days later the call comes recommending surgery. Only then do I experience an intense physiological reaction. This is really happening. Surgery. General anesthesia. Fear, a profound anorectic and as good as atropine for drying the mouth.

Over the next days and weeks I hear and process a lot of information, even though I am often being told facts it seems I must already know, facts with which I have an easy familiarity when they apply to others. But there are times when I am presented with information and hear almost nothing. I am like a deaf person, knowing that words are being said but unable to understand their meaning. I hear words that I have used with my own patients, like "fibrocystic disease," and I am told it is really too common to be a "disease." The surgeon uses another word I have used—"nuisance"—and I know how he means it. That word nuisance, I have used it myself. I think (but do not say), tell me about this nuisance, this nondisease that scares a person half to death and results in surgery.

In the context of having the best care for a minor surgical procedure, I marvel at what my patients must go through. How are my words understood? How many questions go unasked? . . .

Three days after the surgery there is another phone call. I hear the two words I need to hear, and to his credit (because I do not hear the rest), he says them first. "Totally benign."

THE HURTFUL HEALER

It's always a surprise to doctors who find themselves or their family members on the receiving end of the health care system to discover how little in the nature of true healing their profession offers. I have read many moving letters as well as articles and books by doctors who have had this experience. No one has said it better than Dr. Hans H. Neumann, whose article "Why Have We Stopped Comforting Patients?" written shortly before his death, contains a lifetime's worth of wisdom.

First he tells about the callous treatment he himself received four years before, when he was recovering from a myocardial infarction. "You know, I feel remarkably well considering it's been only forty-eight hours since my coronary," he made the mistake of remarking to a young resident. "Don't let that deceive you," was the response, "you're in serious danger." The intern and the staff physician on duty echoed these dire messages—in marked contrast to Neumann's own physician, whom he calls "a member of the older, more compassionate school of medicine." Instead of alarming his patient unduly, his way of explaining the situation was to say, "Barring any unforeseen developments, your chances are excellent. Your ECG shows the expected evolution, and you're making progress."

Neumann tells an even more horrifying story about what happened to a member of his family. Given a diagnosis of inoperable liver cancer, she was treated with a brutality almost inconceivable unless one assumes the doctor reacted that way out of an inability to confront his own mortality and limitations.

Take the case of Mildred, a relative of mine. When exploratory surgery revealed her liver cancer, she was referred to an oncologist. She told me that after the doctor read her pathology report, he reached into his desk drawer and withdrew a slender stick.

"This is what you need," he said, waving it in front of Mildred and her husband.

"What is it?" asked Mildred.

"It's a magic wand," the oncologist replied. "That's the only thing that can help you now."

When she recounted the incident to me, Mildred said, "The man actually grinned when he said this. Did he think I would find it funny?"

Since he kept the "wand" in his desk, the doctor apparently used this technique quite often. Yet he never mentioned—to Mildred anyway—that periods of remission were possible, even predictable, in cases like hers. The encounter had a devastating effect on her, doubling the burden of her disease with iatrogenic depression.

Stories like this and the one I told earlier about the doctor who wanted to prove to his former patient that laetrile is quackery can only be understood as expressions of the essential destructiveness and sickness of many doctors. In *The Vital Balance,* psychiatrist Karl Menninger quotes a British colleague as saying that "the need to cure is . . . nearly always a reaction-formation against destructive needs and wishes, and that is why the need to cure is so dangerous within psychiatry." Then he goes on to say, "It does not matter in surgery; but in a mental hospital the patient may never react to what is on top in the doctor, but to what is underneath." There I would have to disagree, however. The doctor's underlying feelings are just as important in oncology and surgery as they are in psychiatry, because, as these stories show us, those feelings always end up being expressed, one way or another. If there is a compulsion to cure, which is frustrated, out come the destructive tendencies, and doctors destroy what they cannot cure. Doctors who treat their patients like this send them straight into the arms of the quacks. The medical profession needs to accept responsibility for its role in promoting quackery by removing hope.

As Neumann says later in his article, "a doctor who provides the patient only with textbook translations of lab reports is, at best, a competent scientist." At worst such a doctor is a destroyer. If you've ever witnessed a patient's reaction to his or her own pathology report, then you know what I mean. My friend Joe Kogel, who was diagnosed with malignant melanoma over five years ago, is a professional actor and writer. He has a one-man show in which he reads aloud from the pathology report that revealed his metastatic melanoma, letting us see the incredible emotional impact that medical terminology can have on a patient. Lab reports and statistics too often are used to take away hope. But I like what the receptionist in my office told the woman who announced that "statistically" she was supposed to die soon: "Statistics are for dead people. You're not dead." Wouldn't it be nice if those two were teaching a communications course at medical school? I also liked the approach one of my patients took to statistics: When I told him he had cancer, he said, "I guess that means I have five or ten thousand miles left." Don't let statistics tell *you* when to die.

I'm not suggesting that we ignore lab reports and statistics, just that we recognize that they are only one aspect of the picture. I tell my patients who have illnesses for which the statistical outlook is poor that we will use statistics to help select the best treatment options for them. Then I try to complement the benefits of the medical, mechanistic approach with those of the symbolic and spiritual approach. It is important to realize that these approaches need not be mutually exclusive.

That's the point of a course I teach called "Surgery: Mechanical or Healing Art," in which I describe the techniques I use in my clergical practice. But nobody at medical school knows what to do with a course like that. It straddles too many boundaries of things they think should be kept separate. Words like "dreams" and "drawings" scare surgeons, as do certain four-letter words like "hope" and "love."

The letter the associate dean for educational and student affairs sent me about the course states the dilemma very clearly: "As you know, all courses taught at the School of Medicine must be authorized by and become the responsibility of one of the established departments. Your course has been listed under your Department of Surgery. I recently received a letter from the Chairman of the Department of Surgery, indicating that he did not think that the course should be surgical. He suggested the Department of Psychiatry."

I wrote back to them and enclosed several of the letters I have received from students who are crying out in despair at the mechanical nature of what they learn in medical school. I could also have quoted Lewis Thomas to them: "Medicine is no longer the laying on of hands. It is more likely the reading of signals from machines. If I were a medical student or an intern just getting ready to begin, I would be apprehensive that my real job, caring for sick people, might soon be taken away, leaving me with the quite different occupation of looking after machines."

THE HEALER IN TRANSITION

Yes, I react strongly when it's suggested that my course be taken out of the surgical department. But it really makes very little difference whether they support what I do, because the students keep coming and the course will go on, whether it's listed in the Yale Medical School Bulletin or not.

I love the Quaker statement "Speak truth to power." The truth lies in people and their stories, not in statistics, which can be used to say whatever anyone wants them to say. If I continue to speak the truth and live it by example, my patients will do better and the establishment will eventually respond. Which they are both doing.

That my patients do well was most recently confirmed to me when an oncologist called to say "I want you to know that your patients live longer." That the establishment is responding I know because I've been invited to speak at so many medical school graduations and hospitals that I can't accept all the invitations. So perhaps the new medical students will not accept the old teachings any longer. Maybe in the future doctors will feel free to express their emotions, and won't be embarrassed to be seen coming to my workshops or buying my books.

When I speak to physician groups they often sit quietly and rigidly. I used to think they were bored; but then I noticed that when I was done they all lined up single file to talk to me. I realize now that they are in fact very interested, but uncomfortable about letting a roomful of their colleagues know. However, I am encouraged that more physicians are asking questions in these meetings and coming to workshops. My work is becoming better known and accepted, and therefore it is safe to speak openly about it. As one man said, "Even if I disagree with you, half of my patients have your book under their arms, so it's important we talk."

Love, Medicine and Miracles stirred the waters and created change. That's why there is music in virtually every operating room in New Haven today, although when I first brought in my tape recorder I was considered an explosion hazard. And that's why I expect hospitals will in the future use closed circuit television in patients' rooms to provide preoperative preparation, meditation, healing imagery, music and laughter. Sooner or later they'll see that this will help patients heal faster, and reduce hospitalization costs. Wellness is cost-effective.

The fact is, there seems to be a movement today to reintroduce medical students to their patients as human beings, not diseases, and I think that movement will spread, because it will be successful for both patient and doctor. If nothing else, today's consumer-conscious patients will pass the word among themselves, and the doctors who have gotten the message will get their business.

THE ACTIVIST PATIENT

My friend Jake, whom I mentioned earlier, was a real champion among patients. He found inspiration to fight the overwhelming odds against him in what he had learned from years of participating in Outward Bound expeditions. Diagnosed in August 1985 with an inoperable malignant brain tumor, he took two days off to cry and then decided to "get off the pity pot," as he put it. He remembered that he had mobilized the students he taught at a special school for dyslexics by sharing with them the philosophy of Outward Bound Movement founder Kurt Hahn: "Your disability is your opportunity." Now he put that philosophy to work on his own disability.

Jake went through radiation, came to one of my workshops and embarked on a very active Strategy of Wellness that he devised for himself. Two years after his diagnosis he had a CAT scan that showed his tumor to be half the size it had been when it was first discovered.

But refusing to lie down and die quietly can make you unpopular. In a study done at Yale there was a direct correlation between an active immune system and a negative opinion of the patient by the head nurse on the ward. What that means is that if I come on the ward and say I'm going to draw a blood sample from Mr. Smith, and the nurse says, "That old s.o.b. won't take his clothes off, is never in his room and probably won't let you draw his blood without asking you five hundred questions about why you're doing it," then there is a 100 percent chance of an active immune system. Whereas, if I come on a ward and say to the nurse, "Today it's Mr. Jones's turn to have his blood drawn," and the nurse says, "What an angel. Yesterday he had a barium enema by mistake because we have two Joneses on the floor and he never complained a minute"—well, you just know what that says about Mr. Jones's immune system.

Other studies have verified these findings. Unfortunately, most doctors want their patients to be submissive. In fact, the word "patient" *means* submissive. To be a "good" patient means to be docile and fit in and do what the system wants. But that is not good for survival. We need to look to another word, "curious," for survival techniques. "Curious" has the same root as "cure," and that means that doctors should be glad when patients come in with a list of questions, a request for options and an insistence on knowing how they can participate in their own healing. But the patient who does that is not a good patient. I have created a new word for people like that—"respant"—which stands for "responsible participant."

My prescription for becoming a respant requires people to ask themselves the five questions discussed earlier, in addition to sharing the symbolic and unconscious aspects of their true selves. I also ask them to undertake a five-part therapeutic program that you'll read about in chapter 6.

Not exactly a "good patient," a respant is what Bobbie calls a "good/bad patient." Respants get emotional, make noise and may seem difficult to deal with. They fight the submissive role because they are fighting for their lives, so I naturally encourage them in that behavior. The result is that my patients tend to get reputations.

The other day a radiologist called to tell me that a patient had come in to see her with earphones on, a meditation recording on her tape player, a list of questions in one hand and a list of her many allergies in the other—and she knew right away that this lady was a Bernie Siegel patient. Sure, I get teased a lot by my colleagues, but I also get notes like the recent one from an oncologist who told me that my patient was doing beautifully and that he would be sure to provide her with her music and the room with a view of the sky I had requested for her, because he's seen how these things can diminish side effects. I'm gradually making converts in the medical profession, or perhaps it would be more accurate to say that my patients make the converts with their success stories.

More and more patients are learning to participate in their own healing. It's no longer uncommon to hear patients say, "I have interviewed several doctors and now have a team made up of people who passed the interview test." One woman didn't even grant a doctor an interview until she visited a number of different waiting rooms and finally found a cheerful one. Only then did she make an appointment to meet the doctor and evaluate him. So you might think about using waiting rooms as part of your selection process. I love to hear about people who do things like that, and I also love to deal with patients who are direct about their needs and preferences—like the woman who came into my office with two typewritten pages entitled "This Is What I'm Like," and two more typed pages of questions. At this point, I enjoy these patients. Yes, they're difficult, yes, they take time, but they are wonderful survivors.

Recently a preoperative patient who had a lot of questions for me found a nonconfrontational way of asking them. She began each of her requests for information by saying, "Tell me about. . . ." I recommend this technique to all of you when you are talking to your doctors, because it is so nonthreatening.

The following letter, written by a woman to her surgeon, is a perfect example of a patient taking responsibility for her life as I am suggesting, something most people won't do.

I would like to tell you something about myself, what kind of person I am, what qualities I can bring to these rather unusual circumstances.

I bring you a strong, healthy body, equipped with a good heart and lungs and better than average endurance. I bring you someone who runs, swims, plays tennis and bikes. I bring you someone to whom the outdoors is terribly important. . . . I bring you someone who loves life.

Yesterday I felt as though I was being put in a box car and shipped to Auschwitz to rendezvous with the Mengele brothers. I felt as though all "these procedures or protocols" were going to be enacted on me, with my having no say in the matter. I need to be heard, to have you know my fears and expectations.

One of my many concerns is bodily impairment. I want to be able to use my legs as I have in the past. My small incision has been somewhat restrictive, although I feel today that I could go out and run, maybe a mile. To the point, I do NOT want a radical inguinal lymphadenectomy (if I understand it correctly). . . .

This is what I want from the surgeons who are in my hire: I want/need to be consulted if possible, to be in on any decisions that are to be made in my behalf. Once in the operating room, I want the most highly qualified and skilled professionals (surgeons and staff) operating (so to speak) on my behalf. I want someone who sees alternative solutions and is not thrown by the unexpected. I want someone who when making decisions keeps in mind the spirit and life-style of the woman lying helpless and inert on the table.

You are the right person for me. I bring to the situation my strong mind, a sturdy body and a fierce desire to continue my life.

P.S. I want to be sewn rather than stapled.

Some of you may be amazed at this woman's willingness to confront authority and express such strong opinions about the kind of surgery she is willing to have. But she had researched her options, and was careful to leave the door open to further discussion if necessary ("if I understand it correctly," she noted, in reference to the surgical procedure she was opposed to—thereby inviting the surgeon to remedy any possible misapprehension).

If I received a letter like this, but felt strongly that the procedure the patient was rejecting was the right one for her, I would explain my thinking, perhaps by telling her how I would treat the same condition in my wife or myself. But I would never make her feel that if she didn't do what I said she couldn't return to my office. If we were unable to reach an agreement about her treatment, I might say, "I care about you, so let's see you again in two weeks and find out what progress you've made. If what you've chosen works, fine. If it doesn't, maybe you will want to look at some other options." No matter what happens, I don't give ultimatums. I always think of one woman of my acquaintance who, when a doctor told her that he was "captain of the ship," said, "Yes, but I have to decide if I want to get on your ship."

My patients stay with me because I let them know that we are working together as a team. On the other hand, by the time they get to me, some of these people have an entire breast invaded by cancer, or a malignant melanoma as big as a melon, because in their past experience they've found doctors even worse to deal with than the disease. These are intelligent people whose response to physicians who screamed, yelled and tried to play God was to walk out on treatment. They had made the choice that they would literally rather die than return to the medical profession. I can only say to those of you who are having similar experiences—keep looking for the doctor who is right for you. Don't walk away from the medical profession. It has too much to offer to be discarded. To doctors I would say, please accept these people and continue to see them no matter how much you may disagree with them. When you do, 100 percent will ultimately accept you and your therapy, because they will know that you care. It has worked for me with all the wide variety of patients I see.

Surgery can be a healing experience, as can chemotherapy, radiation and other treatments, if you see them that way. They can be gifts from God—in fact the Greek word *therapeia* means "doing God's work." That's what I wrote in answer to a letter from a lady who said, "I decided after reading your first book that I'd let God heal me. So I stopped taking my medicine for high blood pressure and dizzy spells, fell down in the bathtub, banged my head and spent a week in the hospital. Why is God slapping me around?" She had misunderstood what I was trying to say in *Love, Medicine and Miracles*. I told her in my letter that I thought God may have sent her the blood pressure pills. There's no reason to reject God's gifts and set oneself such stern tests of self-healing. To cite Ecclesiastes again, "Give the physician his place, for the Lord created him." Medication can be a gift from God, as well, according to the Bible.

HEALER AND HEALED

It is sad that so many doctors and patients now see each other as adversaries rather than as joint participants in a healing process to which each brings special qualities of mind and heart. In my desire to put a stop to the adversarial relationship, I have talked a great deal to medical students and other health care professionals about what they can do for their patients, and to patients about what they can do for themselves, but I've not given enough emphasis to what patients do for their doctors. However, I have been so continually renewed and healed by my patients that I do not think the doctor's indebtedness can possibly be overstated. The letter that best summarizes what I am trying to say about how the healing flows back and forth—and beyond—is one a patient received from her surgeon. After hearing that her doctor had just been diagnosed with cancer, this woman and her husband had sent him a copy of my book. He responded by writing this letter:

I want you to know how deeply I appreciate *Love, Medicine and Miracles*. This book continues to be a source of strength and optimism for me, and I have been telling my patients about it, so others have also had the benefit of your thoughtfulness and generosity to me. . . . Siegel brings out the power of love and hope.

Indeed, getting a cancer that has metastasized already showed me the enormous importance of a family, with brilliant clarity. I also experienced some depths of pure love which was unbounded and unqualified, as I know you have, from what you have done together. Being a card-carrying cancer patient has also shown the caring and the ties among us all. Each of us finds out by ourselves how long a night can be at 3:00 A.M., and how shattering this experience is.

None of us knows where this is leading. I see my role as more or less of a medical ministry; I have the opportunity to share my patients' experiences more than ever, and this is a rare privilege.

You and many other wonderful people have shared love and concern with me and I have felt humble and uplifted as a result. As you have reached out to me, I will reach out to others.

The longer I practice medicine, the less sure I am of the dividing line between healer and those in need of healing. Patients whose overwhelming physical problems made me feel useless have taught me volumes about the true nature of my calling, thereby restoring my faith in myself as a doctor. Patients who feel they owe their lives to me have returned the gift in full, enriching my life immeasurably by the wisdom they gained from their illness and passed on to me. As students who have worked with me can testify, whenever I am having a really hard day, one of those days that means I have gone into "cure mode" and am therefore feeling defeated by my own limitations, I go into the intensive care unit and sit with my sickest patient. Invariably that person will teach me again what I need to know—that patients ask only for my care, not my cure—and I leave feeling better, restored to my humanity, accepting of my limits.

I suggest to all physicians who are feeling the despair of being unable to cure that they too go to their sickest patient, perhaps with an excuse like "I'm waiting for a lab report, do you mind if I use the chair next to your bed while I wait?" and then sit there for half an hour. I guarantee that your patients will heal you in the time that you are sitting there, by their strength, their courage, and the fact that they don't ask you for a cure but are healed by your care.

The healing I have done as a doctor has always come back to me, tenfold. So who is the healer, who the healed? This is not a question that ever gets looked at in medical school. Students therefore miss out on one of the fundamental truths of the doctor-patient relationship—the fact that their greatest resource will be the people they take care of. The physician who knows this can tap into a never-ending source of loving energy. I have learned that I can always be sure of receiving the gift of renewal at the hands of those who might seem to have the least to give.

In a way, I could even say that I owe many of the extraordinary blessings that have come to me in the last few years, during what I might call my own medical ministry, to the patients in ECaP, the cancer support group I organized over a decade ago. At that time I was so unhappy with the way I was practicing medicine that I was considering alternative careers as a psychiatrist or a veterinarian. However, I realized that becoming a psychiatrist would remove me from the hospital and the whole system I was hoping to change, and though veterinarians work with pets who can be hugged, a veterinarian friend reminded me that people bring the pets in, which would mean I'd still be facing the same problems. My ECaP patients taught me how to remain a doctor by letting me know how to have a success-oriented practice that would help people to live between office visits.

As people who are ministering to those facing life-and-death issues every day, we doctors are privileged to be in a position to benefit from the hard-won wisdom of our patients. The men and women—and children too—who have looked death in the face, are often those who know most about living. Their message is: "I learned I was going to die and so I decided to live until I died." They interpret their diagnosis not as a sentence but as a message to live. Their mortality is accepted, not seen as a verdict. How few of us know how to do that!

Another lesson I learned from watching them is to live one day at a time, suffering and rejoicing for whatever that day brings. But then Evy McDonald taught me about living ten minutes at a time. I've written so much about Evy in this book because she is a veritable scholar and sage of suffering—and of the wonderful things that can come of it. This lady used her illness to turn her life around in such a way that there is nobody, sick or well, who could not learn from her story. Like all exceptional patients, she knows about living in the moment.

Patients really are our greatest resource, and when I think of the doctor I met once who told me that diseases are wonderful, but patients are a problem, I can only say that the loss is his. I feel sorry for him because he is missing out on the many gifts that always flow from the patient to the doctor who is prepared to receive them.

Neal Sutherland, an oncologist friend of mine in Hawaii, is eloquent about the nature of those gifts. In a recent letter he shared with me his thoughts about the spiritual healing and renewal he has experienced because of the people he has met in his practice:

Bernie, I have chosen being with cancer patients because I felt that if I were with them enough, I could find the secret of living one day at a time and why some cancer patients are able to find such phenomenal inner peace through their disease. . . . I think I now understand that inner peace and the transformation that leads to that inner peace. From my perspective it seems that it involves being willing to give up life as we normally perceive it and view life only as a moment by moment occurrence of opportunities to give love. In the giving of love, there is also the receiving of love, and this cycle grows endlessly and without bounds.

Again I would ask: Who is the healer, who the healed? In the chapters that follow, about exceptional patients who have confronted AIDS, multiple sclerosis, cancer and a whole host of other diseases, this is a question you may find yourself asking again and again.

The people who have chosen to take on those diseases and live as fully as possible in the face of them give a gift to all those whose lives they touch, whether it is their health care providers or their families. And from them we can learn not just how to fight illness, but how to live, and what healing really means.

Ten years ago I thought I knew something about living and offered to help others learn. I became the student and have been taught by these incredible and exceptional human beings. If you want to learn how to live, hang a sign in your living room window saying "I give lessons in how to live, 8–10:00 P.M., Wednesdays." You can even charge for it. When the people come, you have one job. Don't say a word; just listen. In three months they will thank you for your help and wisdom. In six months they will call you a genius for changing their lives. That's what's happened to me. I get a lot of credit for sharing what others have taught me.

5

*It all depends on how we look at things, and not on
how they are in themselves.*

—CARL JUNG

*Everything can be taken from a man but one thing:
the last of the human freedoms—to choose one's
attitude in any given set of circumstances, to choose
one's own way.*

—VIKTOR E. FRANKL, *Man's Search for Meaning*

It's never too late to have a happy childhood.

—SLOGAN SEEN ON A T-SHIRT

Healing the Child Within

Earlier in this century, the medical profession's interest in
diseases replaced its interest in the people suffering from those
diseases. In recent years, however, the culmination of several
decades' worth of studies at leading universities has begun to
turn our attention back to the emotional factors implicated in
the development of disease. These studies have set in motion
the slow process of converting "anecdotal" evidence—evidence based on first-hand observation but unsupported by
tightly controlled statistical analyses—into the kind of data the
medical profession will accept as scientific. Dr. George L.
Engel of the University of Rochester, one of the people carrying out these studies, believes in the value of anecdotes, too,
and has collected newspaper items from around the world on
the phenomenon of sudden death. He found the following
account of a loving couple of particular interest in his effort to
understand what makes us vulnerable to illness and death at
particular times in our lives:

This concerns a couple, Charlie and Josephine, who had been
inseparable companions for thirteen years. In a senseless act of

violence Charlie, in full view of Josephine, was shot and killed in a melee with the police. Josephine first stood motionless, then slowly approached his prostrate form, sank to her knees, and silently rested her head on the dead and bloody body. . . . She never rose again; in fifteen minutes she was dead.

Now the remarkable part of the story is that Charlie and Josephine were llamas in the zoo! They had escaped from their pen during a snow storm and Charlie, a mean animal to begin with, was shot when he proved unmanageable. I was able to establish from the zookeeper that to all intents and purposes Josephine had been normally frisky and healthy right up to the moment of the tragic event . . .

I cite this example to indicate that we are dealing with a general biological phenomenon, not simply a process peculiar to an occasionally oversensitive human animal.

EMOTIONS, PERSONALITY PROFILES AND DISEASE

In the 1950s, internists, psychologists and psychiatrists at the University of Rochester began conducting studies on what they eventually named "the giving up–given up complex." This is a state of mind, generally temporary and often related to changes in life circumstances, that was found to be a factor affecting susceptibility to many kinds of illness. In fact, their research showed that in 70 to 80 percent of the cases they studied, which included the full range encountered on a general medical service, the giving up–given up attitude preceded development of the illness.

Characteristics of this attitude include a feeling of giving up, experienced as hopelessness and helplessness; a depreciated image of the self; and a loss of gratification from existing relationships or roles in life. Dr. Engel explains that this failure of normal mental coping mechanisms is thought to activate "neurally regulated biological emergency patterns," which lessen the body's ability to fight disease.

Feelings of hopelessness and helplessness can be triggered by events of all kinds, some obviously traumatic, some not so obvious, at least in the eyes of an observer. Having suffered a heart attack on the last day of the period of formal mourning for his twin brother, who had himself died of a heart attack, Engel knows from personal experience how even the anniversaries of traumatic events can have devastating physical effects. As he notes, however, it isn't so much the event itself that matters, but the way the individual responds to it. We can exercise considerable control over our thoughts and attitudes, and can choose how we use adversity and the so-called useless events in our lives.

That's the message we hear over and over again in *Man's Search for Meaning,* psychiatrist Viktor Frankl's recounting of life in the concentration camps of World War II. At one point his spirits were at particularly low ebb. But then, in the midst of the horrors on which he was dwelling:

> I forced my thoughts to turn to another subject. Suddenly I saw myself standing on the platform of a well-lit, warm and pleasant lecture room. In front of me sat an attentive audience on comfortable upholstered seats. I was giving a lecture on the psychology of the concentration camp! All that oppressed me at that moment became objectively seen and described from the remote viewpoint of science. . . . Both I and my troubles became the object of an interesting psychoscientific study undertaken by myself.

And so he survived another day. He *chose* to take a different attitude, which is something we all can do. Often we may not feel that this is an option, however, because our personalities have been shaped by negative experiences in early life that have made us feel incapable of exercising that "last of the human freedoms." These early experiences can have consequences for both our mental and our physical health, because who we grow up to be, psychologically, will have its effect on what happens to us, physiologically.

INFLUENCES FROM OUR EARLY YEARS

The greatest disease of mankind is a lack of love for children, leading to their psychological and sometimes even physical abuse, which predisposes those children to a hopeless-helpless attitude and to disease later in life. We cannot keep blaming physical poisons or genetic defects for every disease. We have to realize that there are social and psychosocial poisons in our own homes that predispose us to disease by creating certain attitudes and feelings within us.

Internist Caroline Bedell Thomas of Johns Hopkins Medical School began her research on the relationship between psychological characteristics and disease in the 1940s, preparing personality profiles and family medical histories of over 1300 medical students who graduated from Johns Hopkins between 1948 and 1964. In the decades that followed, she continued to track their health, until the mid-1970s when she began compiling the results.

To her surprise, the study confirmed that there were psychological correlates not only of heart disease, suicide and mental illness, which she had expected, but of cancer as well, which she had not. In fact she had assumed the opposite—that her research would show that cancer, in contrast with heart disease, hypertension, mental illness and suicide, has no psychological antecedents. But the cancer patients, like the suicides and the mentally ill, were much more likely than the other subjects in the study to have had unhappy childhood relationships with their parents, and to have reacted by repressing their emotions in the years since. Recently, in an article written over forty years after she began what is known as the "Precursors Study," Thomas summarized and confirmed these earlier findings about life patterns and attitudes and how they predispose to disease. She's looking forward to the day when her research can be confirmed at the molecular level:

Forty years ago, the term "molecular biology" had not been coined and mechanisms connecting youthful psychological characteristics with disease states had not been envisioned. But today, with the burgeoning of neuroscience, it is not unduly optimistic to predict that the pathways leading from habits of nervous tension, family attitudes and interpersonal relationships may be understood in the near future, and perhaps even the molecular structure of some of their components identified.

A new study, which I feel supports Thomas's conclusions about cancer, compared the medical histories of almost one thousand adopted Danish children born between 1924 and 1926 to those of both their biological and their adoptive parents. The study indicated that there was a genetic component to premature death from heart disease and infection. Cancer was a significant exception, as indicated by the fact that there was no correlation between adopted children and their biological parents with respect to premature death (before the age of fifty) by cancer; conversely, there *was* a strong correlation between the children's developing cancer and their adoptive parents' dying of cancer before the age of fifty (but not if a parent dies after sixty or seventy).

Of course it's possible to speculate that this correlation was the result of carcinogens in the adoptive home, rather than psychological influences, but to me this is like saying that the carcinogen is in the kitchen. (I'm referring to a study from the University of Oregon School of Public Health showing that housewives had a 57 percent higher incidence of cancer than the female population as a whole and 154 percent higher than that portion of the female population working outside the home. They looked for a carcinogen in the kitchen, but there wasn't any. The possibility that the housewife's feelings of being trapped might be contributing to the higher rate of cancer was never considered—though it should have been, since domestic help had lower rates of cancer than housewives.)

Again and again we see the medical profession insisting on a mechanistic view of things that ignores the emotional realities in people's lives. I say that we have to look at feelings of hopelessness and helplessness engendered within the home environment. We have to start looking beyond the question of chemical poisons and consider the possibility of psychological poisons. How does a child feel and relate to the world when his or her parent dies at a young age? How does this create vulnerability to disease and early death in the child?

Thomas's conclusions about family background, youthful personality traits and the impact of these factors on physical health in later life have been reconfirmed in a 1988 follow-up study on the same group of subjects by psychologists Pirkko L. Graves and John W. Shaffer, also of Johns Hopkins. The psychological patterns and attitudes formed in early life were found to continue to have a significant influence on the subjects' physical health as they aged. For example, the study showed that "Loners," a group defined by bland, emotionless exteriors and inner loneliness, were sixteen times more likely to develop cancer than the group described as "Acting Out/Emotional," consisting of people who were prone to depression, emotional upsets and anxiety—in other words, people who both felt their emotions intensely and expressed them.

If you want to change your emotional style, you might want to follow the advice given by a man who came to one of my workshops. A computer expert, he said he'd learned from computer programming that if you put garbage in, you get garbage out; but if you put the garbage out, love comes in. A man with lung cancer had similar advice: Instead of smiling on the outside when you are really hurting on the inside, he said, you need to turn yourself inside out. Yes! Let the pain and garbage out, take the smiles and the love in. That's the best description I've heard of the kind of therapy we do in our exceptional patients' groups. When you put your feelings outside, you may heal inside. And you will certainly heal your life, if not your disease.

For some people, however, that can be an extremely difficult lesson, because it goes against lifelong emotional habits. The inexpressive emotional style is learned very early on, as a reaction to parents who don't respond to the infant's expression of its needs. When the emotions are either ignored or actively rejected or punished—for example, by a mother whose own needs are threatened by her infant's neediness (and remember, babies are *very* demanding creatures)—the infant may simply shut down emotionally and become withdrawn, blaming itself for the lack of attention. The resulting stoic, self-denying personality is the most commonly cited psychological factor in the development of cancer.

A lack of love in early infancy can have dramatic physiological effects not just in later life, but in childhood too. I can recall being at a conference where Dr. Ashley Montague got up before an audience of physicians and nurses and asked a question nobody in the room could answer: How can you demonstrate lack of love on an x-ray? Montague, an anthropologist who has written books on the subjects of touching and love and how healing they are, explained that when children aren't loved, they don't grow. The evidence for this is the dense lines that can be seen in x-rays of their bones, indicating periods when love was lacking and growth did not occur.

What is now known as the "failure to thrive" syndrome, seen in infants who haven't received enough attention and love, can result in severely undersized and underweight babies, exhibiting the kind of withdrawal seen in chronic depression. Ultimately such love-deprived children may die. Just as lack of love and physical attention can be damaging, the reverse has been shown to be healthful, helping to explain, for example, why breast-fed infants gain more solid weight than those who are bottle-fed and why they have less cancer later in life. Again, scientists rush to see what is in the milk. I say it is the way the milk is delivered that is significant. Touch is physiologic and love is scientific—they change our internal environment.

For those of you who weren't loved adequately, however, there can be psychological or physical consequences—or both. Lonely, unhappy childhoods and the resulting depressed, repressive personality styles Caroline Bedell Thomas describes had earlier been noted by psychologists Lawrence LeShan and R. E. Worthington in their studies of cancer patients in the 1950s. Other evidence of psychological components of disease includes predictive studies in which it was possible to identify, on the basis of drawings people did, Rorschach readings and other kinds of psychological testing, which of the individuals in a group would have cancer. Caroline Thomas did some of the early work on the use of psychological indicators (drawings and Rorschachs) to predict not only incidence but type of disease.

Interestingly enough, what the psychologists have learned through the results of their studies, many medical personnel know intuitively, if not "scientifically." I had a letter from an operating room nurse, for example, who said that, on the basis

of a few minutes' conversation with a patient prior to exploratory abdominal surgery, she could always tell which instru-
ments to add to the table—those for cancer or those for stones.
"The patients were different. I still cannot tell you how."

Claus Bahnson was one of the psychologists who did predictive studies, and he too drew a profile of cancer patients
that showed a sense of alienation stemming from early childhood experiences. In his 1975 survey of the relevant literature,
Bahnson notes that psychological studies of cancer have
focused on two main themes: a personality configuration
"characterized by denial and repression as well as strong inter-
nalized control and commitment to social norms"; and feelings
of loss and depression as antecedents to the disease.

I think the first part of that description is what I see in my
patients all the time. They're the people who always tell you
they're "Fine," no matter how they feel. When you ask
"What's wrong?" they say "Nothing." As explained earlier, the
message you give your body when you deny your needs, act as
though everything is fine and refuse help, is a "die" message;
the result is, your body helps you do what it thinks you want
and allows you to get sicker and die sooner. I think we need
to institute a grading system for those who have trouble expressing feelings. If someone walks up to you and says "How
are you?" you can respond "C minus." It doesn't sound too bad
and won't upset people. One hospital has even put up posters
saying "If you're anything less than a B plus, let us know and
we'll give you a hug." You could ask your friends and family
to do the same.

A woman wrote me that she has her own approach to
dealing with cancer—secrecy. Then she shared with me the
secret that she had had cancer surgery six years before. When
a friend saw her while she was still in pain from the surgery
no one but a few members of her family even knew she had
had, she never let on that anything was wrong. Although this
approach may have worked for her, it seems to me a terrible
drain of energy that would have been better spent in healing
not just her disease but her life. Now she must devote energy
to the keeping of a secret that prevents her from asking or

receiving help from friends and family. To have a lie accepted as oneself and then to have to live that lie may be poetic justice, but it certainly is a harsh punishment.

Ideally, people should be able to use the knowledge of their own mortality to break out of their prisons of self-denial and punishment, to become authentic, to affirm themselves— but unfortunately not everyone understands that they can break those early patterns. I met a woman in my office who was incredibly involved in covering up her disease. She had just been to her college reunion and was very proud that she had not let on to anybody there that she had extensive cancer. Her husband and her children are not allowed to speak about it, and even her death is to be kept quiet—no obituary. I asked her whether she planned to have herself propped up in her living room window so nobody would ever find out she was dead.

This was a woman who had been given very negative messages by her parents. Her legacy from them is a terrible lack of self-esteem—which I fear will be her legacy to her children as well, for children learn by example. Please don't do this to yours. Accept your mortality and live your life, reach out for the help you need and accept it. To do so is a gift to those around you. You become their teacher and healer. What happens in sick people is often the opposite, however: They feel so guilty about the suffering they are causing their loved ones that they won't ask anything for themselves.

I was on rounds at the hospital one Christmas when I discovered that one of my patients had been left totally alone that day while her family went out to a holiday dinner. If that had been her last night on earth she would still not have said anything about it. When I see my patients denying themselves as she did, I have to wonder what happened to them in their childhood that would make them want to punish themselves this way. What guilt has been instilled in them to make them long for the multiple crucifixions brought about by self-hatred and denial? I'm concerned because I know that emotional repression prevents the healing system from responding as a unified entity to threats from inside or outside.

DEVELOPING A SURVIVOR PERSONALITY

Researchers in the new discipline of psychoneuroim-munology (PNI), a modern-day synthesis of the four previously separate disciplines of psychology, neurophysiology, endocrinology and immunology, are looking into the links between learned emotional patterns and illness. Dr. George F. Solomon was one of the earliest researchers in the field; in fact, it was he who suggested the term "psychoimmunology," in 1964, when he was studying the impact of stress on the immune system. Dr. Solomon and his colleague Dr. Lydia Temoshok, from the Department of Psychiatry at the University of California, have defined what he calls an "immunosuppression-prone" personality pattern in AIDS patients, which has much in common with the "Type C" coping style that Dr. Temoshok has observed in her work with cancer patients. "Compliance, conformity, self-sacrifice, denial of hostility or anger, and non-expression of emotion" seem to be related to an unfavorable prognosis in cancer patients, and possibly to cancer suscepti-bility as well, they note, and they speculate that a similarly repressed personality type may be particularly vulnerable to AIDS.

Temoshok and Solomon are currently studying long-term AIDS survivors. On the basis of studies by themselves and others (including Sandra Levy, Keith Pettingale, Janice Kie-colt-Glaser, George Engel and David McClelland, who are all cited in this book), they have tentatively identified a number of personality traits that actively enhance survival: a sense of meaning and purpose in life, a sense of personal responsibility for one's health, an ability to express one's needs and emotions and a sense of humor.

In the latest article I've read by Dr. Solomon, however, he says that there is one simple question AIDS patients can ask themselves to gauge their chances of long-term survival: Would you do a favor *you didn't really want to do* for a friend who asked you to? If the answer is no, according to Solomon, that has more positive significance in predicting long-term survival than any of the elaborate lists of personality character-istics they have been able to develop. At my lectures, I tell audiences to imagine that they have AIDS or cancer and only six months to live. A friend calls to ask a favor on a day when they have a wonderful activity planned. Would they say yes or no to their friend? I find that less than half, and sometimes as few as 10 or 20 percent, say that they would respond with a no; but the people at patient workshops are much more likely to say no, which indicates to me that those who choose to attend such gatherings have already learned a lot about survival.

Psychotherapy is one of the techniques that can assist people in making health- and survival-enhancing changes in their lives. Beginning in mid-1983, Solomon gave psychotherapy to an ARC (AIDS-related complex) patient in order to see if psychological intervention aimed at reducing depression and enabling the man to feel and express emotion better could improve immune function. Although immune status indicators, which were being measured, did *not* improve as the patient became less depressed and more assertive, his symptoms—night sweats, fever, severe genital herpes—did. Within nine months of embarking on psychotherapy he was able to return to work full time. However, his immune system's helper T cell count continued to drop, even though, to the surprise of his doctor, he continued to feel well and did not progress to AIDS.

When he did suddenly become very ill and was diagnosed with a lymphoma in late 1985, it appeared that he had only days or weeks to live. But he responded to chemotherapy and, as of 1987 when Solomon reported on his case, was feeling relatively well, working on unfinished projects, seeing friends and family (who were very supportive), traveling, using alternative therapies and continuing to hope. Solomon ends his account by affirming that it was the man's "attitude, determination, 'fighting spirit' and social support" that enabled him to do so well for so long in the face of such dire illness.

Letters from and meetings with other long-term survivors and those who have reversed their blood tests indicate that there are many more stories like his. These accounts are valuable because of what they tell us about psychological characteristics that can be useful in the struggle with illness. More important, they remind us that we can acquire those qualities, even at an age when most of us think our character, for better or worse, is set in stone. If change were impossible, there would be no point in talking about which attitudes are more life- and health-enhancing than others, because you wouldn't be able to do anything with that knowledge. But this "last of the human freedoms" is yours, if only you will choose to exercise it.

Let me share some quotes from the February 1989 conference "AIDS—Defying the Odds: A Case for Optimism," organized by Dr. Donald Pachuta of Baltimore: "Getting sick is hard—denying who we are for years. Getting well is more natural." "My illness was all there was that was not me." "AIDS has not been the disease; it has been the cure." Read the book *Beyond AIDS: A Journey into Healing,* by George Melton with Wil Garcia.

ATTITUDES—HEALTHY AND UNHEALTHY

Peace of mind is the goal to work for as you seek change. If, as Candace Pert has said, your body is the outward manifestation of your mind, peace of mind is what you want it to manifest. That doesn't mean suppressing your feelings. As we've discussed, people think that anger, for example, is a "bad" emotion, so they may try not to allow themselves to feel it when they are told that they have a life-threatening disease. But it's okay to be angry—even with God. As one of our group members said, "I fired God a long time ago." Anger, anxiety, depression, fear and many other feelings are unhealthy only if they remain buried inside, unexpressed and not dealt with.

When you value yourself you express all your feelings, and then you let them go. Letting people know who you are and where you are in life means that fewer conflicts occur. One result is that your relationships improve and even business improves. If you're uncomfortable about expressing anger, do as one of my students suggested and think of it as righteous indignation, which even Jesus displayed.

In *Surviving and Thriving with AIDS: Hints for the Newly Diagnosed,* from the New York People With AIDS Coalition (available through the PWA Coalition office at 31 West 26th Street, New York, NY 10010), I found a very comprehensive listing of all the good and bad things you can do to yourself emotionally, whether you have AIDS or not. Though the author has called his rules "Steven James's Totally Subjective, Non-Scientific Guide to Illness and Health," there's plenty of good science to back him up, and more accumulating every day. Since people in various stages of health will read this book, we have something for everyone—one list to help you get sick, one to help you get sicker and one to help you get well—or stay well.

HOW TO GET SICK

1. Don't pay attention to your body. Eat plenty of junk food, drink too much, take drugs, have lots of unsafe sex with lots of different partners—and, above all, *feel guilty about it.* If you are over-stressed and tired, ignore it and keep pushing yourself.
2. Cultivate the experience of your life as meaningless and of little value.
3. Do the things you don't like and avoid doing what you really want. Follow everyone else's opinion and advice, while seeing yourself as miserable and "stuck."
4. Be resentful and hyper-critical, especially towards yourself.
5. Fill your mind with dreadful pictures, and then obsess over them. Worry most, if not all, of the time.
6. Avoid deep, lasting, intimate relationships.
7. Blame other people for all your problems.
8. Do not express your feelings and views openly and honestly. Other people wouldn't appreciate it. If at all possible, do not even know what your feelings are.
9. Shun anything that resembles a sense of humor. Life is no laughing matter!
10. Avoid making any changes which would bring you greater satisfaction and joy.

HOW TO GET SICKER (IF YOU'RE ALREADY SICK)

1. Think about all the awful things that could happen to you. Dwell upon negative, fearful images.

2. Be depressed, self-pitying, envious, and angry. Blame everyone and everything for your illness.

3. Read articles, books, and newspapers, watch TV programs, and listen to people who reinforce the viewpoint that there is NO HOPE. You are powerless to influence your fate.

4. Cut yourself off from other people. Regard yourself as a pariah. Lock yourself up in your room and contemplate death.

5. Hate yourself for having destroyed your life. Blame yourself mercilessly and incessantly.

6. Go see lots of different doctors. Run from one to another, spend half your time in waiting rooms, get lots of conflicting opinions and lots of experimental drugs, and start one program after another without sticking to any.

7. Quit your job, stop work on any projects, give up all activities that bring you a sense of purpose and fun. See your life as essentially pointless, and at an end.

8. Complain about your symptoms, and if you associate with anyone, do so exclusively with other people who are unhappy and embittered. Reinforce each other's feelings of hopelessness.

9. Don't take care of yourself. What's the use? Try to get other people to do it for you, and then resent them for not doing a good job.

10. Think how awful life is, and how you might as well be dead. But make sure you are absolutely terrified of death, just to increase the pain.

HOW TO STAY WELL (OR GET BETTER, IF YOU'RE NOT SO WELL TO BEGIN WITH)

1. Do things that bring you a sense of fulfillment, joy, and purpose, that validate your worth. See your life as your own creation, and strive to make it a positive one.

2. Pay close and loving attention to yourself, tuning in to your needs on all levels. Take care of yourself, nourishing, supporting, and encouraging yourself.

3. Release all negative emotions—resentment, envy, fear, sadness, anger. Express your feelings appropriately; don't hold on to them. Forgive yourself.

4. Hold positive images and goals in your mind, pictures of what you truly want in your life. When fearful images arise, re-focus on images that evoke feelings of peace and joy.

5. Love yourself, and love everyone else. Make loving the purpose and primary expression in your life.
6. Create fun, loving, honest relationships, allowing for the expression and fulfillment of needs for intimacy and security. Try to heal any wounds in past relationships, as with old lovers, and mother and father.
7. Make a positive contribution to your community, through some form of work or service that you value and enjoy.
8. Make a commitment to health and well-being, and develop a belief in the possibility of total health. Develop your own healing program, drawing on the support and advice of experts without becoming enslaved to them.
9. Accept yourself and everything in your life as an opportunity for growth and learning. Be grateful. When you f—k up, forgive yourself, learn what you can from the experience, and then move on.
10. Keep a sense of humor.

Please pay particular attention to the last ten items.

CHOOSING THE RIGHT REACTIONS

Scientists can confirm the value of Steven James's list. One of the personality characteristics relevant to a number of his rules—what psychologist Suzanne Kobasa has called "hardiness"—is actually a configuration of several complementary traits, which came under scientific scrutiny in the 1970s and 1980s.

Kobasa and Salvatore Maddi were part of a group of University of Chicago behavioral scientists who studied two hundred middle- and upper-level executives at Illinois Bell Telephone. All of the employees were under a lot of stress due to changes in management during AT&T's divestiture. Half had experienced a number of ailments, half were healthy. Why, if stress influences health, were half of this group so physically unaffected by it? The answer, according to the Kobasa research team, lies in the three C's: control, commitment, challenge. Telephone company executives and others who stayed healthy in the face of stressful life circumstances felt in *control* of their lives (as opposed to helpless/hopeless), *committed* to lives in which they found meaning both at home and at work, and *challenged* by events that other people might find threatening. These are the qualities that constitute the hardy personality, and they are what we see in the exceptional patient.

They also resemble the characteristics that helped people endure the concentration camps. According to Viktor Frankl, after the initial "selection" (which allowed those judged capable of working to avoid the crematoriums), it was the people who were somehow able to find meaning in their suffering, who saw in it an opportunity to meet their destiny with courage and dignity, who did not simply give up and die. "Suffering had become a task on which we did not want to turn our backs. We had realized its hidden opportunities for achievement." In this way they reclaimed control over their inner lives.

How we explain the events of our lives to ourselves—what psychologist Martin Seligman of the University of Pennsylvania calls "explanatory style"—is what matters. Hans Selye, the endocrinologist responsible for much of our current thinking about stress and disease, gives the example of what happens when you encounter an abusive drunk on the street. If you just figure he is not worth responding to and go on about your business, there won't be any physiological consequences to the encounter. If, on the other hand, you feel your honor has been insulted by something the fellow said and you respond with violence, either verbal or physical, "you will discharge adrenalines that increase blood pressure and pulse rate, while your whole nervous system becomes alarmed and tense in anticipation of combat. If you happen to be a coronary candidate, the result may be a fatal heart accident." A clear case of "choosing the wrong reaction."

Let us choose the right reactions. When you think about it, it's amazing how much power we allow events to have over us. One minor example is the phenomenon of the odd sock. We tend to think that the washing machine ate its mate, and maybe curse the machine, right? Well, that wasn't the way one of our ECaP members saw it. After doing the wash she told her husband with great delight that she now had several "extra" socks. We are in control of our thoughts!

A teenager named Susan moved to a new house and her

mother insisted she do volunteer work during the summer. She went to the local nursing home, where they asked her to read to Mr. Johnson. Susan went to his room and introduced herself to him and asked him how he was. "I'm alright so far," he told her. "What does that mean?" she asked him. "I'm like the guy who falls out of a window at the top of a thirty-story building. Each floor you go by, people lean out and say, 'How are you,' and you say, 'I'm alright so far.'"

I'm alright so far can get you through a lot of things. It helped Susan as she stood at the door of her new school that fall. While pessimists have a more accurate view of the world, optimists live a lot longer and have a better time. So in the end, both can be said to have seen the truth about their own lives— in fact, to have created that truth.

I see many people who make life-affirming choices about how to respond to events. There was a maintenance man at a local hospital whom I noticed because he always seemed to be smiling and giving love. My thought was, Here is a guy who is an exception to the rule. Great life, no problems, and that's why he is this way. Then I was invited to speak to a group made up of the parents of children who had died. When we each introduced ourselves, that same man told how his two-year-old had just died of leukemia, and I realized what a beautiful, powerful man he was. He had made a choice about how he was going to live his life.

Seligman's research explores how developmental experiences enable us to choose the "explanations" that give us a feeling of control over events or, conversely, make us feel powerless. For over twenty years, Seligman has been studying how a sense of helplessness develops. For example, he did animal studies in which dogs that had been allowed no control over shocks administered to them were unable to function in a new situation where control *was* possible. They had "learned" helplessness and no longer knew how to exercise control, although dogs that hadn't been conditioned to help-lessness were soon able to learn how to avoid the same shocks.

Similarly, people may learn helplessness if they have had repeated experiences of being unable to change external circumstances through their own efforts, especially if this sense of helplessness was learned early on from parents who gave them very little autonomy and had no personal sense of autonomy in their own lives. The result is a "What's the use of trying" philosophy, a kind of fatalism that will be applied to all the events that befall them in a lifetime. An oncologist I know is so convinced of the significance of early life experiences that he comes to my workshops to find out how to raise his children, and has suggested that I write a book on the subject.

When people feel pessimistic about their lives and about the possibility of changing them, it can affect everything from their professional success to their health. Seligman and his colleagues at the University of Pennsylvania rated explanatory style in 172 undergraduates and were able on that basis to predict which students would be sick most often, both one month from then and one year later. They also found that explanatory style was more useful than the immune system's NK (natural killer) cell activity in predicting the survival rates of thirteen people with malignant melanomas.

Seligman's term "explanatory style" means much the same thing as psychiatrist George Vaillant's "adaptation to life"—how people master the stressors they encounter in their lives. To speak of a minor one, Vaillant describes what his own response would be to riding a roller coaster, in contrast to the pleasure he watched others find in the same experience:

> I contemplated the physiologic wear and tear that would ensue were I to make the ride. Undoubtedly, the experience would sequester calcium in my bursae, erode the lining of my stomach, deposit cholesterol in the intima of my arteries, compromise my immune system with an outpouring of corticosteroids and, metaphorically at least, take years off my life. But as I watched the excited passengers gather speed, sweep up the loop and hang suspended upside-down with their arms waving, I saw that for them the experience was one of joy, release and even relaxation. By what alchemy had their central nervous system mitigated an experience that should have been noxious to their health? The difference between them and myself, had I ventured to join them, would not have been the external stress and the imposed helplessness. The difference would have been in the ways by which our minds distorted the experience.

When he watched the people on the roller coaster, Vaillant was reflecting (in 1979) on the results of a forty-year study of the relationship between mental and physical health. The study had begun with over two hundred healthy Harvard undergraduates in the early 1940s, who were followed through annual or biannual questionnaires and an occasional interview. When the results were assembled as the men grew into middle age, the study indicated that "positive mental health significantly retards irreversible midlife decline in physical health." Of the fifty-nine men with the best mental health, as assessed from their twenties to their forties, only two had become chronically ill or died by the age of fifty-three. But the forty-eight men with the worst mental health had a very different health picture: Eighteen of them had become chronically ill or died by that age.

In 1987 Vaillant and Seligman and psychologist Christopher Peterson published a study updating the results on ninety-nine of those men. "The men's explanatory style at age twenty-five predicted their health at sixty-five," said Dr. Seligman, confirming the results Vaillant had begun to see ten years earlier. "Around age forty-five the health of the pessimists started to deteriorate more quickly," according to Seligman, who is convinced that changes in explanatory style can be brought about through cognitive therapy.

One example of a cognitive change you can make is to interpret the side effects from your medications not as just another of your afflictions, but as evidence of something positive happening. Perhaps as a result of chemotherapy your hair falls out when you are in the shower. You can see it (and yourself) as "going down the drain" with all the symbolism implied, or you can see it as a sign that the drugs are working, allowing you to uncover and reveal your true self.

DISEASE AS FAILURE

What is suggested by the Harvard study and a growing body of similar work is that our mental attitudes affect first our susceptibility to disease, then our ability to overcome it. Does this mean that sick people must bear the burden not only of their illness but of responsibility for having gotten sick in the first place? Are they "guilty" of repressing their emotions, harboring resentments that turn against them when not allowed expression, feeling helpless and hopeless, having insufficient fighting spirit or not enough "divluv" (to use David McClelland's terminology)?

Viewing disease as a sign of personal inadequacy or culpability is both cruel and false. A letter from a woman who had been diagnosed with cancer two years before describes the dilemma very well. After telling me about how hard she has worked to heal her life and disease, through surgery, meditation, visualization, chemotherapy, love, psychotherapy, spirituality and altruism, she had a terrible experience with her chemotherapy and "recovered extremely slowly from the surgery, [which] really shook my belief system":

I might add that some of the things that people have said to me in the past two years have been really cruel even though they were intended to be caring. One friend suggested that I must have spent my time in therapy avoiding, because if I'd been working I wouldn't have gotten sick. A number of people reminded me that we create our own reality and therefore I should look at why I created my cancer. And this summer a workshop leader told me that "it wasn't enough to cut off my breast and put a bunch of chemicals in my body." Until I could say: "I created my own cancer" and be full with that, I would get sick again.

God's gifts sometimes come in strange packages. My experiences have helped me to get really clear that I am not in control of the outcome. I am in charge of my attitude and what I give to my life and how I treat my body. But I am not in control of the outcome of my illness. It has been a very long time growing to this understanding, and letting go of my sense of failure. I kept turning back on myself, thinking that I must be doing something wrong, or I wasn't trying hard enough or maybe I was somehow sabotaging myself. Because after all, if I was doing it right I wouldn't be sick, be in pain, bleed, etc.

This has been a long way of getting to what I wanted to say to you. . . . Please, please take care not to set a new standard for failure. So much of what you say offers hope for a better way of living. But it is so important to *work for goals which are attainable. I can hope for a miracle but I can't make one happen* and I'm not a failure or a bad person if one doesn't happen. I *can* work for peace of mind and I have a lot to do with attaining peace of mind. I *can* choose to live each moment fully. I *can* choose to love and be loving. But—at least in my experience—when I choose to not have side effects from chemo, not bleed, not be in pain, shrink my tumour, drive cancer from my body, not have a recurrence—these are outcomes I'm less in charge of attaining.

You remembered to point out that the mortality rate [for the condition known as life] is 100 percent. Please also encourage us to hope and work for the best outcome and then to love and accept ourselves no matter what happens. When the outcomes are less than we want, loving ourselves is even more important. The Universe/God will provide everything I need—not everything I want. So teach that when I don't get what I want I'm not a failure—and I'm not necessarily doing something wrong. As a patient I really needed to hear that. And I needed for some of my friends to hear that too.

There is no need for me to teach this lady anything, because she has found it out for herself, and said what needs to be said so eloquently. I hope this message gets through, not only to patients and their loved ones, but to doctors, too. I hope all therapists, doctors, family members, and friends never make people feel like failures, or make them feel that they are still ill because they have not changed enough, achieved enough or made significant enough existential shifts. That is why I focus on teaching people how to live, not how to not die, for that is something that is always within their ability. If you see all of this as work you are on the wrong track and setting yourself up to fail.

The point is, as the lady who wrote the letter knows, you have to know what to fight for and what to leave to God. Your rights and your individuality are things you owe it to yourself to fight for, by saying that you will not be a doormat, by insisting that your doctor treat you with respect, by making sure you get answers to your questions, by wearing your own clothes in the hospital, by participating in decisions that need to be made about your treatment. But there are other times when you must have faith and trust, when you must allow God to handle the burden so that you can be at peace.

At such times you need to take a "We'll see" attitude and understand that some problems can turn out to be spiritual flat tires. One of our friends was in the hospital complaining that his 8:00 A.M. CAT scan had been delayed. I said to him, "Didn't you hear, the cable on the elevator broke at eight, and it crashed to the ground? Good thing you weren't on it." "Did that really happen?" he asked. I said, "Nooooo. But maybe if you get your CAT scan at eleven you will meet somebody in the x-ray waiting area you wouldn't have met at eight who will become helpful to you. Then you'll be glad it was at eleven instead of eight." Stop and let go of things. Leave your troubles to God when there is nothing you can do to change them. This combination of a fighting spirit and a spiritual faith is the best survival mechanism I know.

A doctor who had heard me speak about fighting spirit asked, "Is life extension or peace of mind your primary goal? If the angry, hostile patient lives longer, won't helping such a patient find peace of mind shorten life expectancy?" Perhaps the best answer to this is to be found in the Serenity Prayer, which was written by Reinhold Niebuhr, the twentieth-century theologian, and has been adopted, in the shorter version that I quote here, by Alcoholics Anonymous: "God grant me the courage to change the things I can, the serenity to accept the things I cannot, and the wisdom to know the difference."

As my correspondent above explained, the outcome of the disease may be beyond the limits of our power, and we must learn, as she did, where those limits lie. But that doesn't mean abdicating all responsibility. Responsibility and guilt are not the same things. Neither are disease and failure. All that I ask of the people who come to me for medical treatment or counseling is that they be "respants"—responsible participants in their own care. To ask that they not die is to ask the impossible. We all die; that's no failure. Not living fully is the only failure. Remember, there are probabilities and possibilities, statistics and individuals.

DISEASE AS PUNISHMENT

Another of our misconceptions about disease is that it is a punishment for our sins. Generally this guilt has no basis in reality but has been instilled in us by parents, teachers and other authority figures in our lives. As a result of the guilt, we long for the multiple crucifixions we think we deserve. My hope is that if we view disease this way, we can use it to open us to the possibility of resurrection.

Freud described this function of disease when he talked about symptoms expressing and gratifying a triple wish. One of the triple wishes has to do with the pleasure-seeking needs of the organism (and that's why I ask my patients to think about what needs of theirs are being met by the disease), the second with aggressive intent toward others (as when we use our illnesses to manipulate those around us) and the third with self-punitive measures as a means of atonement. Karl Menninger relates in *The Vital Balance* that at first he was dubious of this theory—who after all "would crave even a minor discomfort, to say nothing of a more serious one?" But his practice taught him the wisdom of Freud's theory, he says. Menninger illustrates the longing-for-atonement theme with the example of a man who had killed his child and then suffered a nervous breakdown. When the man later lost an arm in an accident, he became emotionally healthy again, because he felt he had atoned for what he had done to his son. The loss of his arm meant that he had suffered enough.

This way of looking at disease is another of the things I wish we would teach in medical school, because every doctor will encounter people who are sick for reasons that are not physical. People may go blind because there is something they do not wish to see, may lose the use of their limbs because they do not want to move, may become helpless because they don't know how else to get the help they need. We doctors need to be trained to look for the reasons behind illness, even when the reasons are psychological rather than physiological in nature.

In the Bible there is a gentleman whom Woody Allen called a very well-adjusted only child. For those of you who don't recognize him from this description, his name was Jesus.

Jesus was a healer but he was a terrible doctor: When he saw a man who was paralyzed he said, "Your sins are forgiven," not "Rise and walk." Any good doctor would have tried to get the man back on his feet by applying braces or operating, or at least referring him to an orthopedic surgeon. When people asked Jesus why he took this other approach, he said, "Which is easier, and which would you rather have?" Jesus knew the importance of a healed life, and he knew that a cure is often the by-product of healing. He healed and cured through forgiveness and faith.

By speaking of the need for forgiveness, I do not at all mean to imply that you are sinners, nor do I think that that was what Jesus meant. Before Jesus healed the blind man he was asked, "Who sinned, this fellow or his parents?" and he said, "Neither." The healing of the blind man was not an issue of sin but of manifesting God's healing gifts, which exist in us all. But many of you feel that you have brought your diseases on yourselves through sin, and Jesus knew that, which is why he knew the crippled man needed forgiveness.

Often this is what our patients need too—not our forgiveness but their own. If they can forgive themselves, they won't need sick minds and bodies. If they can't find enough self-love to grant themselves this forgiveness, then disease can be the atonement that finally releases them from guilt, after which they can finally allow themselves to get well.

I had a psychotherapist in my office one day who just couldn't accept what I was saying about people needing multiple crucifixions and using their disease as punishment. As often happens, God helped out by sending him a patient to explain it to him. She attributed her extraordinary survival to the release from guilt she achieved through illness:

The guilt was so overwhelming that I didn't know how I could continue living unless I found a way to suffer. I felt that I was a bad person and that I didn't deserve to continue living without some sort of suffering in my life. There was no forgiveness. I just couldn't overcome that until I had the cancer. Then, once I had the cancer I said to myself, it's o.k., you've suffered enough. Now you can do something positive for yourself.

Her resurrection can now occur. The healer's role is to guide people into self-forgiveness so they will no longer feel that they need to atone, to get them to understand that they are not sinners and to provide a path to self-healing and self-love.

SELF-LOVE

I've heard so many of these stories about self-punishment that I'm considering running for the presidency. My reason for wanting to be president is to enact two vital pieces of legislation: One is a law that will say you must love yourself, and my administration will enforce this by having love patrol officers in purple and yellow uniforms walking up and down the streets of every city asking each citizen, "Do you love yourself?" Anyone answering no will be fined severely. It will be too expensive not to love yourself.

The other major item on my administration's agenda will be to set up a true social security system. You will be assigned a number that puts you in a group that meets for two hours every week. There you will receive the love and discipline that your family does not provide. This is what our exceptional patient groups do now, and what groups like Adult Children of Alcoholics also do. But there are no "wellness" groups—for people who love life and want to live to be a hundred. Until now, if you wanted to join a group, you had to have cancer, AIDS, scleroderma or some other affliction, or be a drug addict, alcoholic, divorced, overweight or fit into some other recognized problem category. Recently, however, someone gave me a flyer for something called the Radical Self-Love Group. Maybe this is the start of a new movement. Maybe we won't have to hurt before we begin to live.

I hope that the group membership will help with what I see as the biggest problem in my work—getting people to want to live and undertake the necessary changes in their lives. It is all well and good to talk about the healing system and how to activate it, but when you realize what condition our society is in, you begin to understand that this information is not going to make a difference immediately. What is important is creating a society in which self-love and love of others are present. Recently I read an article by Ushanda io Elima about the Efé Pygmies, who live that way. According to Jean-Pierre Hallet, who grew up among the Efés and administers The Pygmy Fund (Box 277, Malibu, CA 90265), which is dedicated to their physical and cultural survival, they are very expressive of their feelings for each other.

There is a great deal of touching and affection among all the Pygmies. Babies and small children are held and carried. Older children and adults often touch one another. They frequently hold hands or sit with an arm around a friend or place their head in another's lap. Anyone feeling the need for reassurance may touch someone briefly or go for a hug. There is also a great deal of cuddling.

The result of this upbringing is a society in which "Pygmies concentrate their attention on the betterment of their personal relations, which are based on trust." There is no crime, no infidelity, no stigma against sexuality, and great respect not only for each other, especially the elders among them, but for the forest in which they dwell. If we would love one generation of the world's children as the Pygmies love theirs, the planet would change, and our problems disappear.

If you doubt the damage caused by the lack of self-love in our lives, you have only to look around you. Notice how many people commit suicide, overtly or otherwise, with accidents and untreated illnesses. We're so self-destructive there have to be laws—what I call please-love-yourself laws—even to get us to wear seatbelts or helmets. We poison and numb ourselves with cigarettes, tranquilizers, drugs, alcohol and unhealthy diets, and we seek out relationships that can never work in a desperate attempt to convince ourselves of our own value. No relationship in the world can make us feel worthy if we don't know that we are.

Without self-love it's hard to fight for one's life. When we give advice to someone about how to live, it's fine if it falls on the ears of an individual who wants to live. But if it falls on the ears of someone who does not love life, there's no point to it.

Why live longer if one does not enjoy living? I think the message needs to be "I love you and I hope someday you will love yourself." Criticizing doesn't help; it will only destroy a relationship and create feelings of failure.

If you have not been given love in your early days so that you know that you are lovable, it can be an incredibly difficult journey to try to find it within yourself. Don't think it can't be done. It can. You are capable of changing and finding your true self. That's what groups are for, what psychotherapy can help you do. Alternatively, a bit of what Martin Seligman would call "cognitive retraining" can be useful. That's what was needed by a woman with multiple sclerosis who first wrote to me several years ago. She admitted that many of her problems, physical as well as emotional, were related to her lack of self-love, but said she couldn't seem to stop the negative feelings. In one of her early letters she asks:

How can I love myself when there is one self-disappointment after another? If I were another person trying to love me, I would turn to greener pastures because of the "well today–sick tomorrow" characteristic of M.S. How can you love someone so lacking in dependability? You trade in your car when it stops being reliable. You divorce your spouse when he keeps disappointing you. I'm locked up in here with this belligerent self that I would have ordered out, traded in or divorced a long time ago if I could have. Am I supposed to learn to love this?

In my reply I told her about Evy McDonald sitting in front of her mirror, and tried to get her to see that the limitations of our bodies need never limit our ability to be loved or to love ourselves. But change doesn't come overnight. It's hard work. In a letter written almost a year after the one quoted above, this lady compared the process of learning self-love to that of acquiring any other skill, a subject she knows something about from her years as a schoolteacher. Reviewing her progress in what she calls "Loving and Accepting 101," she explains what it is that still holds her back: "I do have the cognitive capability. I am motivated. I am listening. But I'm having some problems getting my assignments completed."

Well, as the professor in this course of study she is pursuing, I feel sure that one of these days this hard-working lady will indeed graduate, as she says she hopes to, "Magna cum love!" Self-love can be acquired, even late in life, no matter what your circumstances. If you read *The Velveteen Rabbit* you will learn what it is to be real, and will understand that it doesn't matter if "most of your hair has been loved off, and your eyes drop out and you get loose in the joints and very shabby," because "once you are REAL you can't be ugly, except to people who don't understand."

I can recall visiting a woman at her home one evening. Due to extensive head and neck cancer, radiation and surgery, her head was enormously distorted and enlarged with retained fluid and had to be held tilted to the side so that one eye could remain open. Her tongue was swollen and protruding, so she could not speak. When I went into her room I wasn't even sure, with all my years of surgery, if I would be able to stay there five minutes, because of her appearance and odor. She couldn't speak, but she wrote some words on a pad and handed it to me; I wrote an answer and handed it back to her. She wrote on the pad and handed it to me, and I read, "You can talk." I broke out into a big smile and fell in love with her at that moment. She became real and beautiful. An hour later I held her in my arms and gave her a big kiss.

One of my most exceptional patients—and friends—is a woman named Susan Duffy who has scleroderma. We've had a correspondence for many years, through which I've learned much about her family history of alcoholism, suicide and abuse and about how brave you have to be to opt for life in defiance of a background like that. A while ago she wrote:

I have come from generations of repeated patterns of suicide, premature death, all forms of terminal illness—you name it, they had it. My mother and my father both committed suicide, within five years of one another. The message that I heard the loudest was "DIE, KID, DIE . . ." We all need something from our parents, whether it be positive or negative. Sometimes I feel that I am holding onto my illness to stay close to my parents. It is the one thing, somehow, that keeps me feeling a part of them. We all crave identity of some form.

I have broken out of the mold or pattern, but it has been a battle and a half to do so. I have had to fight so against the natural inclination to go the way of my forefathers, so to speak.

Over the years, however, Susan has grappled successfully with her past, her illness and her faith. Her correspondence with me provides a remarkable record of hard-won spiritual growth:

I see my experience of life as this: I live in a prison. I had no control over the circumstances which I was born into. I had no control over the parents who raised me. I had no power over the circumstances that I was exposed to. When my prison was so dark that I could not see, and the pain so great that I did not want to see—I heard a knock on the door and I had the courage to open it. As I opened the door—in walked LOVE. As LOVE walked in, I then had the courage to forgive. I then had the ability to accept. As LOVE walked around my prison, it touched every negative item in it, meaning the experiences in my life—and transformed them into something meaningful. . . .

I still find myself stumbling over some of the items in my prison. As I fall, I can feel the hand of LOVE as it picks me up. As I hurt and cry, I can feel its tender touch upon my heart. As I struggle on, I can feel its tender guidance guiding me, as it lightens my way. As I struggle to understand, I can hear its tender whisper, "It will be all right." And when I die, LOVE will gently lead me out of my prison and take me home with him where there are no prisons.

There is nothing easy about this process. She has healed herself emotionally and spiritually, not so much despite the pain she has experienced as because of it. As Susan says in another of her letters:

It was in the darkness that I found the light. It was in the pain that I found the gain. It was in the dying that I found the life. It was in the aloneness that I found the need of prayer. And it is through the love of God that I found meaning in my life.

This may all sound beautiful, heavenly and spiritual, but the price that I have paid to receive this illumination has been at times overwhelming! But again, it comes to me that through loss of any kind, there is something of a greater dimension to be gained.

The self-love that Susan has struggled so hard to find, through the exceptional patient groups and other groups that she's joined, comes much more easily when it is a natural consequence of the love given us by our first and most intimate group, the family. Like Susan, however, many of us didn't get the love we needed from our parents, who didn't get it from theirs. If we follow this back we get to Adam and Eve, and we can all blame them for not doing it right. Since each generation tends to pass on its legacy of lovelessness to the next, I'm afraid it will be several generations before we can phase out the love patrol and the social security system I'm proposing, unless we choose to stop this cycle now and love ourselves, our children and each other. Let us begin the process of change by allowing our diseases to redirect our lives. Once we've acknowledged, in the words of Elisabeth Kübler-Ross, that I'm not okay, you're not okay, but that's okay, we can decide to stop passing along our pain to subsequent generations and start loving.

OVERCOMING THE PAST

Now the idea that our parents didn't love us well or sufficiently is one that creates enormous resistance in people. Better to believe the fault lies within us, because then at least we maintain the illusion that we can win their love if only we: cut our hair, take a bath, become a doctor, marry the right person, earn more money, call home more often—you fill in the blanks to fit your situation. The point is that most of us are the products of conditional love (and some of us the products of no love at all, or even of abuse). If you come from a family that loved you unconditionally, you are in the minority, which is why so few of us feel that we are lovable.

At workshops I ask people who consider themselves unlovable if they think they were born that way, and I have yet to meet anyone who hasn't felt lovable at birth. My next comment is: Then someone else made you feel unlovable; it's the messages you received from authority figures that have made you feel this way. When love is conditional we feel imperfect and unlovable.

A story was told to me of a young man who wanted to become a violinist but was pressured into becoming a lawyer so that his parents could be proud of him. As an adult he developed a brain tumor and was told he had a year to live. At that point he said, "Then I will play my violin for a year." A year later he had a job as a violinist in a concert orchestra and no brain tumor. I know many stories like his and I wish the same thing could happen to all of you. That's why I ask you to give yourself the unconditional love your parents may have been unable to give. Forgive them, accept yourself and live your life. Here's a simple test: If, when you're dying, someone else's life flashes before your eyes, you've done it wrong.

I was recently rereading Tolstoy's novel *The Death of Ivan Illich* and I came across this sentence: "Ivan Illich led a life that was most simple and most comfortable, and therefore most terrible." Later as he lies dying he asks himself if anything in his whole life was real or true. How painful it must be, for someone near death, to have to wonder if he ever lived.

I know what lies within us, within the unconscious. I know what the unconscious is capable of doing if we set it free. What stands in its way? Both guilt and failure feelings are due to authority figures who made you feel that way and whose judgment you've never been able to escape.

Parents are hypnotic, just as teachers and doctors are, but all too rarely therapeutic. Children need unconditional love, and discipline rather than punishment. Give them messages such as "Life is full of problems and hurdles. Whatever happens you'll overcome and live to be a hundred." Or "Yesterday's gone, tomorrow isn't here yet, so what is there to worry about?" I also like the child-rearing advice given by Elida Evans, one of the first Jungian therapists, who over sixty years ago saw that there was such a thing as a cancer personality. Parents "should above all else teach perseverance to their children, and if the children cannot get what they want, teach them to take a substitute and make the most of what they have. There is interest and opportunity and beauty always possible to some degree, and I am not sure the degree is ever limited in any life."

Perhaps the best advice of all comes from the Swiss psychoanalyst Alice Miller, who has written four books on parents and children: *The Drama of the Gifted Child, For Your Own Good: Hidden Cruelty in Child-Rearing and the Roots of Violence, Thou Shalt Not Be Aware: Society's Betrayal of the Child* and *Pictures of a Childhood.* She told an interviewer that she would like us to be free to enjoy our children for themselves— "not as creatures to manipulate or change." Too often, however, we do the opposite, and try to mold our children into something they do not wish to be, making our love conditional upon their obedience. The resulting self-denial and repression can be contributing factors in illness. But I certainly do not think it is the case that everyone who is sick had unloving or neglectful or abusive parents.

I get letters from people who are angry with me because they think I am blaming them for their children's diseases. Why did my three-year-old "need" this illness, they ask; what did I do wrong? When the mother of a child with cancer calls me and says that I'm making her feel guilty, I believe that her guilt stems from something in her background, from the way she was brought up by her parents. It's not coming from me, though it's being projected onto me.

I don't want to create guilt in anyone, however, so if that's the message that is getting through, I want to clarify it. Yes, I do think there may be things happening in a child's family life that can contribute to illness. I say that not to assign blame but to empower people, to give them insight into positive ways of dealing with illness if there are family problems they can do something about. I want them to respond with love, not guilt; I want to turn on the repair mechanisms, not create further breakdown.

Of course, as a physician I also recognize that there's much more to illness than what parents have done to their children. Genetics and environment can both play major roles in disease. You may look at your family and not be able to see any serious psychological problems that could have been factors in your child's illness. Fine. Now turn the question around and start looking not for what you did wrong in the past, but for what you can do to make things better now and in the future.

Perhaps instead of urging you to let illness redirect your lives, it would be more to the point to say that illness *always* changes lives. Let it change yours in positive ways. There are wonderful stories of the love and healing that have come about and affected entire towns because of a child's sickness, as you will see when you get to the last chapter and read about Kelly Carmody.

I know that there are children—and adults—who have been loved by their parents and nonetheless become ill. I'll repeat: We all die someday. I know too that a child sometimes has inaccurate perceptions about a parent's real feelings. The overworked, overextended parent may be seen as unloving, but may simply be exhausted, as I've had occasion to learn in my own family life. One night my son Keith accompanied me to a Candlelighters meeting (for the parents of children with cancer) where I had been invited to speak. I always give my children the opportunity to speak if they want to. He elected to share what it was like growing up with a father who worked long hours and whose time at home was often disrupted by emergency calls, and a mother who worked equally hard taking care of five children born in the space of seven years (Keith being a twin). He didn't spare me in his recounting, making it clear that he would have liked a lot more from me than I had had time or energy to give in those days. We embraced after he was done.

A woman who was present at the meeting wrote me a note later complimenting me on the courage it took to be willing to have such information presented and thanking me for helping all of them listen to their children. I wanted them to know that I empathize with the feelings of anxiety and insecurity that all parents feel about whether they are bringing up their children properly. I know how hard it is to have those doubts, and I know what it is to make mistakes and see my children suffer for them.

When we run into troubles in our family, for example, I don't always handle things well. I'm still learning and growing. Once I got what I call a "Dear Hitler" letter. In case you don't know what that is, it's a letter telling you all the things you need to be forgiven for and, at the end, forgiving you for them. The problem is, it's painful, and it doesn't really help, to read about everything you've ever done wrong. Since nobody trains you for the job of being a parent, it's bound to be a long list. Who you are as a parent has to do with who your parents were and your parents' parents and so forth. If we trace this far enough, we are back to Adam and Eve again. We wouldn't be having all this trouble if they had done it right. Forgiveness is the key issue here, not continuing to blame generation after generation. Parents need to be forgiven for their mistakes and to forgive themselves. I could have done without the list, but I really needed the forgiveness. Our relationships have now evolved and changed so that we no longer need to write those letters. Our children are our teachers, as yours can be if you listen.

My heart goes out to all imperfect parents, which is what we all are. But ultimately it is the child within each of us who has the greater claim on my feelings, the child who comes into the world "trailing clouds of glory," as Wordsworth said. If we would all honor that child (while forgiving our parents), we would be on our way to reclaiming the love we owe ourselves. Only through loving the child within us can we insure that love will be the legacy we leave to our own children. Otherwise we will pass on the pain we still feel, the needs that were never met, just as our parents passed theirs on to us, and their parents before them *ad infinitum.* I want to stop the cycle.

From the self-hatred I see among my patients, however, I have to conclude that many remain victimized by the ambivalence if not downright hostility that so many parents feel toward their children. As Alice Miller says, there is a tendency to view the child as a little savage who must be tamed and civilized, often forcibly, "for his own good." Jean Houston's image is that of the child who is born as a Stradivarius but turned into a cheap plastic violin. Having had the "child within" throttled by our parents (whether psychologically or physically or both), we don't like seeing it reborn in our children. Thus the cycle of self-alienation and self-hatred continues, which is why our exceptional patient groups must spend so much time on issues of self-esteem.

But it's never too late to find the self-love we didn't experience as children. This is the meaning of the last words of *For Your Own Good:* "For the human spirit is virtually indestructible, and its ability to rise from the ashes remains as long as the body draws breath."

*The world breaks everyone and afterward many are
strong at the broken places. . . .*

—ERNEST HEMINGWAY, *A Farewell to Arms*

*Compared to what we ought to be, we are only half
awake. Our fires are dampened, our drafts are
checked, we are making use of only a small part of our
mental and physical resources.*

—WILLIAM JAMES

Finding Your True Self

This chapter introduces you to what I have learned since *Love,
Medicine and Miracles* about exceptional patients and how to
become one. The word "exceptional," however, creates a fear
in those people who have so little self-love they don't think of
this quality as something they can aspire to. Becoming your
true self may sound more accessible, and means the same
thing. The truth is, you're all lovable and exceptional. I'm an
authority figure and I'm telling you so.

You started out life as a fertilized egg, when a particular
sperm and egg met to become you. As was discussed earlier,
somewhere within that fertilized egg there was a set of instructions, a blueprint, a path laid out to guide you and show you
how to achieve your full potential and uniqueness before you
let go of the Tree of Life. Biologically, it is your destiny to be
similar to every other being on this earth in your basic compo-
sition, at the same time that your DNA makes you as unique
as your fingerprints. That is why every drawing I look at, every
dream or life story I hear, every disease I see is different, at the
same time that they share certain collective themes common
to all humanity. God gave us all certain gifts, but it is up to us
to decide how to use them in such a way that even the Being
who gave them to us will look down one day in admiration and
say, "Hmmm, I never thought of it that way before."

There's always room for expressing our uniqueness and love and changing the world with it, no matter what our position in life. I saw on the news a New York City subway conductor who sent out poetry, love and messages of good cheer over his loudspeaker system instead of the usual "Stand clear of the closing doors." A bus driver in Santa Monica looked in his rearview mirror and saw two men pull guns. He stopped the bus, went to them and said, "I love you" and sang "You Are My Sunshine." They put their guns away and have been riding as monitors on his bus ever since. These people are true originals. So are you—if you will simply learn to express your originality. Share your life with those who are also on the journey and you will change the world. If you don't like being a bus driver or a subway conductor try elevator operator—and realize we all have the opportunity to love and heal others. It's even easier if you have a trapped audience.

Discovering the ways in which you are exceptional, the particular path you are meant to follow, is your business on this earth, whether you are afflicted or not. It's just that the search takes on a special urgency when you realize you are mortal. Healer Barbara Ann Brennan says in her book *Hands of Light* that health, from the point of view of the healer, "means not only health in the physical body, but also balance and harmony in all parts of life. The process of healing is really a process of remembering, remembering who you are." To remember who you are means rediscovering your path. This is a chapter about people who have done that—exceptional people.

As you read about them, you will realize that, whether they have cancer, lupus, multiple sclerosis or AIDS, all people who have dared to defy the statistical odds against them tell some version of the same story. If their stories had nothing in common, then maybe we would say that these people were just lucky or had errors in diagnosis, spontaneous remissions, weak AIDS viruses, well-behaved cancers and all the other euphemisms that doctors use when they don't understand something and simply refuse to see it because it confronts their belief system. These people do share something. They all are manifesting the same basic qualities: peace of mind, the capacity for unconditional love, the courage to be themselves, a feeling of control over their own lives, independence, an acceptance of responsibility for decisions affecting their lives and the ability to express their feelings.

Few of us live up to the potential of our own uniqueness. In fact, for many of the people you will be reading about, it took their illnesses to put them on the path to self-realization. Their bodies had to get sick to make them aware they had stopped living their lives. They had wandered from the path and something had to awaken them. This gets us back to the ideas of Russell Lockhart, the Jungian psychotherapist, who would substitute the word "individuation" for "self-realization," or "remembering who you are":

Perhaps cancer [and I would say that the same could be said of any illness] is an experiment in the creation of greater personality, urging it on to the frontier of its existence, in order to constellate there the meaning and purpose of one's destiny previously denied. Jung said, "It was only after my illness that I understood how important it is to affirm one's own destiny." And it was after his illness that his most creative work was done, by his own admission.

. . . Sickness can be a road to individuation, holding within it the confused mass not yet transformed. Sickness pulls consciousness to ever deeper recesses of the self.

As a woman in one of my workshops said recently, some of the most exciting opportunities of our lives come cleverly disguised as insoluble difficulties. My friend Joe Kogel, who had a malignant melanoma and used this experience to help heal his life and cure himself, calls this the "Kogel Effect"—meaning that the worst things in your life have within them the seeds of the best. Joe reminds us that the Chinese symbol for crisis includes the signs for both danger and opportunity.

DISEASE AS A GIFT

We're used to the idea of disease as a punishment or a failure—but a gift? Think about what I call spiritual flat tires, and you may begin to understand what I mean. Something that happened to a friend of mine recently reminded me once again that nothing is good or bad in and of itself.

This gentleman has a farm. He loves the old-fashioned way of doing things, so he doesn't have any mechanical equipment and plows his fields with a horse. One day as he was plowing his field the horse dropped dead. Everyone in the village said, "Gee, what an awful thing to happen." He just responded, "We'll see." He was so at peace and so calm that we all got together and, because we admired his attitude so much, gave him a new horse as a gift. Then everyone's reaction was, "What a lucky man." And he said, "We'll see." A few days later the horse, being strange to his farm, jumped a fence and ran off, and everyone said, "Oh, poor fellow." He said, "We'll see." A week later the horse returned with a dozen wild horses following it. Everyone said, "What a lucky man." And he said, "We'll see." The next day his son went out riding, because now they had more than one horse, but the boy fell off the horse and broke his leg. Everyone said, "Oh, poor boy," but my friend said, "We'll see." The next day the army came to town taking all the young men for service, but they left his son because of his broken leg. Everyone said, "What a lucky kid," and my friend said, "We'll see."

We too have to learn to step back and start saying, "We'll see." Instead of judging the events in our lives as good, bad, right or wrong, we must recognize that of itself nothing is good or bad, and everything has the potential to help us get back on the universe's schedule. This does not mean that we have to like what happens, simply that we must remain open to the uses even of adversity. A disease may serve as a redirection— or, as I often describe it, a reset button (which starts you up again the same way the reset button works on a jammed garbage disposal). Which reminds me of something that a man at one of my exceptional patients group meetings said: "I'm here because my 'We'll see' button got me through the night and my reset button is waiting to be pushed." If you remember very little else from this book, remember those two words.

When you learn to live your life with a "We'll see" attitude, you will understand how it is that disease can be considered a gift. You will know why it is that people asked to describe their illness have called it a beauty mark, a wake-up call, a challenge and a new beginning. The beauty mark was a malignant melanoma, the wake-up call was breast cancer, the challenge and new beginning can be anything from amyotrophic lateral sclerosis to lupus.

Now when I tell an audience of five hundred people with AIDS that they have a gift, they don't throw shoes at me or get up and run out yelling "What are you telling us?"—because they know. They understand that illness can help heal their lives, that it can bring new meaning to relationships with lovers, family and friends. In some cases it has enabled critically ill young men to find love in a home from which they had been rejected because they were gay. It has brought a community together to love and support each other. And so they do say, "My disease is a gift." That doesn't mean they don't wish to be well, but that they wouldn't give up what they have achieved because of their illness.

Does it take courage to be open to this kind of healing? Sure. Do I have the right to tell you your disease is a gift? No, I do not. The gift is yours only if you choose to create it—as I've seen thousands of others do. Listen to the people who have lived the experience, and realize you are the source of your healing.

In the midst of chemotherapy and radiation treatments one woman took time to write me: "I consider my cancer to be such a blessing because through it we have learned so much about how to handle our lives, how to speak out our feelings to each other, how to throw away the junk forever and have more contentment in our lives."

Almost identical sentiments were expressed by a man in an AIDS group:

If I beat this disease, AIDS will be the best thing that ever happened to me because it has been a gigantic, cosmic kick in the ass. It has made me ask, Who are you? What is your life? Are you happy with who you are and what your life is? Sometimes when I say that it comes out sounding like I reduced AIDS to an EST seminar or something. But however it sounds, that's how I feel.

A twenty-two-year-old man who, with the aid of his doctors, is healing himself of brain cancer, says:

> I've learned to live. I love living. I love my family, my
> friends, my job, everything. And everyone. Every day I wake up
> and I feel alive! At peace. . . . Please excuse this outburst. I get
> carried away sometimes.
>
> I've been dealing with cancer for more than a year now. I'm
> almost glad I got it. It's changed my whole outlook on living. I
> *live* from day to day. I make the most out of every day.

Stephen Levine, author and counselor, who has worked with hundreds of sick and dying people, once met someone who told him that cancer is the gift for the person who has everything. She was a beautiful fifty-year-old woman who had had a double mastectomy and she got up at a workshop to explain what she meant:

> Three years ago, I was graced with cancer. I looked my
> whole life for a teacher, and it wasn't until I got cancer that I
> really started to pay attention to the preciousness of each breath,
> to the momentum of each thought, till I saw that this moment is
> all. All my other teachers gave me ideas. This caused me to
> directly experience my life. When I got cancer, it was up to me
> to get born before I died.

Feelings like these may be hard to believe in if you haven't personally experienced a serious illness—or even if you have. A young medical student I had worked with was in an automobile accident that left her paraplegic. She said in a letter to me that she now knows her paraplegia is a gift to her—but "I can't believe I'm really writing this." And yet it's the message I hear all the time. Why? Because the great lesson people learn from life-threatening illness is the difference between what is and is not important.

Love is high on everyone's list of the important things. In the face of illness, this can sometimes mean healing a marriage gone bad, at other times letting go of one that is beyond repair and going on to new things. A woman who had cancer wrote me a letter describing how she arrived at the decision to seek a divorce after her diagnosis: "I felt, at the time I came down with breast cancer, that I could not live another moment without the love I had so craved my entire life. I felt that love was more important than my next breath of air." After her surgery, as she records in a diary she sent me, she committed herself to life and love:

I am going to regain my positive attitude toward life, enjoy every day as if it is my last, and have a beautiful love affair. I need to make love and I'm going to do it. . . . In the oddest possible way, this experience has lifted me up out of my despair and isolation. . . . I only hope I can have the strength and will to walk with confidence into the new light that has been shed on my dark road. . . . Human love is the most important thing in life.

Within the year she had a new husband and a horse—the latter "a present I have waited for every Christmas of my life since childhood. I finally got it! A person should never give up hope. . . . I find a difference in myself: I am not willing to settle for less than the life I desire. . . . I realize the value of living and incorporate that realization into my daily life. . . . I want to live!"

This letter reminded me of a woman at one of my workshops who said that when her doctor told her she had cancer and would have to have a mastectomy, she decided to get a divorce too—and give up a tit and an ass! This is much healthier than deciding you're going to make your marriage work if it kills you.

On the other hand, disease can be the catalyst that enables some couples to find the life and love they need within their marriages. A husband and wife came to my office and when I asked them each to describe his disease, the wife said she saw it as a blossom, an opportunity for growth, the husband said it was eating him up alive. Now when for one it is a blossom and for the other it's a destroyer, you know these are two people who need to communicate better—and the miracle was that from then on, in the time they had left together, they did.

He had been a man who never expressed his needs but

kept everything inside of him where, as he said, it was devouring him. But after that conversation in my office things were different. As his wife explained when she told her story several years later at a workshop, this previously quiet, unassertive man started speaking up about his needs as they headed to the parking lot—and he didn't stop. First he told her exactly where he wanted her to bring the car to pick him up, then he told her what route he wanted her to take to get home, how fast she should go, and how to get him from the car into the house with the least possible discomfort to him.

That night they stayed up all night talking about their life together, going through a lot of garbage, as she put it, and a lot of wonderful things too. The next night he insisted that she sleep in the narrow hospital bed with him, even though his doctors had said he needed his rest and should sleep alone. Then he asked her to bring in all of his close friends so that he could pick one of them to mount what he called his halos— beautiful concentric mahogany rings he had carved and gilded in earlier years, as part of his work as an artist. Not long afterward he died beneath those golden rings, with the sun pouring in through the windows and his wife at his side, whispering to him that he would be with the angels. The days they had together after they finally learned to listen to each other were a gift to both of them, one that they might never have had without his illness.

The closing of a piece that appeared several years ago in the *New England Journal of Medicine* is typical of what I call "last paragraphs"—the place where you see the summing up of what a person has learned and accomplished through the experience of illness. These last paragraphs all sound alike, which says to me that the process of healing one's life is the same for all of us, in that we are all members of the same species. Surgeon Robert M. Mack, in his summation of what having cancer has meant to him, says:

I am very grateful just to be alive. I am very glad to have been permitted to learn to live with, rather than simply die from, my cancer. Mostly, I am glad to measure my life not in terms of what it once was or what I might have wished it to be but in terms of how wonderful it is now. I am glad to recognize each day as a splendid, unforgettable miracle, a wonderful gift for me to savor and enjoy as fully as I can, and when my days are no longer nourishing and good, I hope that I can simply let go and allow myself to rest in peace.

A woman in a self-created remission from ovarian cancer writes of the joy she too has discovered in the simplest daily activities:

What an experience having cancer is. My whole life will be different for it as long as I live, and, yes, I am one of those who wants to live to be a hundred. An exceptional nurse at the hospital told me to "live each day to the max." Do you know what the max turned out to be once I was up and around again after two surgeries in five weeks' time? It was hanging up laundry in the sun with a cat rubbing against my leg.

Finally there are the words of a woman who has done many years of self-healing. When I first met her about eight years ago she had extensive breast cancer and was using a walker; now she is teaching school and running workshops: "I imagine someday I'll die of cancer. I don't know what I'll die of, whether it's cancer, a heart attack or a car crash. I don't really think about it any more, I'm too busy living my life."

DISEASE AS AN AGENT OF TRANSFORMATION

Some people discover through illness strengths they never knew they had. One woman passively suffered through nineteen years of treatment for musculoskeletal illness until the day her doctors told her that she would have to be on "heavy-duty painkillers" for the next two years, after which they would consider whether to do hip replacements. She knew that she could not accept this fate, and when she happened, on that very same day, to see me on television, she decided she didn't have to. When the program was over she walked on her canes down to a bookstore where she bought my book, then devised her own healing program based on works by Norman Cousins, Joan Borysenko, Dr. Steven Locke, Dr. Herbert Benson and me—although even holding a book was so painful she would have to read for ten minutes and lie down for an hour afterward.

> I am no longer on any medication, I walk three miles a day, work out four times a week, and my family and I have our lives back—a whole new life together. Last week I was in China and walked straight to the top of the Great Wall. Within me there is a peacefulness and a joy and a great confidence in what the human spirit can do.
>
> I know that this is all just a process—there is no cure, this is a conditional gift—one that I hope to work and grow with for the rest of my life—my new life. . . . At times I felt, how much easier to lie in bed and take a pill than to be here in the struggle—but how much greater the reward—and the joy to come.

Again I am reminded of the words of the Twenty-sixth Psalm, "Examine me, O Lord, and try me." Disease is surely one of the ways in which we are tried by life and offered the chance to be heroic. Though few of us will win Olympic gold medals or slay dragons, disease can be the spark or gift that allows many of us to live out our personal myths and become heroes.

Disease can be the catalyst of change for people whose entire lives have been spent denying their own needs. A woman who was an abused child and later an abused wife writes of all the things she has been able to achieve now that she has accepted her mortality.

> I was given my death sentence two and a half years ago when I was sixty-two. . . . My life since then has improved one hundred-fold and I have enjoyed my life more than ever before. I have traveled widely, I have visited thirty or more museums, I go away for weekends of dancing, swimming, flirting, etc. and most important, I have a wonderful boyfriend who takes me out to dinner and the movies and with whom I have a fulfilling sex life.

I make plans for the future. Wonderful things are happening in my family—weddings, births, etc.—and I expect to be here for all of it. I am an active member of a cancer support group and have been able to help several people. I could probably continue working but I don't want to waste a minute of my precious time. I have always wanted to be a teacher so now I am a volunteer tutor in high school and also in the library's adult literacy program. . . . Incidentally, my recent CAT scan showed a slight reduction in the size of the cancer. . . . My doctor said, "These things happen sometimes; we don't know why." I said, "I know why. I made it happen."

People find God, too, a God who is an enduring part of their new found identity as spiritual beings. This was the experience of a woman who recovered from breast cancer over ten years ago. She felt so strongly about the importance of the spiritual issues in her recovery, and was so determined to help the medical profession understand that aspect, that she eventually wrote a master's thesis exploring the psychology of six women who had gone through the breast cancer/mastectomy experience.

The pattern common to all these women was that recovery, which the medical profession views as a return to the predisease condition, was in fact a transformation into something new. In my experience, the disease often opens one to a spiritual reality previously unrealized.

The sense of our mortality and our reason for being stares us in the face. What is real? How can we do something real before we die?

In that moment the long trip from head to heart occurs and the intelligent, loving light shines on our path and lights our way. We contact something that goes beyond all our previous experiences and are aware of an order in the universe that includes darkness and disease. However, it is all spiritual and part of life and leads us to a rebirth and reawakening to a new reality. When one reawakens to this potential in each of us the resources that come with this are incredible. We know we can survive events that are full of pain because we have a constant source of renewal.

Cancer, death or loss are not the issue but love and healing are and we finally see that in the pain lies the opportunity to love and care even more. As Mother Teresa has said, the greatest disease of mankind is the absence of love. There is only one treatment for that, to let in the loving light and to heal your life.

And another letter from Susan, the woman from a family background of alcoholism and suicide, who has suffered for years from scleroderma:

> I am growing so in a spiritual sense that it makes it all the more worth it to hang around this world. Had I not grown so spiritually I would have left a long time ago, saying who needs this grief. Which is what I think life is about on many, many levels. For me it is like sitting in a garbage heap, but oh the light I can see. . . . One thing I love about growing in the spirit is that it is eternal and you never really stop.

SAVING YOURSELF: HOLDING ON, SPEAKING UP, REACHING OUT

A lot of people call me up and say, "I learned I have cancer. I want to start a group to help cancer patients." Then they go on about how they're going to save everybody else with cancer. They've got missionary zeal. What I always say to these people is "Stop. You'll wear yourself out saving everyone else. Go to the mirror. Look in it, and save the person you see there. That's your client." I do this because people who have cancer, as well as many other diseases, tend to be people who have always put others first. They need to be liked.

But co-dependency is a disease and an addiction. These people usually don't do well unless they make changes in their lives and learn to save themselves before saving the world. Sometimes this means learning to stand up for yourself and your own needs by saying no to family and friends after a lifetime of saying yes, which is particularly hard for some women to do. I can see how much Bobbie's example means to the women at our workshops when they see her "making me better." Many women and some men have thanked her for being there, showing them how two people can interact and still love each other. One woman learned to do this in her own family after she became ill and realized that she couldn't continue to be the "perfect" wife and mother she'd always tried to be until then:

I have become more assertive with my family. I have tried to teach my four children to be responsible for themselves and not to be so dependent on their mother. They are learning quite well. My husband is having more difficulty adjusting, but I do know that if I am to stay alive and well, I can not go back to being the pleaser, appeaser, "little woman." So I wait for him to accept the changes.

I heard poet Robert Bly share a story of three brothers who go out in the forest to chop wood. Each morning one stays in the cabin while the two others are out gathering wood. One day a dwarf appears at the cabin while the oldest brother is there alone and asks to share what's left of their breakfast. The brother says "Yes." The dwarf starts to eat but drops his food and asks the brother to pick it up. When he bends down the dwarf hits him on the head with a club. The next morning, the middle brother is left alone in the cabin, and again the dwarf comes by, asks for breakfast, drops it, asks the young man to get it for him and clubs him when he bends over. The third morning the youngest brother is there, and the dwarf appears and asks if he may eat something left over from breakfast. "Yes," he says, "there's bread on the table. Help yourself." But when the dwarf drops it and asks the young man to get it for him, he says, "No, if you can't handle your own bread you're not going to survive. You pick it up." And the dwarf then thanks him and asks him if he would like to know where the princess and the treasure are.

The point of the story is, please, give others responsibility for their problems: Let them learn to hang on to their own bread and take care of themselves. They will grow—and you won't get clubbed. In fact, they will thank you. The children of the lady who wrote the letter, for example, will be grateful for having learned independence and for having as a role model a mother who has learned to express and take care of her own needs, because these personality traits get passed on from generation to generation—just as the opposite ones do.

Take the example of Ray Berté, who was diagnosed with "terminal" cancer in 1977 but couldn't understand why his disease had gotten its start in his voicebox, since he had never been a smoker. The event that opened his eyes to the meaning of his disease was a terrible crisis with his fifteen-year-old son, Keith. After hearing of Ray's terminal diagnosis, Keith suffered a hemorrhage from a blood vessel in the roof of his mouth. He had to have surgery eight times in six days before it finally stopped bleeding. As Ray recounted the events that followed:

> I understood something then. After Keith's surgery everyone kept saying the kid was *tough!* They said it was just fine that he never cried, even after he'd found out I had cancer. Suddenly this gave me gooseflesh because I realized that Keith had learned a macho message from me. He kept his feelings inside, and then they literally burst out of his mouth. My son was almost destroyed.

Once Ray realized what had happened to his son, he held him in his arms and gave him a "live" message, telling him that it was all right to express his feelings and ask for help when he needed it. In the process of helping Keith, he helped himself, for he realized that he too had always kept his feelings inside. This was the lesson that he had learned only too well from *his* father, who was always telling him to shut up. In fact, he began to realize, his inability to verbalize his feelings meant that they had gotten stuck—in his throat. His cancer now made a certain terrible sense to him.

Ray used this new understanding to make profound changes in his life. Once a man who prided himself on controlling his feelings, he gave himself the same "live" message he gave his son and decided that he would no longer be destroyed by keeping things inside: "I cry. I trust my instincts. Everyone should." With his "terminal" diagnosis nine years in the past, and a life transformed by the experience, he proclaims: "If the cancer comes again, I'll fight like hell again. But I've already beaten it, because I've blossomed into a new person."

Part of Ray's blossoming was learning how to ask for the help he needed. People want to help, but often they don't know how, and they may withdraw from you as a result. Don't let that happen. Tell them what you need. If you've never spoken up about your own needs before, you may be amazed at the reception you get.

This was certainly the experience of one woman, a social worker, who wrote me a long list of the things she had done once she discovered her husband had cancer. Many of the items on her list, which is too long to quote in full but every word of which is useful, focused on how she asked for and got the help she needed from family, friends, colleagues, even her husband—and herself. For, like the person with the illness, those helping to care for him must also learn how to reach out for what they need. We all, sick or well, must learn to live the same message.

- I "called in the troops." I told my family, Joe's family, and friends.
- I asked people to let us know about, or introduce us to, cancer survivors, and I asked them what they thought helped them survive.
- I got psychotherapy as fast as possible.
- I continued my exercise.
- I hugged my cat a lot. I hugged friends, family and my therapist. I hugged myself. I wore soft fuzzy clothing and took bubblebaths.
- I trusted what felt good. One thing that felt good was continuing to dress well and use makeup. Looking good felt good.
- I tried to eat nutritious food. Sometimes I could only swallow liquids. Sometimes only chocolate tasted good. [If you want to eat chocolate with no ill effects, break the bar and hold the broken ends down so the calories run out. Then visualize celery as you eat it.]
- I predecided, immediately, that no matter what happened, including Joe dying, we would be going through this entire

experience together, that I would come out winning from this experience, and that I would use whatever happened to make a contribution to others.

- I maintained contact through my work with aspects of myself which were not linked to being Joe's wife.
- I sought medical information, and got friends and family to do research for me.
- I asked people to pray.
- I screened Joe's visitors and callers.
- I accepted support.
- I took breaks. Joe has wanted me to be well, and taking an occasional day off has affirmed both my own life and Joe's ability to be independent. Even when he has been very ill, he has had the opportunity to give back, by giving me freedom.
- I let go of the past. Our lives were irrevocably changed with Joe's diagnosis. Comparisons of our present life with our cozy past became irrelevant energy drains.
- I let go of trying to control my emotions.
- I let go of nonessential tasks.
- I let go of Joe's course of healing. My job as Joe's wife is to love him; his job is to heal.

My experience was clear: *people couldn't wait to show their love!* Some just wanted guidance on how best to do that. All I had to do was communicate my situation and people took the opportunity to be human and loving.

Asking for help when you need it can be a good thing not just for yourself but for the people who are asked. I heard of a social worker with cancer who did an inventory of the practical ways in which people could help him. He sent it to all the people in his life, asking everyone who received it to get together and share the tasks. The people he asked were so honored and felt they had learned so much that they still get together every year for a community lecture and party.

Another woman formed an official "healing network," made up of friends and family as well as medical and psychiatric professionals. She relied on them for everything from child care to chauffeuring, errand-running to massage, medical research to transportation. (I provided the surgery.) Two years after her successful recovery from advanced breast cancer, she interviewed the members of her network for a research paper in support of her candidacy for a master's degree in counseling. How did they feel about having been part of the network? "Honored," "grateful," "great [because] it meant you felt close to me," "better than just sitting scared," "lucky to be part of the experience. I felt that it nourished me. . . . I had a great sense of feeling included, feeling needed, feeling a part of something which was a large part of someone's life."

You will discover that once you share your pain, it makes it easier for others to share theirs. One young woman, a teacher with breast cancer who had not revealed this at school, had to ask for a ride to an ECaP meeting when her car broke down. The principal offered her a ride and she discovered that he had been operated on by me. The next week her car was still in the shop so she asked another of her colleagues for a ride, and when they started to talk it turned out that he had cancer too. Soon they had a group therapy session going at school. People who have given rides to members of our exceptional patients groups have been known to keep coming to the meetings long after their passengers no longer felt a need to attend. "I still need to come," they say.

Some of us are taught early on to keep quiet. That happens when parents don't respond to our cries, or respond negatively. If we don't learn the lesson as infants, then we may be taught it shortly thereafter, when we are told to be "good little soldiers" or "big girls." I see people like this all the time—they do drawings of themselves in boxes, because they feel trapped. If we are raised that way, it can be very hard to break out and give voice to our feelings. One woman sent me a poem on that theme called "Shh, Listen"—with the comment that it had taken her years to learn to do what the poem asked:

listen   to who
to yourself   I can't hear my voice
shh
listen   to who
to yourself   no one will love me

shh	
listen	to who
to yourself	
you'll love yourself	what about the others
shh	
listen	to who
to yourself	
do you scream	no, not in years; I have to again
go ahead	will it be all right
yes	
listen	to who
to yourself	

As the poem says, you must listen to yourself, hear the sounds of your inner voices. Only then can you learn to sing your own song, as Larry LeShan puts it—or scream your own screams. This has nothing to do with selfishness. It is self-love and self-esteem, not selfishness, and in the end these qualities will allow you to give more to the world as well, as you discover your own way of loving that world.

MANAGING YOUR OWN HEALTH

If you listen to yourself, you will also be able to make decisions about your health care that are right for you. This can be difficult, however, if the very qualities that contributed to your susceptibility to illness prevent you from trying to fight it on your own terms. The woman who got a new husband and a horse in the year after her cancer diagnosis noticed during her hospital stay the extremely repressed, often submissive nature of her fellow breast cancer patients. One of her roommates came out of anesthesia to discover that she had had a breast removed, without her doctor having made it clear to her ahead of time that that was a possibility. The first she knew of it was when she returned to consciousness. "Since then, she has not been able to cry; anger, rage is all she feels. She is a warm, soft person. So many of these people are shy and kind.

I wonder at all that is kept inside, not released—where does it go? What does it do to the human being?"

Very observantly, this woman intuited from what she saw of her roommate's behavior what people like Russell Lockhart and Arnold Mindell have theorized about people with cancer—that the cancer, being a kind of growth gone wild, lives something of the life that is unlived by those with repressed, constricted personalities. It is almost as if the absence of growth and excitement externally leads to its internal expression. All that energy that is kept inside seems to fuel the cancer, for it has no place else to go.

Participating in your own medical care can be the first expression of yourself and your energy. You will want to form a team with your physician and play an active, responsible role in your treatment, getting second opinions, making choices and becoming the expert only you can be about your life and your disease. Don't let your doctors be the only experts on your case. It isn't their life, and experts don't know everything. This was the point of a letter from a man who had been cured of his lymphoma with a very aggressive form of chemotherapy, which none of his doctors had chosen to tell him about:

After several medical consultations, I learned that the proposed "standard treatments" . . . had a recovery rate of *one half* that of the new protocol developed, tested and recommended by the National Cancer Institute. I also learned that the reason many physicians were reluctant to use or even recommend the latest protocols was in part due to the increased risk of side effects to the patient. Most doctors, understandably, would prefer to see the results of ten and fifteen year studies before administering a new and advanced protocol that does not have the benefit of many years of testing. . . .

It can take hard work to investigate every option. If you don't feel up to doing it yourself, ask for help from family and friends. Of course not everyone will feel that such a thorough investigation is necessary, and in many circumstances it is not. But for some people it is the best way of maintaining a feeling of control. For the man who wrote the letter, an attorney accustomed to "fighting battles," as he put it, anything less than being fully informed about all the options available to him was not acceptable. He goes on to recommend, as I do to many patients, that anyone wishing to research all his options begin the search with a phone call to the National Cancer Institute's hotline number: 1-800-4-CANCER. There are also hotlines for nontraditional therapies, and when appropriate you can become informed about them too. I don't make my patients' choices for them; I can only provide advice and opinions. If there's one thing I've learned from my years as a surgeon, it's that we must all find our own route to healing. I can only be a facilitator and share with you my knowledge and feelings.

I recall being at a conference where someone stood up and said he'd listened to people who had gotten well with radiation, chemotherapy and a variety of diets and other alternative techniques. He didn't understand how it was possible that all these things worked, because they seemed to contradict each other. I said to him, "It's the body that heals, not the medicine." Each person's body makes use of different healing agents. You have to decide which ones are right for you. That's why I do so much work with symbols and drawings, trying to help my patients discover their true feelings about the different therapies available.

At an intuitive level, there is in each of us knowledge of what is therapeutic for the individual. Not everyone dealing with lymphoma, for example, would make the same choice as the man who wrote the letter. Even if presented with the same information about all the options, someone else might reject as too risky the chemotherapy that seemed promising to him. One woman I worked with drew her doctor giving her chemotherapy as the devil giving her poison. If that's how you feel about your treatment, then you need to change either your therapy, your doctor, or your mind. (She changed her mind, once she was able to make her own choices instead of being pressured into them by her family and her doctor.)

One of the questions I ask people trying to decide about their therapy is "How would you feel if, after the course of therapy you are considering, your disease came back?" If the answer is "I'd be outraged that I didn't do something more," then that choice is wrong for you. You need to choose therapies you can live *and* die with. There should never be a moment when you look in the mirror and say, "Dumbbell, why didn't you give yourself a better chance at getting well?"

However, you should never have the feeling that the treatment is worse than the disease. We are making choices about healing, not assaulting ourselves. To take a specific example, I've seen families where the wife of a cancer patient was making everyone eat a macrobiotic diet. One man did a drawing of this situation showing the kitchen turned completely upside down, his wife looking depressed because she'd spent the whole day preparing the meal, the children in the family looking miserable because they didn't want it, and himself yelling "Why do I have to eat this garbage!" He would have preferred chemotherapy. Meanwhile in other families the macrobiotic life-style made everyone feel better about themselves because they were participating in a healing process.

While I know that some diets are healthier than others, I also think you have to do what feels right for you. A man with cancer who attended one of my workshops took issue with my having said that vegetarians get less cancer. In a letter, he explained his history:

> I just can't seem to let go of the fact that for eighteen years I was a vegetarian and natural hygienist and lived such a pure life (raw foods, exercise, meditation) and this should happen to me. In the Torah there is a saying that goes "Man plans and God laughs." I once was on a radio program with Nathan Pritikin. We were debating the merits of which diet or way of life was better—his or mine. It wasn't really a debate but a shouting match. . . . He said don't eat nuts—I said nuts are a good source of protein. He said only eat the whites of the egg—I said only eat the yolk—etc. etc. etc. He died of leukemia. I contracted cancer. Two schmucks arguing over how many angels can sit on the head of a pin.

When he stood up in the workshop and asked what was the point of being a vegetarian if you could still get cancer, I told him that he'd eaten vegetables for the wrong reasons. The vegetables may have prevented him from getting cancer ten years earlier—I don't know. But I do know that joggers and vegetarians die too. If you eat vegetables and get up at 5:00 A.M. to go jogging because you feel better when you do, that's terrific. If you're just trying not to die, however, you're going to be damned angry when you discover you're going to die anyway. That's when you'll wish you'd slept late and eaten an ice cream cone. The point is to find a life that's enjoyable to you and live that life. It may be longer or it may be shorter than someone else's life, but if it's not a life you enjoy, you can be sure it will *seem* longer. Better to feel that our lives are "over much too quickly." The important thing, as Joseph Campbell says, is to follow your bliss.

I would say the same thing about drinking and even smoking as about diet and exercise. Lately there have been articles about women who drink having more breast cancer. But you have to look at the life-style of these women—their emotional life, nutrition and childbearing history—not just their drinking habits. You also have to look at drinking in a cultural context. In many cultures where people live to be a hundred, there is significant alcohol consumption. Alcohol is part of their society, part of their enjoyment of life, but it is not abused or misused.

It's been shown that married men can smoke three packs a day to the single man's one without having any more cancer, which shows that it takes more poison to kill a lover. In fact, statistics show that single men earn less money, go to jail more often, have more illnesses, kill themselves at a greater rate and die at an earlier age. But when a happily married man pointed that out, a confirmed bachelor drew the only conclusion obvious to him: If he wanted to live a slow, lingering death, he could get married.

As Jung says, the shoe that fits one man pinches another. Only you can choose the way of life—or, in the case of illness, the therapy—that is right for you. So make the choices that feel right for you. You are the expert in your case.

At the same time, you need to keep an open mind and open ears, for there may be messages and options coming your way with something valuable for you. One woman who had fought and prevailed over her doctors on a number of other issues was equally determined about her decision not to have chemotherapy. She had read that Jimmy Carter's sister, Ruth Stapleton, was going to try to heal herself of pancreatic cancer with faith, and she decided that faith in God would see her through her illness as well. The next day, however, she saw in the newspaper obituaries that Ruth Stapleton had died. That was message enough for her: When her family doctor pleaded with her to keep her faith but have the chemotherapy too, she finally accepted his arguments. He might have pointed out to her that no less a source than the Bible tells us medicine is a gift.

Sometimes, however, it may not seem like such a gift— when the chances of its being a success are small, and the time gained is going to be of poor quality because of side effects. As one woman wrote, about why she had chosen not to have chemotherapy and radiation treatments for her metastasized lung cancer: "The decision was so simple! The six to eight months' time would surely be of better quality than the twelve to eighteen months with heaven-knows-what happening to my body and perhaps preventing my doing and saying what needed to be done and said. I had a lot to do, and not much time for doing it, so I had to stay in control as long as possible."

She was decisive from the beginning, about this and everything else. "I guess my acceptance was rather quick. But any problem presented to me has always started my thought process toward what to do about it now, and where to go from here." When she wrote her letter, almost five years had passed since her "terminal" diagnosis and refusal of medical intervention, and she was thriving, with no sign of the cancer.

How to account for her healing? She mentions what she did and what happened to her along the way but doesn't single out any one from among the very large number of factors that might have made a difference. The most important factor, however, was that she knew what she wanted and was willing to accept the consequences, including the reactions of those around her. Her mother thought she should take the treatment the doctors were recommending. She gently reminded her mother that she had always been raised to make her own decisions. Acquaintances were horrified and expressed disapproval of what she was "doing to" her husband. Her husband didn't agree with her choice, but stood by her, defending her position to others by saying "I can only tell you what Jean would say if you asked her."

Medically speaking, what she did was to "build up" nutritionally. Probably more important than the food supplements and multivitamins were the changes she made in her emotional life. She developed a closeness to her husband, her sons and her daughter. As a result, "These have been the most interesting years of my life." She reached out to people, both to give and take, and found many new friends, while renewing relationships with old ones. She appreciated the things friends did for her and forgave the ones who didn't know how to help—the "beautiful cowards," as she calls them. "They care deeply, too, but they don't know how to say it, and they're fearful of doing anything wrong. I learned about these people long ago, so I spoke the dreaded word first, giving them permission, in a way." She attended a cancer support group at her local hospital and would like to continue going to offer her support to others, but stays away because she feels her unorthodox approach has given offense to some of the people there.

She gave away most of her household treasures to her children rather than having them shipped down to the new home she and her husband had recently moved to—not out of a feeling of hopelessness about the future but because "I had arrived, finally, at the realization that things are really not important." She was almost converted by a born-again Christian but decided she preferred the beliefs she had developed herself over the years and "came full circle" back to them.

She also mentions that she quit her forty-five-year smoking habit on the day of her cancer diagnosis, which a nurse friend of hers thinks could have caused such a shock to her system that it "turned things around." Or perhaps her body is creating its own hyperthermia treatment, she speculates, since her "entire body will suddenly become extremely hot, for no apparent reasons." And there's the fact that she's "rather adept at avoiding stress and fatigue. Too much time is spent worrying over that which one can't change."

This woman is a walking catalog of healthy attitudes: She was definite about what she wanted in terms of medical care, she's loved and loving, she has peace of mind, control over her own life, confidence in her own decisions, willingness to face the consequences, a strong personal philosophy, the belief that both life and death can be meaningful. She saw her illness not as a death sentence but as a door to life. At the moment, she's too busy living to die. She ends her letter by saying: "I feel so good about myself, and proud of the manner in which I have 'managed' my situation, so far. . . . Thank you for reporting how it really is possible to maintain dignity totally, by choosing when to go on. I'm not even close to having to make the choice, but knowing that it is a definite possibility is a lovely thought, and I will try my best, when that time comes."

One can find in this letter almost all of what my chiropractor friend Jeff Rockwell and his wife call the "Symptoms of Inner Peace." As listed in his "Spinal Column," they are:

1. Tendency to think and act spontaneously rather than from fears based on past experiences.
2. An unmistakable ability to enjoy each moment.
3. Loss of interest in judging self.
4. Loss of interest in judging other people.
5. Loss of interest in conflict.
6. Loss of interest in interpreting actions of others.
7. Loss of ability to worry (this is a very serious symptom).
8. Frequent, overwhelming episodes of appreciation.
9. Contented feelings of connectedness with others and nature.
10. Frequent attacks of smiling through the eyes of the heart.
11. Increasing susceptibility to love extended by others as well as the uncontrollable urge to extend it.
12. Increasing tendency to let things happen rather than to make them happen.

Rockwell warns, "If you have all or even most of the above symptoms, please be advised that your condition of PEACE may be so far advanced as to not be treatable."

GOING YOUR OWN WAY

One characteristic of people who have achieved peace of mind is their independence. They trust their instincts. Nobody can tell them what to think if their inner voices say otherwise.

Brendan O'Regan, whose spontaneous remissions study was mentioned in chapter 1, tells about a doctoral student doing a related study who placed an ad in an Idaho newspaper asking if anyone within a 300-mile radius had experienced a remission. Twenty-five people replied, which was quite a large number for such a sparsely populated area. As she started interviewing the respondents, she noticed that many of them were farmer's wives who had in common a strong faith in their own judgment. When she asked one of her interview subjects how she had felt when the doctor told her she had a terminal illness, the woman simply said, "I figured that was *his* opinion." "Would you like to say more about that?" she was asked. "Well," she replied, "we're used to being told all these things by all these experts from the federal government who come in and look at the soil. They say to plant corn over there, but when you do, nothing comes up. They say don't plant it over there because it won't grow, and you plant it and it grows beautifully. So you realize the experts don't know everything. When the doctor told me I was going to die in six months, I said 'What does he know, he's only an expert!' "

It is interesting that, in the United States, the states with the largest number of people over the age of eighty-five are Maine, North Dakota and Minnesota. (And of those people, nearly 70 percent are women.) The point I would make is that these are states where the living conditions are not the easiest, and I think that people from these areas have had to to learn to be survivors from the beginning. They are independent, willing to take on life and used to providing for themselves. (I also believe that people in the smaller, quieter rural communities that are characteristic of these states tend to live lives in which their feelings stay near the surface; whereas people in big cities like New York find it necessary to build a wall around their feelings to protect themselves so that they can survive the pressure and the noise. The result is that those with the quieter life-style are more in touch with their feelings than those who have buried them deep inside.)

I can remember the first time I went to speak in New Hampshire, another state like those just mentioned. Although the community I was visiting was small, the local church was packed with hundreds of people. When I asked where they had all come from, and why, it turned out that many of them were from communities several hours away. One man said, "I have to travel two hours just to get my groceries, so why shouldn't I come here to learn how to be responsible for my health and participate in my life."

These people know they don't have to die based on an expert's opinion. Unfortunately many patients don't know that, and they proceed to die right on schedule—or sooner—once the doctor gives them the statistics.

There was a wonderful magazine article on the subject of statistics by the evolutionary theorist Stephen Jay Gould, who was diagnosed in 1982 with a rare form of cancer known as abdominal mesothelioma. He begins with the Mark Twain quip about the three varieties of dishonesty, each worse than the one before—"lies, damned lies and statistics." This he applies to his own diagnosis, which carries with it a median survival rate of eight months. But as an evolutionary biologist Gould knows that "means and medians are the abstractions. . . . variation itself is the reality. I had to place myself amidst the variations." So he doesn't just disregard the experts, he beats them at their own game by doing a much more sophisticated (and optimistic) statistical analysis of his chances on the basis of his age, the stage of his disease, the excellent medical treatment he would be receiving, and his own state of mind. In the end, however, he discards his own statistics as well, noting that statistics apply only when conditions remain static and that due to the experimental nature of his treatment, the conditions that apply to him are not static. Therefore, he concludes, in the language of the statisticians themselves, "if fortune holds, [I] will be in the first cohort of a new distribution with high median and a right tail extending to death by natural causes at advanced old age." I personally know several mesothelioma survivors who are supposed to be dead. So much for life expectancy statistics!

Dulcy Seiffer is another of these independent-minded exceptional patients who has rejected them. When the doctors told her she had only a 40 percent chance of surviving her ovarian cancer beyond two years, she didn't really listen—though that didn't stop them from telling her the bad news over and over. Then, by one of those "coincidences" that change people's lives, a nurse put her and another woman in the same hospital room because they were both motel owners, and her roommate told Dulcy about ECaP. Writing to ECaP was the beginning for her of a healing journey that would require enormous amounts of determination and optimism in the face of many obstacles, including, of course, the bleak prognosis.

The first practical problem Dulcy had to face was how she could get the chemotherapy treatments she needed and still be able to return to the home she loved in St. Croix, where she and her husband had their guest house. The local hospital was not equipped to handle such a complicated regimen, so Dulcy took matters into her own hands. She interviewed nurses until she found one who was willing to be trained over the phone by an oncology nurse in Boston, where she had had her exploratory surgery. Then she and her husband arranged to have all the paraphernalia and drugs she needed shipped in from Puerto Rico every three weeks.

Using ECaP tapes as her inspiration, Dulcy made ten of her own visualization tapes, "figured out methods to raise my red and white counts, and made tapes of exercise programs for sick days and for well days. Being an artist helps the creative turnout." At the time she wrote her first letter to me, less than a year after her diagnosis, she was already confident that her tumors had disappeared, because "when I do my 'heal yourself' part of the meditation, my army of tiger white cells zoom all over my body but they can't locate any tumors any more." When she went in for more exploratory surgery some weeks later, her intuition was confirmed—not a sign of anything, "after only eight chemotherapy treatments and a lot of meditation and holistic endeavors."

Dulcy also saw a psychiatrist who used hypnotism to help her deal with her fear. "He'd tell me 'You're going to get well. Soon, you're going to find out you're cancer-free.' I'd come out of his office feeling sure I was going to win." Love, in-coming and out-going, helped too. "The hardest thing for me to do was to love. I'm not a soft, loving, huggy person. . . . But once I found that I had enough self-love to want to take care of myself and listen to all of my own needs, I found that other people gave me more love and support than I could ever have dreamed of." Dulcy enjoyed a remission of almost three years before having a recurrence, after what she called a hell of a year, during which she said she had allowed work and family stresses to get to her. But Dulcy is a fighter, who has used her recurrence as a catalyst to get herself to deal more effectively with her family problems through psychotherapy and membership in a group. She's also continuing her meditations, using those middle-of-the-night sessions of sleeplessness that most of us complain about as an occasion to listen to an inspirational "Nite Tape" she prepared for herself.

It takes a lot of courage to say no to the experts and their statistics, but I see people like Dulcy all the time. One day, at a lecture I was giving, a gentleman came up to me and handed me his card. He was an executive at a publishing firm, but he looked so terribly ill that I never thought his card would be of any use to me. I'd have been surprised if he survived more than five or six weeks.

Five years later I was in a small rural community giving a lecture, and who should walk up to me but this same gentleman, looking perfectly healthy. He had six of his townsfolk in tow and told me he had brought them because what I had said when he'd seen me five years before had meant so much to him. After hearing me speak, he'd quit his support group, which was only depressing him with the bleak pictures the members drew of their lives. Then, as part of the visualization program he started for himself, he gave a name to his x-ray machine and started talking to it, telling it that it had to heal him. His doctor thought he was crazy, and his wife was so upset that *she* had to see a psychiatrist. But here he is, years later, inspiring us all.

One woman wrote to me: "My oncologist had just told me I'd live about a year. After I fired him, the first thing I told my new oncologist was 'I've just fired my last doctor. So please keep your guesses to yourself because I will beat this thing.' " And she did—in the process of redirecting her life, for she didn't just fire her oncologist, but (as she put it in her letter) her husband as well.

The people who probably have the toughest battle fighting off the doom and gloom predictions of the experts are PWAs (people with AIDS). Michael Callen, the editor of a handbook called *Surviving and Thriving with AIDS: Hints for the Newly Diagnosed* (from which Steven James's rules were quoted earlier), has written an article about his own experience. He begins by telling about how a friend's six-year-old son, who hadn't seen him in several months, asked if he were dead yet. That's how prevalent the idea is that AIDS is invariably fatal, Callen remarks—even six-year-olds have picked it up.

Our Surgeon General thinks so too. I've told him, as I'm telling you, that it doesn't have to be—we kill people by saying a disease is 100 percent fatal. There is then no hope. I've asked him to come to one of our workshops to find out for himself, for an increasing number of long-term survivors are beginning to call this "expert" opinion into question. So are some of the health care professionals who work with PWAs and who have a much more hopeful view than the one presented in the media. Callen quotes New York physician Nathaniel Pier, who has a large AIDS practice, as saying: "There's a serious bias in the medical literature as to what's being reported, and it's giving people a distorted picture of what is going on with AIDS. They're not seeing the people who are doing well, the people who are surviving long, the people who have good quality of life, because these people don't go to medical centers and therefore they don't get papers written about them."

When they do get written up, in articles like the one in the *New York Times* entitled "AIDS Mystery: Why Do Some Infected Men Stay Healthy?" there is never any consideration of possible psychosocial factors. This particular article includes coverage of such factors as "virulence" (maybe the AIDS virus in these men is a "nice" one); genetics (maybe some people are just born without susceptibility to the virus); and immunity (maybe there is "something unusual" in the immune systems of some long-term AIDS virus carriers that allows them to remain well). The fact that Dr. George Solomon and Dr. Lydia Temoshok are engaged in a psychological study of long-term survivors, and the idea that there might be factors that AIDS patients *could* do something about, as opposed to factors like genetics and natural immunity about which they can do nothing—these considerations go unmentioned.

Yet in their ongoing study, a number of potentially valuable factors are listed that could inspire PWAs to new efforts in their own behalf. These factors include:

1. Acceptance of the reality of the diagnosis in conjunction with refusal to perceive the condition as a death sentence, at least an imminent one.
2. A personalized means of active coping that is believed to have beneficial health effects.
3. Altered lifestyle to accommodate disease in an adaptive manner.
4. Perceiving the treating physician as a collaborator, not interacting in a passive-compliant or defiant mode.
5. A sense of personal responsibility for one's health and a sense that one can influence health outcomes.
6. A commitment to life in terms of "unfinished business."
7. A sense of meaningfulness and purpose in life.
8. Finding new meaning as a result of the disease itself.
9. A prior mastered experience with life-threatening illness or very serious life event.
10. Physical fitness programs.
11. Deriving useful information and supportive contact with a person with the same diagnosis.
12. Being altruistically involved with other patients.
13. Long-term survivors are assertive and have the ability to say no.
14. Long-term survivors have the ability to withdraw from involvements and to nurture themselves.
15. Long-term survivors are sensitive to their body and its needs.

16. Long-term survivors have the ability to communicate openly, including about their illness concerns.

Not only are the psychiatrists and psychoneuroimmunologists often ignored in articles about long-surviving PWAs, but personal testimonials from survivors like Michael Callen are never cited. Callen's assessment of what makes for a survivor is very close to Solomon's:

If I had to describe in one word the common characteristic of the PWAs I interviewed, it would be grit. These people are all fighters: opinionated, incredibly knowledgeable about AIDS, stubborn, and passionately committed to living, they work hard to stay alive. And they are all involved in the politics of AIDS—some by becoming publicly identified, others counseling or operating hotlines. Politics can be an antidote to the self-obsession that comes with AIDS. To realize that there's someone worse off, whom you can help, is an incredible relief—and maybe even healing.

HAVING A PURPOSE

Whether it's political or personal, a sense of purpose can do wonders for your health. I'm reminded of a story that Elisabeth Kübler-Ross tells of a critically ill woman who was in the hospital and begged the doctors to help her survive long enough to attend her son's wedding. If she could just get to the wedding, she said, it would be all right to die right after that. So they infused her and transfused her to build her up. The day of the wedding all her intravenous lines and tubes were removed. She was dressed up and made up until she looked beautiful, and off she went to the wedding. When she returned to the hospital, everyone was expecting her to stagger onto the ward, lie down and die. Instead, she came back on the ward and said, "Don't forget, I have another son."

There's a wonderful term that was shared with me by a man whose wife I was taking care of—"roundtrippers." "Don't worry," he said to me one day. "My wife is a roundtripper, and

I know she'll make it." When I asked him what a roundtripper was, he explained: "When I was in the service and we were caught in a foxhole without supplies or ammunition, we would only send out the men we knew would come back. You could always trust them to do what was necessary, so we called them roundtrippers."

Purpose, like hope, is physiologic. It makes for roundtrippers. Health psychologist and counselor Jeanne Segal writes that a student who was working with her in a program for cancer patients did a survey to determine whether there was a statistical correlation between selfless service to others and survival. The answer, Segal says, was a resounding yes! This confirmed on the physical level what she had observed on the psychological level when she was working with a family service agency. There her clients seemed unresponsive to the kind of counseling she had been trained to do, until she discovered a United Way office downstairs from hers that needed volunteers. Whenever she could make no progress with her clients, she would send them downstairs to enlist as volunteers—"and guess what? My clients got better fast! Even borderline individuals improved markedly. Their grasp on reality, self-esteem and purpose for living improved as they gave of themselves in unselfish ways that felt good to them." Volunteers live longer and have fewer illnesses.

Physicians are too rarely aware of their patients' need for purpose and meaning in life, so they often don't know how to account for dramatic improvements in their patients' conditions. However, I know there's always a life story behind the change, some kind of existential shift. Recently I received a letter from an oncologist telling me that a woman with extensive breast cancer, whom we had both cared for, had returned to his office five months after he had sent her to a nursing home for hospice care—and that he had "never seen her looking so well!" No further comment by the oncologist was made. I told the medical student who was working with me to call the woman and find out her story, because I was sure there would be one. The woman told the student that when she got to the nursing home, she found conditions there so unbearable and depressing that she led a revolution among the other "inmates" to insist that they receive better treatment. She spent time talking with the staff about the tenderness and love the patients needed, and she transformed the place. Then she felt so good that she went home and bought herself a new car!

For some people, the challenge of their illness is part of what gives their lives a purpose, as they find new paths to healing and love. One remarkable woman wrote to me about her struggle to rehabilitate herself after a car accident left her a partial paraplegic. "Not Giving Up" is her credo: "The one thing I have found out about this area is, there are too many unknowns. Impossibilities are continually turning into possibilities. I have always felt our bodies and minds can do more to promote our healing than they are allowed or encouraged to do. Tapping into that source is the key." Having been told by her doctors that all she can do is "hope for a cure," she remains determined to take a more active role in her healing. In fact, she was writing to me for suggestions about how she could do visualizations to reverse the paralysis in her spinal cord. Again, "F" is not for failure, but feedback and fighters. She is setting up a challenge, not an opportunity to fail.

Sometimes one of the things that gives people a sense of purpose is the challenge to do the things they love despite the obstacles of illness. I think of John Calderhead, a young man I've been corresponding with, who had a leg amputated in March 1983 due to a sarcoma. He'd been a skier since he was seven years old, and he's now back up on the slopes again, skiing competitively in events for the disabled. "I skiied before the operation, so why should I not ski afterward," he told a newspaper reporter. Here's a man who doesn't accept limitations.

For another man, it's the love of the Talmud. Rabbi Aaron Soloveitchik, whom I read about in the *New York Times,* suffered a stroke several years ago when he was sixty-six. Despite being barely able to walk, every week he commutes from his home in Chicago to a rabbinical class in New York in order to pass on his knowledge of the ancient Jewish texts. "Do you know what it's like to tie my shoes? It's as difficult as parting the Red Sea . . . I'm in constant pain. But when I give a *shiur* [class], I don't feel it as much," he says.

Some people just seem to have limitless amounts of courage and joy. It might be said that their purpose is to teach us how to live. I have a wonderful letter from a woman who wants to share the story of her father-in-law's life:

Mr. Wood contracted the three worst kinds of polio thirty years ago. He was given at most ten years to live at that time and was and is still paralyzed from the neck down. He is in an iron lung at night and his wife has provided for all of his care at home. During these thirty years they have raised seven children, the youngest of whom was born shortly after he became paralyzed. He has seen all of his children graduate from high school. Until the last year or so, he was an active mouthstick artist and has sold many oil painting and countless note cards. He has paintings hanging in our state capital.

Mr. Wood has always maintained an interest in life and greatly enjoys lively conversation with company who come to the house. He doesn't view himself as less fortunate than others. Instead he displays great compassion for other people. He always has something interesting to talk about and has a way of drawing conversation from people.

A few years ago he purchased a late model red convertible and during the warmer months he spends as much time as he can riding around the countryside and visiting family. His wife comes along and they hire a driver/mechanic to take him and of course they have to pack up all of his gear and respirator.

This man has determination. He has a purpose in life and he is an "exceptional" person or, as you say, an "exceptional patient."

To be exceptional doesn't always mean having to perform extraordinary feats, however. It's your attitude about living and loving that makes you exceptional, not whether you can ski one-legged, create mouthstick paintings or heal yourself through visualization and meditation.

A woman came into my office one day with multiple sclerosis. Her accomplishment was that she had taught herself to walk again, because she had an infant at home and wanted to learn to walk before her child did. What courage and beauty! I've known so many incredibly inspiring and awesome people, each one someone who has found his or her own way of being exceptional, of being strong at the broken places. The varieties of exceptional behavior are endless. Find yours.

In the words of Max Navarre, one of the contributing editors of *Surviving and Thriving with AIDS:*

If you have never loved yourself, never really loved yourself, gently and unconditionally, now is the time to do that. Love yourself, forgive yourself, and at the same time, know that there is nothing to forgive. Love other people, and let them love you. You'll never be bored. Unconditional love can do some amazing things, and it's a real safety net. And we can do amazing things when we know that we are safe. Miracles happen every day.

One of these miracles is the love that Max Navarre was talking about. It's love that makes us immortal in the only true sense of the word. I've been on many television programs and had people in the audience stand up, angry, and tell me that one of their family members had fought bravely for life and died anyway, despite doing everything that an exceptional patient is supposed to do. I understand the pain of that. I know that these people want their loved ones back, and that often the people who died would have liked to continue to live and be well. Being an exceptional patient doesn't mean that you can live forever. None of us will.

What it does mean is that, if you choose to be exceptional and confront life's challenges, after you are gone your loved ones will go on living with a fullness, not an emptiness. Yes, there will be grief, but not emptiness. I have spoken around the country at memorial services held by family members of those who have died. And these people are living memorials to their loved ones, because they bring something back to the community, a way of sharing what they have learned about life from the individual who died. It is wonderful to see this happen because it means that life and the message of that person's life have continued.

What we're talking about is taking on the challenges of life, not living forever. Again, it is Evy McDonald who has so beautifully summed up the changes that heal lives, and sometimes cure diseases as a by-product. Evy says that in the months following her "death sentence" she made the following changes in her inner experience of reality:

1. From hating my body to loving it just as it was, a "bowl of jello in a wheelchair."
2. From resentment of my parents to forgiveness of them and myself.
3. From being on the take, believing that life owed me something, to giving freely of my talents and energy to life.
4. From "doing" service for the acknowledgment or reward to practicing the art of "being" service.
5. From being had and tormented by unspoken and unacknowledged emotions to having emotions that were health-filled and consciously chosen.
6. From being afraid of intimate and sexual relationships to embracing intimacy and sexuality as a clear, sacred, ecstatic expression of who I am.

When you affirm your life in this way, you give everyone who comes in contact with you a gift, and you find your immortality in the love you leave behind. Where there has been no love and no life, however, there's only a terrible emptiness after death. Exceptional patients don't leave an emptiness; they leave the examples of their own lives and the love they've inspired in those around them.

SHOPPING LIST FOR CHANGE:
A FIVE-PART THERAPEUTIC PROGRAM

Let me now present you with a list of things I would like to see you do every day to help you become an exceptional human being. In this way you will heal your life as well as the lives of others, and possibly cure any afflictions.

1. Keep a daily journal recording your feelings and dreams. In tests of college students and executives, those individuals who had been asked to keep journals were shown to have a more active immune system and

to develop fewer colds and other illnesses during exam
time and periods of work stress. Even after they
stopped keeping the journals, the immune system
remained more active for up to six months. Including
periodic drawings may also help.

2. Join a therapy group that meets for two hours every
    week, where you will receive love, confrontation and
    discipline. It should not be a victim group. If it is a
    group where everyone complains every week, then
    don't go back. If you can't find a group specific to your
    needs, go to an Adult Children of Alcoholics meeting or
    any other group you like. The affliction doesn't have to
    be the same as yours; it's the attitude that is important.

3. Meditate, visualize, pray, or listen to quiet music, to
    interrupt your day four to six times with healing
    intervals that allow you to refocus, destress and give
    your body "live" messages. These are to relax you, not
    to make you feel you have more work or are not doing
    it well. So pick what feels right for you.

4. Live one hour at a time, based on your feelings. If you
    are close to death, ten minutes might be the time you
    have to focus on. What I mean by that is not to live as
    if you're going to die in an hour or ten minutes, but to
    ask yourself at the beginning of that period of time how
    you feel. If you do not like how you feel, then resolve
    those feelings or let go of them within the time limit.
    This teaches you that you are in charge of your feelings.
    When your time is significant to you, you will make a
    point of not wasting it in feelings that you don't like.

5. Twice a day for fifteen minutes sit or stand naked in
    front of a mirror. Work with the feelings that come
    up—the negativity for most of us—and then learn to
    love what you see in the mirror just as Evy McDonald
    did, progressing from her image of herself as a "bowl of
    jello" in a wheelchair to a part-by-part appreciation of
    herself, beginning with her smile, proceeding to her
    soft hair, and moving on to each of her body parts until
    she had put herself back together and could honestly
    say that she found the whole beautiful.

Now that you've read this list you see why so many people prefer having operations. Only a truly exceptional human being will take on this work. Once you do all of these things, however, you find that you begin to live more and more in the moment, and life becomes a series of moments that you are in charge of. Then joy will enter your life and you will be in heaven without dying.

Doctors don't know everything really. They understand
matter, not spirit. And you and I live in the spirit.

—WILLIAM SAROYAN, *The Human Comedy*

True Healing: Life, Love and Immortality

Arthur Hertzler, who practiced medicine around the turn of the century, wrote *The Horse and Buggy Doctor,* a book that reawakened me to the true meaning of healing. The first chapter begins: " 'Protect us, O God, from diphtheria!' These ringing words uttered by my father at morning prayers were my first introduction to the tragedy of diseases." In the pages that follow, the author's vivid memories of the dreadful diphtheria epidemic of his childhood evoke all the horror of a plague for which medicine at that time had found no remedy: Horse-drawn wagons bearing the bodies of the dead crowding the country lanes; eight out of nine children in one family dead within ten days; everyone filled with fear.

Today, do we feel frightened of diphtheria? No. Do we feel frightened of AIDS? Yes. Fifty years from now, will people be frightened of AIDS? No. Will there be some new disease, with five capital letters? Yes.

It is important that we realize that we can never cure everything. We will never find homes for all the homeless, or food for all the hungry, or cures for all diseases. But we can, as doctors, as family and as friends, care for everyone. And in that caring, true healing will occur—the healing of the spirit and of lives.

CARE VERSUS CURE

In his book *Out of Solitude* the Catholic priest Henri Nouwen tells us what it is to care. He begins by explaining that caring is not the attitude of the strong toward the weak; caring takes place between equals. The word "care" has its roots in the Gothic *kara,* meaning to grieve, experience sorrow, cry out with. The person who truly cares must join with the person in pain. Sometimes that is all that can be done, which is hard for anyone to accept, and especially hard for doctors, trained as we are to be fixers and mechanics, not healers or caregivers. However, Nouwen says, that may be what is most needed:

> . . . when we honestly ask ourselves which persons in our lives mean the most to us, we often find that it is those who, instead of giving much advice, solutions or cures, have chosen rather to share our pain and touch our wounds with a gentle and tender hand. The friend who can be silent with us in a moment of despair or confusion, who can stay with us in an hour of grief and bereavement, who can tolerate not-knowing, not-curing, not-healing and face with us the reality of our powerlessness, that is the friend who cares. . . .

And that is the doctor who can heal, even if he or she cannot cure. What the sick and the dying most need from those around them is an acknowledgment of their shared humanity. The prison doctor I wrote about earlier quotes a passage from Solzhenitsyn's *One Day in the Life of Ivan Denisovich,* in which Ivan the prisoner contemplates his guard and wonders "How can a man who is warm understand a man who is cold?" The doctor wonders too—how can he, a man without AIDS, understand the feelings of men with AIDS? As I said to him in a letter, "You can understand pain. You are a member of the species." If he has nothing to offer medically, he can still offer a hug or a hand to acknowledge the pain of a fellow human being.

I don't mean to suggest that this kind of care is easy, especially when we are caring for someone who may be close to death. To "join with" that person is to confront our own mortality. That takes great courage. It's no wonder that doctors and nurses who every day must deal with the dying try to distance themselves, to protect themselves. But the results of such distancing can be terribly cruel. A student nurse who was dying wrote of the suffering she endured because of the way the medical staff avoided spending any extra time with her:

> I know, you feel insecure, don't know what to say, don't know what to do. But please believe me, if you care, you can't go wrong. Just admit that you care. That is really for what we search. We may ask for whys and wherefores, but we don't really expect answers. Don't run away . . . wait . . . all I want to know is that there will be someone to hold my hand when I need it. I am afraid. . . . I have lots I wish we could talk about. It really would not take much more of your time . . .
>
> If only we could be honest, both admit of our fears, touch one another. If you really care, would you lose so much of your valuable professionalism if you even cried with me? Just person to person? Then it might not be so hard to die . . . in a hospital . . . with friends close by.

Although she is speaking mainly to nurses, it's usually they who *are* willing to spend the extra minute, stroke the forehead, hold the hand, while doctors move on to those cases they can "fix," for they tend to feel helpless with the dying. I see medical histories that begin with words like "Poor unfortunate terminal white female," and I know that the doctors who took the histories did not really know the individual but are trying to deal with the pain they themselves feel when they can't cure. But the doctor who is also a healer knows better than to write off a patient with pity and withdraw. To do that is often to deprive the patient of hope—and life. If you would be a healer, you will continue to offer hope as long as your patient wishes to continue fighting. How long that is must be the patient's choice, not yours. Dr. Karl Menninger, one of this century's pioneers in understanding the inseparability of mind and body, wrote in a letter to our mutual friend Ann Landers:

> Some years ago I was about to put together a book on *Ten Hopeless Cases.* They were all patients who had not been expected to get well. But they all *did.* Some got "weller than

well" as I described it. "Miracles," some said. Of course, it wasn't I who cured them although they (and I) sometimes thought so. . . . Well, I never got that book written and now I don't need to write it because a fellow named Bernie Siegel has written one of the best medical books I have ever read. It is a book that says that hope and love cure people whom medicine and surgery can't. Nobody's *disease* is hopeless, he says, but many people are.

In a later letter to me he said that his book was to contain the same message—"that hope and love are the most neglected remedies. Hope is useful when things are hopeless." I quote Dr. Menninger not to give myself a good review but to show that these ideas have been with us for a long time, even though most doctors today have forgotten them—if they ever knew them.

Hope is useful in many ways. You must remember, however, that the hope referred to is the patient's, not the doctor's. As the "attending" physician, you must learn to pay attention to what hope means to each individual patient. I was reminded of this one day recently when a patient I was visiting reached out her hand to me as I started to walk out of the ICU. She was on a respirator and could not speak and she wrote to me, "You won't leave me?" I said, "I have to leave now because I'm due in the o.r." She wrote again, this time in bigger letters, "But you won't leave me?" Then I understood what she was really saying. I told her that of course I would never leave her, but would always be there when she needed me. That was all she wanted, and that is something I can give her, even when I can help her in no other way.

It is my job to defeat the pain of living, not death. All exceptional patients know this. In our acceptance of our vulnerability is our healing.

DEATH AS A HEALING

Often we find that children are particularly sensitive to the feelings of those who are taking care of them, with a wisdom far beyond their years and a generosity of spirit that allows them to forgive us our inability to cure them. Physician Naomi Remen, the medical director of the Commonweal Cancer Help Program in Bolinas, California, described an incident that occurred when she was running the pediatric ward at Mt. Zion Hospital in San Francisco. She came to work one day to discover a number of the ward's nurses and residents embroiled in a very emotional argument, accusing each other of having lied to a five-year-old boy who was close to death from leukemia. It seemed that someone had told the little boy he could go home that day, for he had announced to his nurse that morning that she needed to pack his suitcase so that he could leave. Of course it was not possible that such a sick child could be released, and the nurse had tried to discover who had been so irresponsible as to make him such a false promise, but everyone on the ward denied doing it. No one, however, had asked the child himself, so Dr. Remen said she would talk to him.

When I opened his door he was sitting on his pillow, facing me, and coloring. I was again struck by how emaciated, how sickly he seemed. Then he looked up from his coloring and our eyes met. At that moment everything changed. The room became very still and there seemed to be a sort of yellow light—and an enormous presence. It was almost as if we had stepped out of time. I became acutely aware that I was carrying a great deal of guilt about this little boy. I had caused him great pain, and, even more important, over the many, many months I had worked with him I had not been able to cure him. But in the moment when our eyes met, I also knew that he forgave me. And even further, in that moment I was able to forgive myself. Not just for this little boy but for all the children I had treated and hurt and couldn't help in the ten years of my career. For me it was a sort of healing.

And then it went on to another level, and I knew that he wasn't a sick little boy and I wasn't a doctor. We were two beings who had played our roles in a painful drama with impeccability—he as a little boy and I as a doctor and there was absolutely nothing to be forgiven. All there was was a deep mutual love and respect. This all happened very suddenly, in a moment.

Then he said, "Dr. Remen, I'm going *home.*" I mumbled something like "I'm so glad for you," and I backed out and closed the door.

I was very confused and shaken by the experience, for at the time I had no context in which to understand what had happened. I went back to my office where the staff was waiting. "What did he say?" they asked me. I told them that I hadn't asked him. I said, "Why don't we just wait a little while and see what happens." A few hours later the child said that he was tired. He lay down, pulled his sheet over his head and quietly died.

The staff's response was one of grief. But they were all relieved that he had died before he found out that he couldn't go home—before he found out that someone had lied to him. My experience, on the other hand, was that he had known, truly, that he *was* going home, in a much more profound sense than the staff was prepared to appreciate.

I had a similar experience with a child. He was a beautiful young boy of two whom I had operated on. But he was now in the hospital to die; active therapy had been stopped. One day he said to his mother, "I'm going to be a little bird soon and fly off. I wish you could come with me, but you can't." And over the weeks he continued to prepare his parents for his departure.

Because I had been his surgeon I continued to visit him regularly, although there was no longer anything I could do for him as a physician. One morning when I went in, instead of the usual request for an ice pop from the refrigerator or some other errand I could run for him, he greeted me by pointing to a chair by his bed, indicating that I was to sit down and join him. He then had his mother put on a videocassette of the Muppets which we watched together for a few minutes. Soon I told him that I had to go, and he did something he had never done before: He pointed at his cheeks, meaning for me to kiss him on both sides. Which I did. I had never been given that privilege before, and when I left the room I felt highly honored by what he had allowed me to do, so much so that it didn't occur to me until later that he had been saying goodbye. Fifteen minutes after I kissed him, he died. This was one of those times that reminded me why I never abandon my patients—they have so much to give. The love that child left behind still sustains me.

Jim McQuade, a medical student who worked with me for a month, did interviews with twenty-five physicians concerning their attitudes about death. At the conclusion of the paper reporting his findings he wrote:

It is important to come to an acceptance of death, not only as an absolute reality, but as part of the natural order of things. When the physician achieves this acceptance he no longer needs to avoid the people who have problems that he cannot solve. [He or she] is then able to remain in a partnership with the patient and to share the common bond of mortality and love that they have between them until the very end. As George Santayana has said, "There is no cure for birth and death save to enjoy the interval." Only through the acceptance of mortality and love can we enjoy the interval.

McQuade closes with a quote from one of the doctors he interviewed, a man who had a reputation for being particularly good at relating to dying patients: "After all it's the dilemma of man, the only subject of interest, and I have the opportunity to participate, I have in a way the opportunity to *practice* dying. The fact that I had the opportunity to spend long hours with a dying patient while he was getting ready to die—that experience alone is just wonderful."

For this doctor the time he spent with his dying patient was a privilege. Yet when I am lecturing to doctors I often ask how many have actually been present at a patient's death. If attempts at resuscitation and other emergency procedures are excluded, close to 100 percent have *not* had that experience. We avoid being with our patients in their last moments because we see their death as our failure. When we can stop feeling like failures, our profession will change and we will become a more genuinely caring group. When we realize that our role is to heal, and that to heal is to alleviate suffering, not to stop death, then we will understand what an honor it can be to share a person's last moments. And when we also realize that people have an incredible ability to die at the moment that is right for them, then we too will be able to see that dying can be the final healing. For we die as we live.

DEATH AS A CHALLENGE AND AN OPPORTUNITY

One day I was visiting a woman in her hospital room and counseling her about what a wonderful challenge she faced in trying to exercise control over her illness, her life and even her death, when I got so carried away with my theme that I heard myself saying "You know, you can even survive dying." There was a moment of silence, she looked at me strangely, and then we both burst into laughter.

I know this sounds crazy—first I talk about illness as a gift, and now it's death as a challenge. To make matters worse, I'm not just talking about death as a challenge for the physician, but for the family and friends and ultimately for the dying person. One of my exceptional patient group members said one day, "Fatal isn't the worst outcome." And I agree completely. In the words of Woody Allen, "There are some things that are worse than death. If you've ever spent an evening with an insurance salesman you know exactly what I mean." Not living is the worst outcome; whereas dying can be a healing, ending a full, rich life for someone who is tired and sore and in need of rest. More important, the knowledge of our eventual death is what gives meaning, urgency and beauty to every day of our lives.

The greatest gift of all is that we don't live forever. It makes us face up to the meaning of our existence. It also enables people who never took time for themselves in life to take that time, at last, before they die. A young woman asked me to see her mother to help her with dying. The daughter said her mother was miserable, had decided she did not want any more chemotherapy and was ready to die, but couldn't seem to do it.

I went to the woman's hospital room to talk to her, and she told me the same thing—that she was sick and wanted to die. Just then the phone rang. She talked for several minutes and then hung up. She told me it was her grandchildren calling to say that they were coming for a visit, and then she said, "Excuse me," jumped up, went to her closet, took out a lovely robe, put on her wig and makeup and prepared to receive her guests. At that point I said to her, "I can see why you're having trouble dying. You're still trying to be the perfect wife, mother and grandmother. It's hard to do that if you're dead."

I continued to visit her, trying to help her let go of all her roles, to detach and separate so that she could die without failing anyone. Two weeks later I was sitting on her bed when the phone rang. She reached for it and I said, "That's a perfect example of what I'm talking about. If you're trying to die you don't have to answer the phone." She picked up the phone and instead of saying, as most people do when a doctor is in the room, "I'll call you back in a few minutes, the doctor is here," she went right on talking. After about fifteen minutes, she handed me the phone and said, "It's my daughter. Now you talk." We chatted for a few minutes and then hung up. I turned back to her and said, "You are putting all your energy into your family instead of yourself and that is why you are having trouble dying."

The phone rang again and I told her she didn't have to answer it. Her hand wavered back and forth with each ring and my saying "Don't answer," until finally it landed on the receiver. Before she could pick it up I said, "I have to go now because I'm due in the operating room, but first I want to tell you—that's a wrong number sent by God to teach you something." As I walked out I heard her pick up the phone, and it was a wrong number, as I'd known intuitively that it would be. A day later she was dead. That wrong number was probably a greater teacher than anything I could have said to her. I do not claim to be clairvoyant, but when you are working with people you care about there are times you "know." I use that knowledge to help them.

It's always sad to see people who are literally on their deathbeds still spending all their energy trying to make the world happy and ignoring their own needs. Despite the fact that they're dying, they're trying to be nice to everyone and ignoring their own feelings.

Just as painful, in a different way, are the people from whom control is forcibly taken away, usually by hospital personnel with their emergency procedures and their machines and their medicines. As I was making my "clergical" rounds one day I walked into a room and asked the woman there how she was doing, and she said, "Terrible, my doctor just told me I'm dying." I said to her, "If you're dying, why don't you get up and get out of here? I wouldn't want to spend my last moments on earth lying here hooked up to all these tubes and machines. Why don't you go home and sit on the porch you and your husband built and have enjoyed for years, and die there?" She looked at me and started beaming and said, "You know, you're right." This totally empowered her. Within four or five days her oncologist said that, for reasons he couldn't understand, her blood count was much better and she could be discharged from the hospital. She went on for many more enjoyable months. When she was ready, she went back to the hospital and died peacefully. She was a wonderful teacher and healer, for her family and for me.

In *JAMA*, Dr. Alvan Feinstein wrote about the quite different experiences his ninety-year-old mother had in the hospital. After being revived from near-death episodes several times, this formerly independent, spirited woman was reduced to a vegetative state that forced her son to question the values of medicine as it is practiced today:

Since the preservation of her life helps no one, and is desired neither by her nor by those who love her most dearly, why could her doctors not be content to let her die in peace and serenity? Why did they pursue a vigorous therapy that could benefit no one except their own satisfaction in thwarting death, regardless of the consequences? I do not know the answer to these questions. But I, the physician son of this woman, weep for my mother and for what has happened to my profession.

Our profession can be incredibly cruel in its relentless focus on keeping people from being dead no matter what the consequences. We have to learn that death is not pathological; it's a natural part of living, which we doctors have rendered as unnatural as possible in the interest of denying our limitations and mortality. I've seen many beautiful deaths, but for every one of those, how many more there are like the one described in this poem by Helen Blitzer.

THE BARRIER

Berta. Berta . . .

my father calls.
My mother waits outside his door.
Doctors, nurses work machines
to pump his lungs with air,
shock his heart to rhythmic pulse.

Wired with electronic plugs, he twitches
still calls for his wife.

Banned from his bedside,
my mother is told
she would be in the way.

Against my father's flesh,
cold metal of defibrillator.
    His life
    one dot
    spiralling the monitor.
Through the whirring humming clicking

    Berta . . .

Silence.

The machines are rolled from his room
to the next ward.

My mother is told.

"Can I see him now?"
No. Says Nurse. We have a special waiting room.

My father grows cold.

His lips
still open
with my mother's name.

How terrible, for both husband and wife, that they were denied the chance to be together at the moment of death as they had been in life, and that his death was robbed of all dignity. Of course, doctors and nurses aren't the only enemies of a good death. Many people die in great anger, leaving behind them a legacy of bitterness, because of an inability to understand that dying is not just a physical process but an emotional, psychological and spiritual transition as well. I received a letter describing two contrasting deaths in the same family, one within the context of traditional medical and religious channels, the other a very different experience because the young man had been given support from a couple who believed in adjunctive healing approaches, including those described in my first book. It was they who wrote the letter.

Both people who died were afflicted with a rare genetic disease, which struck in their thirties, but there any similarity ends. The sister was described as "bitter and withdrawn from early in the illness until the final moments. . . . The way she died, with such anger, made it hard on all members of her immediate and extended family, on her caregivers, and on herself. Bitterness that resulted still exists today." The brother had a completely different experience; he attended one of my exceptional patient support groups, did visualization exercises that had been specially tailored to the needs of his disease and watched videotapes on healing that his friends bought for him.

As a result of these actions, Kevin handled his illness entirely differently from his sister. Of course, he was not a saint and was not always pleasant and sometimes cried. But for the most part Kevin had a beautiful smile for everyone and could still smile

even when he could only indicate "yes" by raising his eyebrows.
. . . He made it easy for all those around him to love him and to
care for him—the hospice volunteers, your support group, his
caregivers at the care center; by so doing he made this ordeal
easier for himself because he could attract love and because his
own viewpoint was positive, hopeful, and, in a way, accepting. . . .
[Although he did not survive] what did happen was still a miracle.

I quote this letter in tribute to yet another of the many exceptional patients with whom I have been privileged to work—
people who have learned how to grow into their own uniqueness when confronted by death. His friends end their letter by
saying "he was a hero in his death. His caregivers have said that
he taught them 'how to die.' "

Wonderful things can happen among families as death
draws them together. I heard about one such family from a
woman I met one day in a small shop on Cape Cod. Bobbie and
I had walked in to buy frames for some photographs I had
taken. A woman was standing in the frame section staring at
me. I had a hat on, so Bobbie removed the hat and said, "Yes,
it's Bernie." The woman came over and introduced herself,
explaining that she and her husband had planned to attend one
of my workshops but that he had died before they ever got the
chance. She was in that shop looking for a frame for her husband's picture which she was holding in her hand. Another one
of those "chance meetings" that lets you know that coincidence is God's way of remaining anonymous, because she had
a story that had to be told. It's a story about the final days of
her husband, Richard Meads, whose name she wanted used in
commemoration of his life. The part of it that I'm going to
share with you begins on an evening shortly before his death
when, drugged with morphine to dull his pain, he called his
wife to his bedside:

"Kathie, come here. I know what it is now. It's not
CANCER." "What is it?" I asked. "It's all ENDLESS LOVE! It's
what I feel for you, Richard and Jeremy and that's GOD! That's
all it ever was. It was always there and I didn't see it. I love you
so much at this moment. It's stronger than love—it's lust," he

said. "I love you from the ends of my toes through my whole body" and he kissed me over and over again. "I love you just as much," I said as I hoped this morphine thing would pass quickly. But it wasn't morphine—he was perfectly lucid. He saw everything that mattered in life very clearly and he saw beyond this life to a greater meaning and truth.

All night he told me how much he loved me. The next morning I went to work but when I got back he looked worse, more disoriented. Our neighbor Linda said, "We better get Dr. Alberts to authorize an ambulance." She left to get him.

Father Mike came in and sat with Richard. When Dr. Alberts arrived he examined him briefly. "Step outside," he told me. "He doesn't have much longer. He belongs here with his priest and his loved ones. There's nothing they can do for him at the hospital that we can't do for him here." I'm in disbelief—THIS IS NOT IT, NOT THE END—but it was. That was Monday at 3:30 P.M.

Soon the house began to fill with family, friends and loved ones. We all held him that night—he was happier sitting up but he wasn't afraid. He was very peaceful and wanted to talk to everyone. It was his turn to say goodbye and I love you to each of them and he did. He slept a few hours. In the morning he was more disoriented. He could no longer sit all the way up. He spoke of sailing his boat—for hours we were sailing. I spoke to him constantly. He always answered me. I asked him at one point, "Are we racing?" He said, "Yes." "Where are we?" I asked. "Way ahead!" he answered. I should have known we would be "way ahead."

Then about thirty-five minutes before he died he started saying "Sun, Sun" but I thought he was saying "Son, Son" meaning Richard and Jeremy. I said, "They're both right here, holding your hand." He said, "No, no—Light, Light—lots of Light." Then I knew and I said "Oh yes, Richard. You see the Light? The Light is God. The Light is Jesus. It's all right to go to the Light." "Okay," he answered, "I'm going—But you be there in half an hour." "Yes," I answered with more love than I've ever felt in my life, "I'll be there in half an hour, my love!"

He wasn't quite ready to leave all of us yet. He sailed a short while longer. I kept whispering to him, "I love you" and he kept softly murmuring back, "I love you." Then he didn't answer me any more but I kept on telling him, "I'm with you. I love you, my love." I know he heard me—he was still right with us. So peaceful. So loving. But he definitely knew where he was going. He led us all there with him as far as he could. He showed us all that he was in some sort of transition. Death was not the end—just the beginning of something new that must have been beautiful in its own right or he never would have left me so peacefully. He took my fear of death away. Whatever this new life is I'll know when he meets me there in "half an hour."

When you meet Kathie and she shares that story with you, you will cry with her, as we did, but you will also know that she and her family and friends, as well as her husband, were extraordinarily blessed to have had such an experience. When Bobbie and I had dinner with Kathie on the Cape later that year, there was such warmth and such a glow in the room that it was clear that she and her family were still sustained by the love they had shared in those final days.

DEATH: THE FINAL FLOWERING

Eli Wiesel, in his book *Souls on Fire,* tells us: "When we die and we go to heaven, and we meet our Maker, our Maker is not going to say to us, why didn't you become a messiah? Why didn't you discover the cure for such and such? The only thing we're going to be asked at that precious moment is why didn't you become *you?*"

Facing death is often the catalyst that enables people to reach out for what they want. You've heard some of the stories: the man who stopped practicing law and started playing his violin when he thought he had only a year to live, the woman who divorced her husband so that she could truly love someone for the first time in her life, the man who finally started speaking out about his own needs when he realized that his illness—and his son's medical problems as well—grew out of unexpressed feelings.

Everyone does it in his own way, and sometimes the fullest expression of selfhood is simply continuing to be the person you always have been. I think in this context of a Jewish mother in the hospital who told her family the cafeteria was closing and to go and have a nice meal—and then died five minutes after they left. This woman didn't die lonely; she died happy in the knowledge that her last act was to do something caring for her family. She lived and died a loving mother.

When you know death may be near, you may finally start to live, and the by-product is sometimes physical healing. One woman I know who was told she had six months to live said, "I raised so much hell, I got better." In fact, my definition of a good hospice is one where the hospice workers do so well helping people get ready to die that some of them start feeling too good to die. They resolve all their emotional conflicts, become "hospice dropouts" and go home.

People who experience spiritual joy can also heal quite unexpectedly. This happened to a man in an intensive care unit who was looking forward to dying because he would meet Jesus and go to heaven. One night he heard his physician announce to the family members gathered around him that he probably wouldn't make it through the night, and he became so overjoyed at the prospect that he recovered. When last I heard from his family, whom I met at a workshop, he had done that three times. My comment to them was that if he's going to die, they'll have to keep it a secret from him.

That may seem like an unusual story, but I've seen many similar cases. Family members who receive a call to come because someone is dying will travel long distances to be with their loved one at the end, then come to me shocked at how good the patient looks. I explain to them it's because these people are at peace finally. No more therapy, no more appointments, no more worries or concerns, just the freedom to be completely, authentically themselves, liberated from all the things that don't matter, honest about their needs and feelings. The comfort that comes with this kind of peace often produces what I call little miracles, or remissions that may last for days or months.

In a wonderful article by Katy Butler of the *San Francisco Chronicle,* three long-surviving men with AIDS talk about how facing the disease has helped them to say yes to themselves and no to everything that does not matter. Bob Reynolds, who had always seen himself as "the quiet guy in the corner," became active in the Shanti Project, a self-help group for PWAs, stood up to his doctors about what kind of treatments he wanted and in general took his life into his own hands:

When one is faced with one's mortality, one has to re-evaluate how one is going to live. I had options: I could get all involved with grief and helplessness and anger. . . . Or I could go out and be motivated by my grief and anger and frustration and accomplish something. . . .

Whatever I think I need, I try to give myself. I don't "make myself wrong" if I'm feeling a little down, or angry, or depressed. Sometimes I'm active at Shanti. Sometimes I need to play couch potato, to come home and read my murder mysteries. Or go out to the back yard and scream.

I try to ask myself, "Am I living how I want to live if this is the last month of my life?"

Another of the men interviewed for the article, Dan Turner, felt that self-expression would enhance his immune system, so he quit his job as a word processor and did what he really wanted to do—write songs. He produced a song a week for a local production. And he too speaks of options: "The musical is what kept me alive. . . . Writing those songs week to week was a joy. . . . People have to know they have an option. You can focus on living in the present moment, or you can get wrapped up in the horrors of the future and let those burden you. If you blame everything on AIDS and become obsessed with it, you create a powerful monster within."

So write (or sing) your songs, play your violins, have your love affair with life, or keep right on being the Jewish mother you've always enjoyed being. Just make sure you're doing what you want to do. That makes the idea of leaving easier. As Ron Carey, the third man in the article, said:

I think I will probably die of AIDS. I've lived a good life, and I've got no regrets. I've made my will, and made a tape for my memorial service: good Walt Whitman poems and country music:

Dolly Parton singing "There's a Calm on the Water"; Juice
Newton singing "You're One With the Spirit, One With the Soul";
and Willie Nelson singing "Amazing Grace."

I've always looked at death as a wonderful adventure. I look
forward to it.

The young men and women who are dealing with AIDS
seem to me to deserve special credit. They have had to learn far
more about life and death than they should have to at their time
of life. But they have met their challenges with great courage.
The support they give each other, their way of coming together, their sharing, their love, and their ability to understand
how they can make their lives meaningful are incredibly inspiring. Their example shows us what we are all capable of.

I think especially of the lessons gay men have learned
about self-affirmation. Leonard Matlovich, an Air Force sergeant who challenged the military's policy of excluding gay
people and won, was a man who had at one time hidden his
homosexuality. When he contracted AIDS he recognized in
the disease a new opportunity to affirm what he had been in
his life, to join with the gay community once again, as he had
in his lawsuit, and feel proud of being a part of it. As he told
his biographer:

If there has to be a disease, and if I have to have it, then this
is the disease I want, because the good that has come out of it is
just incredible. The reality of the situation is that before we meet,
the main thing gay people have in common is our sexuality. Yet
the AIDS crisis allows us to share far more by bringing us closer
together. For this much love, care, and compassion to come out
of this community because of AIDS proves that we truly are a
people of incredible love. We're going to be a better community
because of this.

Matlovich summed up his military experience by saying "I
got a medal for killing two men and discharged for loving one."
He knew before he died that he had lived the life he wanted
to live, loving and living the path he chose. If only we could
all say the same, instead of denying ourselves in this life in the
hope of something better to come in the next.

ON GETTING TO HEAVEN
AND BECOMING AUTHENTIC

I have a secret to share—I can tell you how to get to heaven without dying. From my visits there I have learned that there are three basic differences between heaven and earth: One, a beautiful view, two, the weather is consistently good and three, there is no time element. It is always now, eternity now and forever. Though I can't reproduce the weather or the view, I can help you create heaven on earth by getting you to live in the moment.

One way of understanding what this would mean in practice is to think about what you would do before you left on your next automobile or airplane trip if you knew you would not survive the trip. What phone calls would you make, what letters would you write, what thoughts would you share? That's the way each day should be lived, with the sense that it may be your last.

Some wise words on the subject of living in the moment came from an eighty-five-year-old woman named Nadine Stair, who was confronting death. I've seen several slightly different versions of this poem, but the one I like best is this:

> If I had my life to live over, I'd try
> To make more mistakes next time. I would
> Relax, I would limber up, I would be crazier
> Than I've been on this trip. I know very
> Few things I'd take seriously any more.
> I would take more chances, I would take more
> Trips, I would scale more mountains,
> I would swim more rivers, and I would
> Watch more sunsets. I would eat more
> Ice cream and fewer beans.
> I would have more actual troubles
> And fewer imaginary ones. You see . . .
> I was one of those people who lived
> Prophylactically and sensibly and sanely,
> Hour after hour and day after day.
> Oh, I've had my moments
> And if I had it to do all over

Again, I'd have many more of them.
In fact, I'd try not to have anything
Else, just moments, one after another,
Instead of living so many
Years ahead of my day. I've been
One of those people who never went anywhere without
A thermometer, a hot water bottle, a gargle, a
Raincoat and a parachute [and if she had traveled with Bobbie, a
    tape recorder, an iron and a hair dryer].
If I had it to do all over again,
I'd travel lighter, much lighter,
Than I have.
I would start barefoot earlier
In the spring, and I'd stay that way
Later in the fall. And I would
Ride more merry-go-rounds, and
Catch more gold rings, and greet
More people, and pick more flowers,
And dance more often. If I had it
To do all over again.
But you see,
I don't.

The one thing that's true of all exceptional patients is that they are people who have become authentic. They do not reach the point of death only to find that they've never really lived. Sometimes they only "really live" for a few moments before they die. But they have lived and they are ready to go, as their choice. They know who they are, where they've been and why. This makes it easier for them to let go, and for their loved ones to let them go when they are tired and sore.

If there is a genuine acceptance of the appropriateness of death at a certain point for an individual, that person's loved ones may whisper "If you need to go, it's all right. You haven't failed. We will survive because your love will stay with us." If the time isn't right—as it wasn't for Rachel, the lady with the obstruction, whom I talked about earlier—that won't hasten death; it will simply let the person know that the family can deal with it when they must.

For those like Rachel who are not ready, such a message

will not cause any harm, and it may motivate them to turn things around and start living, start dealing with the obstructions in their lives. For those who are ready, it can be an unburdening. I have seen people take one breath and die when they knew it was all right with their families, which is an incredibly spiritual experience. To watch somebody be given permission to die and just smile and leave makes you know that there is more to dying than the body ceasing to function. You really feel that you have witnessed something leaving.

A nurse recently wrote to me that she had flown to California to be with her son while his lover was dying of AIDS. When she arrived the son's lover was in the intensive care unit, dying. She told her son to tell him he could go. Her son resisted and she said, "Tell him your mother is here to be with you. It's okay to go." Her son repeated these words in the ear of his lover, who took one breath and died.

As you know, I think of God as intelligent, loving energy. So I expect everything in creation to be meaningful. After all, the same messenger molecules that I talked about earlier are in all living things. We find them in one-celled organisms, in plants and in ourselves. A few years ago, in the fall, I was thinking about all this and began to wonder why the leaves turn color every autumn. For that matter, why are we human beings all different shapes, sizes, colors? What is the message in this?

I think that every spring when the leaves come out, if you look closely you'll see that each one is slightly different. Some are reddish, some bright green, some pale, and they have different shapes and sizes too. But picture yourself as a maple leaf coming out. You think of how you can express yourself by manifesting your uniqueness, but the other leaves on the tree say, "Hey, this is a maple tree, fit in. You'll be green and this shape. Do you want people to look at us and point and say 'What a funny tree'?" You want to be liked, so during the spring and the summer, when the sun is shining and you have plenty of food, you turn the same green as everybody else, take the same shape and fit in.

Then the fall comes and it gets cold, and some of the guys

who were telling you how to behave start dropping. You're still hanging on, but you realize that you're not going to be able to hang on forever, and if you're not, then you'd like to let everyone know who you really are before you let go of the Tree of Life. So the green, which is a cover-up, goes, and you become your unique individual beautiful self.

Then you hang on as long as you want. There are still some dried-up scrawny leaves hanging on even in January, just as there are some dried-up scrawny specimens walking the streets. But this is an individual choice—how long you want to hold on to the Tree of Life, how long before you can feel that you've shown your true colors and lived your life. If you have lived and had your moment, then it will be much easier to let go. You will know and your loved ones will know your unique beauty, and it will be something they remember and live with. Then you truly achieve immortality.

When that doesn't happen, however, when you never allow yourself to understand or express your own value, you leave behind a pain that can't be healed, an emptiness that can't be filled. So don't go before you've shown your beauty. When you do that, not only are you immortalized through the love of those around you, but both you and they are healed by that love. This is a healing that can come only from you. I know all this because I've witnessed or been told about such healings. One man wrote me words that his wife, who was too weak to write, had dictated to him:

I think I now realize the true meaning of love. Although I am suffering, I really feel happy, because I am now truly aware of love. Everything moves me, but particularly the love of my family and friends. The wonder of it all . . . trees, birds, flowers, grass . . . inexplicable, marvelous . . . but particularly the love of my darling husband (that is hard for me to write as scribe/husband).

A few days later another letter came—actually two letters, because one of the daughters as well as the husband wrote this time—telling me that the woman had died. Both husband and daughter felt that her last weeks had been a blessing all around:

> Despite the fact that I know I am going to miss her terribly . . . I was able to let her go, knowing that she was at peace with the world and particularly at peace with herself. She finally came to understand how important she was to so many people. . . .
>
> Although her attempts at self-healing were unsuccessful, nobody could have tried harder. [Here I would interrupt and say that, while she didn't cure herself, she did heal herself and those around her, in the truest sense of the word "heal." She failed no one.] However . . . she certainly fought the good fight. This made it easy to be supportive and gave us all hope that a miracle might happen. I do not perceive the lack of a miracle to be a failure. . . . I think in trying she showed such strength and determination that we derived the same qualities from her. . . . The last few weeks were both terrible and wonderful.
>
> Love does heal. Despite our sadness, we are not overwhelmed, but understand that Alice lives on in all of us.

The daughter's letter ended with one of the last things her mother said to her: "Love, that's all that's important—that's what it's all about, nothing else matters."

YOU IN OTHERS: LIVING ON THROUGH LOVE

What is it that allows us to live on after our deaths? What is it that allows those we leave behind us to heal from the pain of loss? It is, of course, love. And it's primarily the one who is dealing with the disease who does the loving *and* the healing *and* the teaching. First must come self-love, as we have said. Self-love is an acknowledgment of the spark of the Divine that is in each of us, no matter what our imperfections. (Remember: We are all perfectly imperfect.) And out of self-love comes the ability to reach out and love and help others.

If you love, you can never be a failure. The great Russian novelists seem to know this better than most. In *The Death of Ivan Illich,* Tolstoy's protagonist realizes before he dies that his small son loves him and that his life is therefore not a loss. That's enough, he sees—to love and be loved—that's what it's all about. Our loved ones are our future and our immortality.

But of course it's not only the great writers like Tolstoy who know these truths. Each of us may come to know them in our own lives. Phil Bolsta sent me a poem he'd written to his wife after her death, entitled "Our Daughter's Eyes." Six years had passed and he'd been waiting to share it with someone. I'll quote from part of it:

And you said, "Look for me in our daughter's eyes,
And you will find me there.
I never will leave you, so honey don't grieve,
It's more than I can bear.
And I thank God for our time together,
And the joy you brought to my life."
And then you closed your eyes, and I whispered "Goodbye,"
My best friend, my woman, my wife.

Well, last night our daughter said her prayers, and climbed into
    her bed.
She lay down on her pillow, and then slowly turned her head.
I gazed into her face as you came climbing through her eyes,
I felt a warm embrace like a breeze from summer skies.
My disbelief gave way to grief, I brushed away a tear,
And then I heard you softly singing, rich and crisp and clear.
You poured your music on my soul, it blossomed like a rose.
Those gaping wounds of empty rooms began to heal and close.
And when at last your music passed, and your caress was gone,
I sat quite still, not moving until I heard our daughter yawn.
I noticed that her blanket had been pulled up to her chin.
She smiled and said, "Goodnight, Daddy. Mommy tucked me in."

It is hard for me to read this without crying. Another wonderful memorial to a loved one came in a letter I received from a young woman who was mourning her mother's death from a recurrence of cancer some months before. Although she was only supposed to have lived for a year after her diagnosis, "She kept saying to my dad, 'I have a husband and three children to go home to and take care of,' " and she stretched that year to seventeen—seventeen years with a lot of suffering in them but also a lot of love and joy:

> As long as she was alive and here on earth with her husband and children she was thrilled. My mom was so proud of me becoming a nurse. She was interested in everything I did. She knew all about my schoolwork, my hospital work etc. She always supported me and whenever I felt like giving up she was there to guide me along telling me I could do it.
>
> . . . I am going to be a nurse in nine months and I know it is what I want, but if I could have one wish it would be to have my mom there to see me graduate on that special day. Now I am not sure what that day will be like, I am not sure if it will be happy or sad. But I do love nursing, and it is helping and caring for patients like my mom that makes nursing so special and rewarding.

To live on not just through your daughter but your daughter's work, to know that every patient she cares for will receive that extra measure of tenderness because of her love for you—what a wonderful way of achieving immortality. This woman has left a legacy not only for her daughter but for all her daughter's patients. Here truly is a living and continuing memorial.

I don't mean to suggest, however, that that mother and her daughter would not both wish that her life could have been longer, that she could have lived on not just in the spirit but in the flesh. I know that often when we talk of living on in the spirit it may seem cold comfort to those on the verge of death, or newly bereaved. It reminds me of a story I once read about a little boy in bed one night who called out to his father to come to him because he was scared of the lightning and thunder. The father, a minister, told him not to be afraid because God would take care of him. The little boy replied that he knew God would, but "right now I want somebody who has skin on." We all want our loved ones "with skin on."

Perhaps no death is harder to accept than that of a child, in part because it seems to us that the child has been cheated not only of life but of a chance at the kind of immortality I've been talking about. But children can achieve much in their short lives. They can become as immortal in the love they leave behind as people who have lived many times their life-span. I think of Kelly Carmody, the nine-year-old boy whose parents helped him fight off his tumors for two years with visualization, a macrobiotic diet, a trip to Hawaii, a visit to a healer in Mexico—and love, in addition to chemotherapy and radiation. At the time of his death, there were people in Hawaii, California and Mexico as well as his hometown of Woodbury, Minnesota, whose hearts had been touched by Kelly. Dozens of people wrote poems to him for a memorial, hundreds showed up for his funeral, sang his favorite songs and released purple balloons. Kelly Carmody will live on not just in the hearts of his parents, Mitch and Barb, but in the hearts of people throughout this country, as you would know if you could read the tributes they wrote to him. A photograph of his beautiful face sits under the glass on my desk—one of the many faces I look to to help me go on with my life.

However, once again I have to say that I don't mean in any way to diminish the pain of such a death. "We are still after six months grieving very hard," his father wrote me in a letter, and the poems he wrote are filled with pain. But he also knows what his son and their whole family accomplished in the two years of their ordeal, and knows, as a poem he wrote says, that it was in their pain that they discovered "the tie that binds all human hearts/to each and one another."

DYING AS A BIRTH INTO
A NEW DIMENSION: ETERNAL LIFE

For each of us, life in the body does eventually come to an end. When I heard about the mother of a friend of ours who died at the exact moment that the public address system in the hospital announced "Visiting hours are over," I thought to myself, That's really what death seems to be—an end to our visit and our ability to touch one another. The skin is gone but it is also a beginning of something else, though we know not what. Jung has said that "our psyche reaches into a region held captive neither by change in time nor by limitation of place.

In that form of being our birth is a death and our death is a birth." And so it seems to me.

Just as I believe that love and laughter and peace of mind are physiologic, so I also believe that in our earthly lives we exist as physical manifestations of the loving, intelligent energy that we call God. David Bohm, the quantum physicist whose word "somasignificance" I cited earlier, is one of many modern scientists, especially physicists, to see the physical and the psychical as different expressions of the same order. Since Einstein we have known that particle and wave, mass and energy, are but different manifestations of the same thing.

The wholeness of the individual is the wholeness of the universe in microcosm. Atomically, anatomically and cosmically we express this unity, whether or not we are conscious of it. I don't know that this is something that can ever be proved, but there are many phenomena suggestive of communication between the spiritual and the material realms that would be hard to account for in any other way. What else could explain why patients who pray and/or who are prayed for heal faster or have fewer complications than others? Several different studies have shown this, as well as our ability to affect the function of machines and communicate with bacteria via our thoughts.

Randy Byrd, a cardiologist and former assistant professor of medicine at the University of California at San Francisco, did a double-blind study of 393 coronary care unit patients at San Francisco General Hospital. When the group was randomly divided into two, half to be prayed for, half not, with neither patients nor doctors aware of who was in which group, the prayed-for group did statistically better in three categories: need for antibiotics, need for intubation, and incidence of pulmonary edema. A study by biologist Bernard Grad of McGill University in Montreal has demonstrated the efficacy of prayer when it is the sick person who is doing the praying and when sick people are prayed for.

Dr. Byrd's study was refused acceptance by two major medical journals, although its methodology appears entirely sound.* That's sad, because we need to open ourselves to all

*I was told the article finally appeared in the September 1988 issue of *Southwest Medical Journal.*

possibilities. What I am sure of is that if the article had been about a new drug that caused those kinds of differences in statistics it would have been printed immediately. But spiritual matters are too disturbing to the beliefs of most scientists—they don't want to give up their addictions. As you saw above, physicists are often exceptions to this rule, perhaps because their work puts them so closely in touch with the ultimate mysteries of the universe that they cannot help being moved to a sense of awe and reverence. Albert Einstein, who considered himself a religious man, wrote: "The most beautiful experience we can have is the mysterious. It is the fundamental emotion which stands at the cradle of true art and true science. Whoever does not know it and can no longer wonder, no longer marvel, is as good as dead, and his eyes are dimmed."

Why am I discussing these matters in a book on healing? Because I think spirituality is part of healing, and because I think death is not just an end but perhaps a beginning as well. From my experience I feel that we do live on in some other form of energy after the body dies. I don't just say this to make people feel better, but because I have seen and heard about such extraordinary events.

I have many letters from people who were very well aware that an individual had died who was at a great distance from them. A voice, a vision, a hand on the shoulder, and then the phone rang and they knew what the news would be. At an unconscious level there is a great deal that we know about the future. Often people know it from dreams. I can sometimes see it in drawings. Whatever you may think about the meaning of such phenomena, it's interesting to note that the National Opinion Research Council found that people who have had mystical experiences are far from being "religious nuts or psychiatric cases" (as Father Andrew Greeley, the novelist and sociologist who is a member of the Council, put it). They tend to rank above the norm in education and intelligence and below it in formal religious involvement. Often they don't even believe, intellectually, in the validity of their own encounters. Many reasonable, sane people are so embarrassed about any mystical moments they may have had that they are extremely reluctant to admit to them.

When you sit in a room full of parents whose children have

died, and listen to some of their mystical stories, you will hear many that they have been afraid to tell anyone. One woman shared with me the story of a young girl whose nurses kept feeling, after her death, that she was still with them. Finally it seemed to them that her spirit left. Not long afterward the girl's mother was driving down the road when a seagull swooped down and sat in front of her car, causing her to slam on the brakes and wait what seemed like an eternity while the bird took its time sauntering across the road. Her dead daughter's favorite bird was a seagull and somehow she felt that it was Patty come to visit her. Her feeling that there had been some kind of divine intervention with that seagull was soon to be confirmed. When she proceeded down the road once the bird had crossed, she found a horrible car accident at the next corner that she would certainly have been involved in had it not been for the dawdling seagull.

Spouses also have stories to tell. A woman wrote to me a few days after Christmas to say:

> So far, Allen has appeared to me as a bright cardinal to cheer me on a run on a dreary rainy morning, a mallard duck who distinctly separated himself from the group tossing in the reservoir in Central Park and quacked at me as I ran, and on Christmas morning as himself, a distinct dream or vision of Al standing at the door all dressed up and wearing something red, a scarf or a cummerbund, and looking very handsome and a bit impish as if he were surprising us for Christmas. He gave me a warm kiss on the mouth and faded gently away. . . . I got up full of good cheer determined to make the day a happy one and it was. As we began our dinner with champagne I told everyone of my vision and we went happily on with the day. . . .
>
> I'm not always so up. The pain is more than I ever could have imagined, but so far anyway I can get myself out on the road and am ever alert to the joy of life and the signs of Allen's love.

DEATH IS NOT A FAILURE

Those who think that it's wrong to tell patients they are responsible for their own illnesses say that to do so will make them feel like failures if they don't get well. I hope by now it is clear that that is not what I am saying. Illness and death are not failures. It is how we face up to our illnesses and how we take on the challenge of our mortality that determine whether we are successes or failures. No matter how sick we are or how close to death, as long as we are alive we have the chance to make something of our lives. When I was running in the New York Marathon not long ago, a woman on a street corner shouted out, "You're all winners." She knows more about life than most and made the entire run worthwhile for me. If we take on the challenges of life, we are all winners.

We have no less an authority than God for the truth of this statement. In a sermon entitled "Keep Trying," Monsignor Arthur Campbell of St. Ann's Church in Nyack, New York, looked to Jeremiah 18:1–6 for insight into God's expectations of us.

In today's scripture we have another one of those instances where God teaches through everyday experience. God told Jeremiah to go down to the potter's house and learn a valuable lesson about life.

Jeremiah watched the potter working the wheel. The potter would gather a shapeless mass of clay, plop it on the wheel and begin turning the wheel by pumping a pedal with his foot. As the wheel turned, the potter shaped and squeezed the lump of clay into a graceful shape. If the potter didn't like the result, he'd simply start again. He would dampen the clay and begin to mold the clay into an entirely different object. He might turn a low, wide cooking bowl into a slim, tall drinking jar. The potter would keep trying until he got exactly the shape and size vessel he wanted.

Jeremiah was quick to understand the lesson. God treats us [as] the potter treats his clay. He molds us into different shapes and sizes. He works some into stout bowls and others into delicate urns. But sometimes he doesn't like what he sees, so he scraps the clay and starts again.

What a wonderful and reassuring lesson about our lives this is. God isn't through with us when things go wrong, when we become flawed by failure or misshapen by events. God is dead set on making something beautiful and useful out of our lives, no matter how long it takes. And because God never gives up on us, we ought never give up on ourselves. The motto and message of the potter is clear to all who see: namely, "Keep trying." The only unforgivable sin is giving up on life when we have made a mess of things.

Those who rise to the occasion will find that no matter what the outcome of the struggle, they have created something beautiful. This is the gift that illness gives us, that the knowledge of our own mortality makes possible. Facing up to death can be the catalyst for the kind of profound internal change that allows us to love, often for the first time in our lives.

Susan, whose letters I've been quoting in the last few chapters, was an incredibly angry woman when I first met her. There was so much rage in her that it was frightening to sit in the same room with her—I was afraid the windows would explode! Coming from a family background of alcoholism and abuse, she seemed a perfect candidate for passing on a similar legacy. But that is not what she has done. In one of her most recent letters to me, Susan says:

> In all honesty, I may die of my illness, and I know that. But the most important thing to me is to leave something positive from it behind. Living, dying, physical healing, and no physical healing—are not the issue. The ultimate goal for me is to walk and live in the fullness of God's love, in such a way that it may be a healing for all.
>
> To live is to love—nothing more and nothing less. I finally learned this.

I hope we can all learn this before our lives are over. If so, we will discover how to live in such a manner that those who love us will say, after we are gone, to quote Sigrid Undset, "Few better will come after"—and then go on living with the example we have lived. If you choose to live and love in the face of adversity, that will be your legacy to your family and friends, the beautiful burden they will then always carry. Those who have borne witness to that kind of courage will go on living their lives after you are gone; to do otherwise would be a slap in the face to the individual who died.

It lies within you to see to it that those you love keep faith with life. No matter how much they grieve for you, they will know that you live on in them. Love defeats death and makes us immortal. In Saroyan's novel *The Human Comedy,* the young hero grieves for his brother Marcus, who has died in the war. Homer feels that with Marcus's death the whole world is different, lacking something, altered for the worse, but a friend gives him good counsel:

"I'm not going to try to comfort you," Spangler said. "I know I couldn't. But try to remember that a good man can never die. You will see him many times. You will see him in the streets. You will see him in the houses, in all the places of the town. In the vineyards and orchards, in the rivers and clouds, in all the things here that make this a world for us to live in. You will feel him in all things that are here out of love, and *for* love—all the things that are abundant, all the things that grow. The person of a man may leave—or be taken away—but the best part of a good man stays. It stays forever. Love is immortal and makes all things immortal."

If you want your life to be a "healing for all," a live message to those you love, you must take on those challenges that God has meted out to you. In this way you will discover the heroism that is yours alone.

The truly heroic know that heroism lies in living, fully and joyously, in each moment that is given us. Therefore, take warning:

WARNING

When I am an old woman I shall wear purple
With a red hat that doesn't go, and doesn't suit me,
And I shall spend my pension on brandy and summer gloves
And satin sandals, and say we've no money for butter.
I shall sit down on the pavement when I'm tired
And gobble up samples in shops and press alarm bells
And run my stick along the public railings

And make up for the sobriety of my youth.
I shall go out in my slippers in the rain
And pick the flowers in other people's gardens
And learn to spit.

You can wear terrible shirts and grow more fat
And eat three pounds of sausages at a go
Or only bread and pickle for a week
And hoard pens and pencils and beermats and things in boxes.

But now we must have clothes that keep us dry
And pay the rent and not swear in the street
And set a good example for the children
We must have friends to dinner and read the papers.

But maybe I ought to practice a little now?
So people who know me are not too shocked and surprised
When suddenly I am old and start to wear purple.

—Jenny Joseph

Commit yourselves to love and life—and start wearing purple!

Meditations

You can record the following meditations yourself, or ask someone you love and trust to speak the words in a calm, gentle voice. You may wish to have relaxing, soothing music on in the background, playing softly. Where I have indicated pauses, do not say them; there should be a period of quiet on the tape, anywhere from fifteen to sixty seconds in length or even longer, depending on the kind of pacing you prefer and the amount of time that you need to experience the images fully. You may want to experiment with different voices, music, and pacing before you find the combination that puts you at ease and feels right to you. Remember, there are no right or wrong ways of doing these visualizations. Do not judge yourself.

MEDITATION 1

Begin by taking some deep breaths. Breathe in peace. Breathe out conflicts and thoughts and fears. Just fill a balloon with them and let them go. And when you're ready, look up and let your eyes close gently if they haven't by now. And now let a wave of peace move down through your body. You might give it a color if you like, or repeat a word like "peace" or "relax" to yourself. Let go of the tension in your jaw muscles, and your neck and shoulder muscles.

I'd like you to try to remember sitting in a school room, a classroom with those old wooden desks, names carved on the surface, the sound of your classmates around you, the teacher at the blackboard filling the board with lessons and chalk writing. When the board was full and the lesson was done the teacher would take an eraser and just erase the blackboard. Do that now. Clean your slate and erase the blackboard of your mind so that you are ready for new lessons and new experiences.

Once you've prepared the slate for new images, words and lessons, we'll go on a journey. You know where we're headed. We're headed for the middle of nowhere, to your corner of the universe, your own special place in the middle of nowhere, with its vivid colors, textures, aromas and sounds. Take yourself to that very special place you have created for yourself. Once you're there, find a quiet little den or nest that you can rest in or curl up in. And take a moment here to absorb the energy of the earth and the sky and to take the time for self-healing. If there is any problem present within your mind or body, see yourself eliminating that problem, with any treatment or techniques that you would like to utilize. And now take another moment for yourself, here in this special safe place that only you know where.

[Pause]

And when you're done I'd like you to follow my voice again, and dress yourself for work. We're going to build a bridge from your corner of the universe to ours, a bridge over a river that will connect with your path through the universe.

So dress yourself for work, and be aware of the weave and fabric and texture of your life, and how that has prepared you for the journey. And if your garments need to be repaired, repair them with love so that you're prepared for your journey and are dressed appropriately to work on your bridge.

Then take a look at the bridge you've built as you walk across it: how wide, how long, how strong? What kind of a connection do you have with the universe?

[Pause]

As you cross the bridge to start down your path to begin your journey, all of the people in your life will be present—family friends, co-workers, people you have all kinds of relationships with. Stop and touch them, and talk to them. See what changes occur in your feelings and theirs as you all come together. All feelings are appropriate. They are simply feelings.

[Pause]

When you have completed that, continue on your path. But if you need to stay you can catch up with us later. As you walk down the path you will see an old house off to the side with a garden and a porch. Walk through the garden, up to the porch steps and into the house, and find the living room. And when you find the living room look around in it for a chest.

Be aware if the chest is in some dusty old corner, or out in a prominent place. Have you looked at it many times before? When you find your chest, open it and see what lies within, what your heart would like to tell you. What gift or message does your heart have for you as you look inside your chest?

[*Pause*]

When you find the message within your chest make it a part of you and then come out onto the porch and back to the garden. Find a place where you'd like to plant a seed to create more beauty. And prepare the soil and take the seed and plant it. And then become that seed, sitting in the dark, paying attention to what it feels like to be that seed. Do you know which way to grow? Do you know which way is up? Which way to put down roots? You can't see here in the dark, but you can feel and you can know.

[*Pause*]

So put down roots to give yourself the nourishment and strength you need to get a grip on things. And then grow, pushing aside problems and obstacles until you break out into the sunlight and then stretch your limbs to the sky. Grow and bloom and blossom. Become that unique beautiful individual that you already are. And just feel the velvety petal, the aroma, the beautiful color. Grow and bloom and blossom where you are.

When you're done make that flower a part of you. And then continue on your journey. You will come to a quiet safe place where I'd like you to stretch out, or sit, and become small enough to enter your own body. Go through your body, opening every cell to light, to love. Harmonize the organs, and listen to what they have to tell you. Go through your body, repairing, rebuilding, recreating. Walk the corridors of your mind and brain, opening doors, cleaning the shelves of old material, turning the valves and switches in the different rooms to create the changes that you want to create in your body, so that you create a new self, a new you, a new I.

Then look in the mirror at this new self, this new creation. And look out of the mirror at yourself. Reflect upon what you see, and embrace yourself, accept yourself. Become one with your new self. And then gradually let this new self come back to the room, back to your breathing. Breathe in peace and alertness. Come back gradually, awake and alert, yet relaxed and at peace, back to an awareness of your chair, or the floor. And when the music and the voice have stopped, come back to the room and open your new eye when you are ready.

MEDITATION 2

Take a few deep breaths. Breathe in some oxygen and life. Give yourself a gift; you deserve it for being the kind of person you are. So breathe in peace and life and love and oxygen. And allow yourself to settle down. When you're ready look up and let your eyes close gently. Let a wave of peace move down through your body releasing the tension in the muscles. Breathe in peace and breathe out conflicts and fears and worries. Then remember what it's like to erase the slate, to clean the slate, cleanse your mind. You know where we're headed.

[Pause]

Once more we'll go off to the middle of nowhere, to your corner of the universe. And each time you visit be aware. Is it different? Are the colors any more vivid, have the sounds changed, the aromas and textures, the feelings you have as you arrive there? Find your nest or den again, and curl up for a moment. This moment is just for you. To absorb the energy of the earth and sun and to heal your body and your mind. Take a moment to eliminate any problems in this special safe place.

[Pause]

When you feel cleansed and ready for the journey, dress yourself. And each time you do this you will see if the weave and texture and fabric of your life have changed any. And if they have, then know you're changing and growing, and that repairs in the fabric of your life can be made continuously with love.

[Pause]

And then cross the bridge that connects you with our part of the universe. Be aware of how strong and long and wide that bridge is, and of any changes in the connection since the last time you were here. And as you start on your path, know you will always take the turns that feel right for you. Wherever the path divides, you will know which turn is yours. Sometimes you may go left and sometimes you may go right, but whichever way you go will be right.

As you walk along the path you will see a child coming toward you and you'll realize that the child is you. Give the child what it needs. Go with the child and be a child. Perhaps you'll find a play-ground or a park. Or you may want to go for a run in the woods or a field. Go wherever your child wants to go to feel free and experience some joy. Take a moment to be a child and have a happy childhood.

[*Pause*]

And then become one with your child and come back on your path. As you walk along the path you'll come to an elevator. It's made totally of glass and if you look out at the numbers marking the floors, you'll see that the elevator is now up in the eighties. I'd like you to take it back from the eighties to the seventies and sixties. Just keep going back through the years, to a floor or to a year that's important for you. And when you get back to that year, stop the elevator and step out into the voices and aromas and sights that are important for you to come back to. For whatever reason, you have decided to come back to this year to relive, to experience, to heal, to love. As you come back to that time and that familiar scene, ask yourself what you feel as you re-enter that scene. Spend the time here for what you need to accomplish and do.

[*Pause*]

When you have completed that, and only then, follow my voice again and we'll step back into the elevator and go down to the ground floor and step out on our path. Know that the elevator will always be there for you, and can go both ways, up and down, into the future and into the past. Then follow the path over a little hill, down to the seashore or the lakeside. And as you watch the gulls, realize how easy it is to fly and to rise above problems. You too can learn to fly, to rise above earthly cares. You know what it's like to bowl, how it feels taking those three steps and releasing the ball, the weight. Take three steps and let go of the weight you're carrying so you rise up and just fly. The weight you've let go of is your problems. Let them go, let them sink out of sight beneath the sea or the lake. Nature will take care of them. And you are rising up, supported by nature, just flying free, enjoying a moment of total freedom and support as you float above it all.

[*Pause*]

When you're ready, just gently come down, down to the shore. Stretch out. Absorb the energy of the earth and sun. Once again open yourself, every cell, to light and love. Harmonize the organs. Create the person, the new self. Go into every cell, every structure, the

DNA. Reprogram the genetic mechanisms, repair, recreate, redo until you're satisfied with what you've done. And when you are just let your light fill the room so that it mingles with our light and our love. And take back into you some of our light and some of our love so that not only will we be with you, but you will always be with us in times of need. Take that light and love and store it inside your chest. When you have it safely inside, allow yourself to be aware of your chest and how it feels, how it moves with each breath. Breathe in that love, and each breath will bring you back a little more alert, while still at peace. Until when you're ready, you'll open your eyes and return to the room, alert and at peace, but with a new view of the world and yourself.

MEDITATION 3

Take a few deep breaths. Take a breath of life for yourself. Breathe in life and energy and peace. Fill your lungs. Feel your chest rise and fall, then settle down. Let the life and energy go all through your body. Let all of the troubles and conflicts and thoughts just go up in a balloon as you breathe them out. If there's any tension in any of the muscles in your body, let it go. Let a wave of peace move down through your body.

[Pause]

Once more let's go back to that classroom. If you run your fingers over your desk you can feel the carvings of people's names and dates, hear the chalk scratching on the blackboard, the sounds from outside the room, sounds from the cafeteria or from kids in the yard. You'll be aware of all of them.

When the teacher has finished the lesson, she cleans the slate. Now clean the blackboard of your mind. Wipe your slate clean, and put up an empty movie screen.

[Pause]

On that great big screen, let's create the middle of nowhere. You are very familiar with it by now and you know where it is, so create it for yourself with all the textures and sounds, the aromas, feelings and sights that make it so special to you. Put it all together and find your safe little quiet place, and curl up there. Take a few moments to heal and eliminate any problems, and heal your life. As your life is healed, see any disease being cured and eliminated.

[Pause]

When you have completed that, follow my voice again. Once more we dress for some work. The weave and texture and fabric of your life may change from day to day. Take a look at the weave and fabric of your garments, feel them, then step on to that connection you've made, that bridge with the universe, with our universe. Come across. You're brave enough to cross all the bridges in your life and start on your path.

Pay attention to your feelings as you go, so you'll know which turns are right for you. Whichever way the path divides, you'll always take the turn which is right for you. And as you walk along you'll come to a lovely pond and garden. Walk to the edge of the pond and slip your things off and enter the warm healing waters. It's not deep at all. Lie down on your back and let the water support you and bathe you and heal you.

[Pause]

Then turn over and look down into the water. Look below the surface. See what lies down there, what is there for you to see and be aware of. Reach down into the depths and see what needs to be brought up that you can learn from and understand. What is at the bottom of all this?

[Pause]

Make what you discovered a part of your awareness and bring it to shore. Dry off in the sunlight and dress again, and continue on your path.

You will come to an outdoor theater. All of the people in your life will be sitting there. You're to go up on the stage and let them know what you want them to know by performing—singing, dancing, speaking. Show them what you want them to see and feel. The stage is yours. It's your show.

[Pause]

When you have completed that, come down into the audience and see how they respond to you. How does it feel? Who do you see there? What have they heard?

[Pause]

When you're done, come back to your path and continue on your way. Off in the distance you'll see a very bright light on your path. You may see a figure coming out of that light, someone coming toward you. As that individual gets closer, you will see more clearly what he or she looks like, what kind of feeling comes with him or her.

Finally you'll get close enough to learn the name of this being, who is your guide. Ask your guide about any questions or problems or conflicts you might be having in your life. But if no one has yet appeared out of the light, turn and look at the shadow which has been created by the light. Look into your shadow, and talk to your shadow, and see what you can learn from your shadow. Take a moment to speak to your guide or shadow, and learn, and receive guidance.

[*Pause*]

When that is done, know that the guidance will always be there when you need it. Continue on your path again, until you come to a quiet safe place where you can stop and pause and fill your body with light and love.

[*Pause*]

Go through your body, creating the new you, the new self, repairing each cell and opening it to light and love, reprogramming the DNA, finding the rooms of your brain and mind where the controls are, and making all the changes necessary to produce the new self, the new you, the new I. Then look at your work in the mirror. And look out of the mirror at yourself. And bring them together, all of the images, to blend in, to embrace, to accept as the new self. Let that new self come back to the breathing, back to the chair, the floor, the music, and my voice. And when you're ready, with each breath feeling more alert and at peace, come back to the room, awake and alert, but at peace, by opening your new eye.

MEDITATION 4

Begin with some nice deep breathing. Breathe in peace and love and light, all the things that fill the room. Just take them in.

Let go of any problems, weights, worries. And look up and let your eyes close gently when you're ready.

Once more, let a wave of peace move down through your body, perhaps repeating a word like "peace" or "relax" with each breath. Then erase the blackboard of your mind, put up an empty movie screen. And once more recreate on that screen your special place in the middle of nowhere. Once more take a moment to stop there before you begin your journey, to restore yourself, to heal, and to give yourself a measure of love.

[*Pause*]

When you have charged your battery and feel that self-love, walk up to your bridge and be aware of any change you have made in it. Then cross your bridge and start on your journey or path. Each step you take is helping you feel more relaxed as you progress on your way.

Soon you'll come to a mountain that the path climbs. I'd like you to start up that mountain. Equipment and tools are there if you need them. Be aware of how you progress and how you overcome obstacles, how you get to the top.

[Pause]

When you do get to the top, enjoy what you've accomplished, and give yourself credit for the effort. Then be aware of a large rainbow-colored balloon with a basket hanging from it. Climb into the basket and release the balloon. It's totally safe.

Rise up over the trees and clouds. The breeze will carry you. You'll feel weightless, trouble-free. Keep going until you have an astronaut's view of the earth. How small problems seem up here. But if there are any problems in your life, use the pencil and pad you'll find right beside you to write them down. List all the problems in your life. And then let them go, out into space, as you sail on trouble-free, weightless. You can now relax and enjoy the freedom.

[Pause]

Come back down gradually, come down slowly and safely. Keep coming, until you touch down alongside the path and climb out of the basket and start on your journey again.

Think for a moment about what you would be if you could be any creature in the world. And become that creature—an animal, a bird, a fish, another person. Who or what would you like to be? A butterfly? Take a moment to enjoy the experience of being what you would like to be.

[Pause]

Then ask the creature what you have experienced and what you can learn from it. And then come back into yourself, and continue on your journey. Look ahead to see where your path goes. Where will it lead? As you pause here, put a message on the blank billboard next to the path. Use this billboard to let people who come this way know whatever it is you would like them to know. You may paint, design, or write anything at all on the billboard. It is your message to those who come this way after you.

[Pause]

When you have completed the message, allow yourself to come back to your path. As you move along, you'll see the path disappearing into a dark tunnel going through to the next mountain. But you can see the light over there, so you will go for that light. It'll be dark in the tunnel, cool, damp. You may find yourself bumping into the sides, stumbling occasionally, perhaps falling down. But if you focus on the light, moving toward it, you'll find your way. Remember what it was like to be a child learning to walk? How many times do you think you fell down? What happened when you learned to ride a bicycle? How many times did you fall off? But you got up and you tried again. You climbed on again. And so you head for the light, just as you learned to walk and you learned to ride the bike. You know how to overcome difficulties.

And eventually you will come out into the light. Once again your family and friends will be there. How do they see you? What will you share with them after this experience? Take a moment to exchange feelings and views and words.

[Pause]

Then bring all your loved ones around you. Just let them love you, and heal you, and feel the change occurring in you as you accept the love and the healing. Now take a look at yourself. How have you changed? Accept this change and bring it back with you, back to the room, back to your life, back to the future. When you have made it a part of you, allow yourself to come back, renewed, restored, recreated. Upon opening your new eye you will see the new you, when you are ready to look.

Notes

CHAPTER 1

The Remission Project of the Institute of Noetic Sciences: B. O'Regan, "Healing, Remission and Miracle Cures," *Institute of Noetic
Sciences Special Report,* May 1987. For an update on the figure
of four thousand, see *Noetic Sciences Review,* Autumn 1988.

as researchers more receptive to this kind of thinking: *Advances:
Journal of the Institute for the Advancement of Health* 3 (4), Fall
1986.

Generally speaking, about one-third or more of the people: On
the figure of one-third, see H. K. Beecher, "The Powerful Placebo," *Journal of the American Medical Association* 159, 1955:
1602–6.

"post-operative wound pain; seasickness; headaches": R. Ornstein
and D. Sobel, *The Healing Brain* (New York: Simon & Schuster,
1987), 78–79.

as a scientific text explains: L. White, B. Tursky and G. E. Schwartz,
eds., *Placebo: Theory, Research and Mechanisms* (New York:
The Guilford Press, 1985).

A quite dramatic instance of the mindbody connection: R. A. Kirkpa-
trick, "Witchcraft and Lupus Erythematosus," *Journal of the
American Medical Association* 245, 1981: 1937–38.

several other miraculous recoveries from lupus: B. F. Solomon and
R. H. Moos, "Emotions, Immunity and Disease: A Speculative
Theoretical Integration," *Archives of General Psychiatry* 11,
December 1964: 657–74.

It appears that the pain-relief reported in so many studies: For stud-
ies illuminating the mechanisms of placebo effects, see J. D.
Levine, N. C. Gordon and H. L. Fields, "The Mechanism of
Placebo Analgesia," *The Lancet* 2, 1978: 654–57; J. D. Levine,

N. C. Gordon, R. T. Jones and H. L. Fields, "The Narcotic Antagonist Naxolone Enhances Clinical Pain," *Nature* 272, 1978: 826; B. O'Regan, "Placebo: The Hidden Asset in Healing," *Investigations: A Research Bulletin of the Institute of Noetic Sciences* 2 (1), 1985.

Brendan O'Regan, whose *Investigations* newsletter: B. O'Regan, "Multiple Personality—Mirrors of a New Model of Mind?" *Investigations: A Research Bulletin of the Institute of Noetic Sciences* 1 (3–4), 1985.

In 1964 Dr. George Solomon: Solomon and Moos, "Emotions, Immunity and Disease."

"Psychosocial Correlates": B. R. Cassileth, E. J. Lusk, D. S. Miller, L. L. Brown and C. Miller, "Psychosocial Correlates of Survival in Advanced Malignant Disease," *New England Journal of Medicine* 312 (24), June 1985: 1551–70; M. Angell, "Disease as a Reflection of the Psyche," ibid. 312 (24), June 1985: 1570–72; Letters to the editor, ibid. 313, 1986: 1354–59.

Candace Pert, for example, is already using Peptide T: "U.S. to Let Bristol-Myers Market AIDS Drug," *New York Times*, March 3, 1988.

When premature newborns are assigned: T. Field et al., "Tactile/ Kinesthetic Stimulation Effects on Preterm Neonates," *Journal of Pediatrics* 77, May 1986: 654–58.

***The Lancet*, a comparable British journal:** K. W. Pettingale, T. Morris, S. Greer and J. L. Haybittle, "Mental Attitudes to Cancer: An Additional Prognostic Factor," *The Lancet*, March 30, 1985: 750.

Sandra Levy, associate professor of psychiatry and medicine: S. M. Levy, "Emotions and the Progression of Cancer: A Review," *Advances: Journal of the Institute for the Advancement of Health* 1 (1), Winter 1984: 10–15.

Levy's latest research has revealed: S. M. Levy, J. Lee, C. Bagley and M. Lippman, "Survival Hazards Analysis in Recurrent Breast Cancer Patients: Seven Year Follow-up," *Psychosomatic Medicine* L (5), September/October 1988.

David C. McClelland, a professor of psychology and social relations: J. Z. Borysenko, "Healing Motives: An Interview with David C. McClelland," *Advances: Journal of the Institute for the Advancement of Health* 2 (2), Spring 1985: 29–41.

Studies have shown that relaxation training: J. K. Kiecolt-Glaser, R. Glaser et al., "Modulation of Cellular Immunity in Medical Students," *Journal of Behavioral Medicine* 9 (1), 1986: 5–21;

J. K. Kiecolt-Glaser, R. Glaser et al., "Psychosocial Enhancement of Immunocompetence in a Geriatric Population," *Health Psychology* 4, 1985: 25–41.

Body and mind are different expressions: Nerve fibers originating in the brain have been found to extend into organs in the immune system, and immune cells have receptors for the messenger molecules that travel across the nerve-ending synapses. It has also been discovered that peptides are not produced only by the brain (in which case they're called neuropeptides), but by the immune system as well. Research done by immunologist Ed Blalock has shown that chemical transmitters produced by the immune system complete the communication loop by going back to the brain. For discussions of interactions between immune and central nervous systems, see J. E. Blalock, "The Immune System as a Sensory Organ," *Journal of Immunology* 132, 1984; E. Smith, D. Harbour-McMenamin and J. E. Blalock, "Lymphocyte Production of Endorphins and Endorphin-Mediated Immunoregulatory Activity," *Journal of Immunology* 135, 1985; J. E. Blalock, D. Harbour-McMenamin and E. Smith, "Peptide Hormones Shaped by the Neuroendocrine and Immunologic Systems," *Journal of Immunology* 135, 1985. For a brief overview of anatomical and biochemical links between immune and central nervous systems, mentioning the work of Karen Bulloch and David Felten (on anatomical links), Janet Kiecolt-Glaser and Ronald Glaser, Sandra Levy and others, see J. L. Marx, "The Immune System 'Belongs in the Body,' " *Science* 227, March 8, 1985: 1190–92.

"They are expressed in the body": C. B. Pert, "The Wisdom of the Receptors: Neuropeptides, the Emotions, and Bodymind," *Advances: Journal of the Institute for the Advancement of Health* 3 (3), Summer 1986: 8–16.

"For Freud and Jung, the unconscious was": C. Pert and M. Ruff, "AIDS Research: A Leading Edge at NIMH," *Psychological Perspectives* 18 (1), Spring 1987: 105–12.

"We know that the same neuropeptides secreted by the brain": Pert and Ruff, "AIDS Research," 111.

as Swami Rama demonstrated: E. Green and A. Green, *Beyond Biofeedback* (New York: Dell, Delta Books, 1977).

Studies performed on rats and mice: R. Ader and N. Cohen, "Behaviorally Conditioned Immunosuppression," *Psychosomatic Medicine* 37, 1975: 333–40.

CHAPTER 2

as Jungian psychologist Russell A. Lockhart put it: R. A. Lockhart, "Cancer in Myth and Dream," *Spring 1977: An Annual of Archetypal Psychology and Jungian Thought,* 1977: 1–26.

Jungian psychotherapist and author Arnold Mindell: A. Mindell, *Dreambody* (Boston: Sigo Press, 1982), 55–72.

"I don't believe that a person actually creates disease": A. Mindell, *Working With the Dreaming Body* (London and New York: Routledge & Kegan Paul, 1985), 13.

"The physical disorder," as Jung says: C. J. Jung, *The Structure and Dynamics of the Psyche,* trans. R.F.C. Hull, vol. 8 of *Collected Works* (Princeton: Princeton University Press, 1960), par. 502.

In a study done at Ben-Gurion University: *Psychology Today,* June 1987: 10. This is a report on a study by D. Bar-On in *Human Relations* 39, 1987: 917–31.

"The purpose of sickness, the meaning of affliction": Lockhart, "Cancer in Myth and Dream," 7–8.

"Not only patients but doctors also": H. Sabini and V. H. Maffly, "An Inner View of Illness: The Dreams of Two Cancer Patients," *Journal of Analytical Psychology* 26, 1981: 149.

"One cannot say that every symptom is a challenge": C. J. Jung, *Letters,* vol. 1, 1906–1950, ed. Gerhard Adler and Aniela Jaffé, trans. R.F.C. Hull (Princeton: Princeton University Press, 1973), 429.

"When I began studying dreams of illness": Meredith Sabini, "Imagery in Dreams of Illness," *Quadrant,* Spring 1982: 102.

"Not infrequently the dream shows": Jung, *Psyche,* par. 502.

"for a few timeless hours": A. Huxley, *The Doors of Perception* (New York: Harper & Row, 1970).

Dr. Caroline Bedell Thomas: M. Harrower, C. B. Thomas and A. Altman, "Human Figure Drawings in a Prospective Study of Six Disorders: Hypertension, Coronary Heart Disease, Malignant Tumor, Suicide, Mental Illness, and Emotional Disturbance," *Journal of Nervous and Mental Disease* 161 (3), 1975: 191–99; C. B. Thomas, L. W. Jones and D. C. Ross, "Studies on Figure Drawings: Biological Implications of Structural and Graphic Characteristics," *Psychiatric Quarterly Supplement* 42, 1968: 223–51.

Jungian therapist Susan Bach: S. R. Bach, "Why We Do This Work: A Short Introduction to the Reading and Evaluation of Spontaneous Pictures," *Psychosomatische Medizin* 9, 1980: 120–23.

Psychologist Joan Kellogg: J. Kellogg, M. MacRae, H. L. Bonny and
F. Di Leo, "The Use of the Mandala in Psychological Evaluation
and Treatment," *American Journal of Art Therapy* 16, July
1977: 123–34; J. Kellogg and F. B. Di Leo, "Archetypal Stages of
the Great Round of Mandala," *Journal of Religion and Psychical
Research* 5 (1), January 1982: 38–47.

"At that moment I knew": Mindell, *Dreaming Body*, 8, 7, 27.

CHAPTER 3

A recent report by the National Institutes of Health: Lena Williams,
"Influence of Pets Reaches New High," *New York Times*, August
17, 1988, sec. C, 1.

In support of her ideas, Achterberg cites: J. Achterberg, *Imagery in
Healing* (Boston: Shambhala, 1985), 114–15.

appears in Ernest Rossi's book: E. L. Rossi, *The Psychobiology of
Mind-Body Healing: New Concepts of Therapeutic Hypnosis*
(New York: W. W. Norton and Co., 1986), 110. See also E. L.
Rossi and D. B. Cheek, *Mind-Body Therapy: Methods of Ideody-
namic Healing in Hypnosis* (New York: W. W. Norton & Co.,
1988).

"Even under adequate anesthesia": R. Rymer, "What You Hear
Under the Knife," *Hippocrates*, May/June 1987: 100–102.

An interesting comparison of thirty patients: E. B. LeWinn and M. D.
Dimancescu, "Environmental Deprivation and Enrichment in
Coma," *The Lancet* 2, 1978: 156–57.

In a review of the professional literature: D. B. Cheek, "Awareness
of Meaningful Sounds Under General Anesthesia: Considerations and a Review of the Literature 1959–79," paper presented
November 17, 1979, at the annual meeting of the American
Society of Clinical Hypnosis in San Francisco and reprinted in
Theoretical and Clinical Aspects of Hypnosis, 1981. The study
referred to is L. S. Wolfe and J. B. Millett, "Control of Postoperative Pain by Suggestion Under General Anesthesia," *American
Journal of Clinical Hypnosis* 3, 1960: 109–11. See also D. Hutch-
ings, "The Value of Suggestion Given Under Anesthesia: A Report and Evaluation of 200 Consecutive Cases," ibid. 4, 1961:
26–29.

A recent article in *The Lancet:* C. Evans and P. H. Richardson, "Improved Recovery and Reduced Postoperative Stay After Therapeutic Suggestions During General Anesthesia," *The Lancet,*

August 27, 1988: 491–92. See also H. L. Bennett, "Behavioral Anesthesia," *Advances: Journal of the Institute for the Advancement of Health* 2 (4), Fall 1985: 11–21.

Some intriguing research: Marcel and Hilgard studies are reported in D. Goleman, *Vital Lies, Simple Truths: The Psychology of Self-Deception and Shared Illusions* (New York: Simon & Schuster, 1985), 67–69, 87–89.

a number of psychological studies have shown: D. B. Cheek, "Areas of Research Into Psychosomatic Aspects of Surgical Tragedies Now Open Through Use of Hypnosis and Ideomotor Questioning," *Western Journal of Surgery, Obstetrics and Gynecology* 70, 1962: 137–42.

"The specific functions that have been attributed": Achterberg, *Imagery*, 122.

Dr. Dean Ornish, a cardiologist: Dean Ornish, private communication, August 1987, and news release from the American Heart Association, Dallas, Texas, November 14, 1988.

Relaxation training has also helped asthma sufferers: On Fuller-von Bozzay, see S. Locke and D. Colligan, *The Healer Within: The New Medicine of Mind and Body* (New York: New American Library, Mentor Books, 1987), 201. For Lehrer, see P. Lehrer et al., "Relaxation Decreases Large-Airway but Not Small-Airway Asthma," *Journal of Psychosomatic Research* 30 (1), April–May 1986: 13–25.

"Not only is there a reduction in level of anxiety": A. Meares, "A Form of Intensive Meditation Associated with the Regression of Cancer," *American Journal of Clinical Hypnosis* 25 (2–3), October 1982–January 1983: 114–21.

"1. Take a few minutes in the morning": S. F. Santorelli, "Mindfulness and Mastery in the Workplace: 21 Ways to Reduce Stress During the Workday," *Buddhist Peace Fellowship Newsletter*, Fall 1987.

Harvard psychologist Mary Jasnoski has done research: Daniel Goleman, "Relaxation: Surprising Benefits Detected," *New York Times*, May 13, 1986, sec. C, 1.

In an interview with Ernest Rossi: M. H. Erickson and E. L. Rossi, "Autohypnotic Experiences of M. H. Erickson," *American Journal of Clinical Hypnosis* 20 (1), July 1977: 36–54.

Dr. Karen Olness of the Children's Hospital in Cleveland: Karen Olness, "Teaching Mind/Body Skills to Children," *Noetic Sciences Review*, Spring 1988: 13–14.

CHAPTER 4

A group of oncologists, psychiatrists and medical school workers: Michelle Vranizan, "Dramatize Nuances of Telling Patients They Have Cancer," *Medical Tribune,* September 3, 1986.

Another training program I've read about: "Effort Grows to Create Sensitive Doctors," *New York Times,* April 8, 1986.

Recently I read about: Dick Roraback, "Patients for a Day," *Los Angeles Times,* San Diego edition, July 5, 1988.

a survey reported a few years ago in *JAMA:* Jules Older, "Teaching Touch at Medical School," *Journal of the American Medical Association* 252 (7), August 17, 1984: 931.

A recent contributor, a seventeen-year-old girl: J. E. Matthews, "My Dream," *Journal of the American Medical Association* 258 (21), December 4, 1987: 3112.

Wellness is cost-effective: A study of eighty people in the Harvard Community Health Plan that compared patients enrolled in wellness groups (where they received training in visualization and relaxation) with a control group showed that those who received the training reduced their use of health plan services by 47% in the six months afterwards, yielding a savings of $171 to $252 per person. This is reported in Joan Turkington, "Help for the Worried Well," *Psychology Today,* August 1987, and Daniel Goleman, "The Mind Over the Body," *New York Times Magazine,* September 27, 1987.

CHAPTER 5

"This concerns a couple, Charlie and Josephine": G. L. Engel, "A Life Setting Conducive to Illness: The Giving-up–Given-up Complex," *Annals of Internal Medicine* 69 (2), August 1968: 293–300.

Engel knows from personal experience: G. L. Engel, "Emotional Stress and Sudden Death," *Psychology Today,* November 1977.

Internist Caroline Bedell Thomas: C. B. Thomas and K. R. Duszynski, "Closeness to Parents and the Family Constellation in a Prospective Study of Five Disease States: Suicide, Mental Illness, Malignant Tumor, Hypertension, and Coronary Heart Disease," *Johns Hopkins Medical Journal* 134, 1974: 251–70; C. B. Thomas, "Precursors of Premature Disease and Death: The Predictive Potential of Habits and Family Attitudes," *Annals of Internal*

Medicine 87, 1976: 653–58; C. B. Thomas, K. R. Duszynski and J. W. Shaffer, "Family Attitudes Reported in Youth as Potential Predictors of Cancer," *Psychosomatic Medicine* 41, 1979: 287–302; C. B. Thomas and O. L. McCabe, "Precursors of Premature Disease and Death: Habits of Nervous Tension," *Johns Hopkins Medical Journal* 147, 1980: 137–45.

"Forty years ago, the term 'molecular biology' ": C. B. Thomas, "Cancer and the Youthful Mind: A Forty Year Perspective," *Advances: Journal of the Institute for the Advancement of Health* 5 (2), 1988.

A new study, which I feel supports: T.I.A. Sorenson, "Genetic and Environmental Influences on Premature Death in Adult Adoptees," *New England Journal of Medicine* 318 (12), March 24, 1988: 727–32.

a 1988 follow-up study on the same group: E. Smith, "Fighting Cancerous Feelings," *Psychology Today,* May 1988: 22–23.

Touch is physiologic: For an overview of some of the research on touch and mental and physical well-being, see D. L. Goleman, "The Experience of Touch: Research Points to a Crucial Role," *New York Times,* February 2, 1988.

psychologists Lawrence LeShan and R. E. Worthington: L. LeShan and R. E. Worthington, "Personality as a Factor in the Pathogenesis of Cancer: A Review of the Literature," *British Journal of Medical Psychology* 29, 1956: 49–56; L. LeShan, "An Emotional Life-History Pattern Associated with Neoplastic Disease," *Annals of the New York Academy of Science* 125 (3), 1966: 780–93; L. LeShan and R. E. Worthington, "Some Recurrent Life History Patterns Observed in Patients With Malignant Disease," *Journal of Nervous Mental Disorders* 124, 1956: 460–65; L. LeShan, "Psychological States as Factors in the Development of Malignant Disease: A Critical Review," *Journal of the National Cancer Institute* 22, 1959: 1–18.

Caroline Thomas did some of the early work: P. L. Graves and C. B. Thomas, "Themes of Interaction in Medical Students' Rorschach Responses as Predictors of Midlife Health or Disease," *Psychosomatic Medicine* 43 (3), June 1981: 15–225.

In his 1975 survey of the relevant literature: C. B. Bahnson, "Emotional and Personality Characteristics of Cancer Patients," paper delivered May 14, 1975, at the American College of Physicians as part of "The Patient With Cancer" and reprinted in *Oncologic Medicine,* ed. A. Sutnick (University Park Press, 1976).

Dr. Solomon and his colleague Dr. Lydia Temoshok: G. F. Solomon and L. Temoshok, "Psychoneuroimmunologic Perspective on AIDS Research: Questions, Preliminary Findings, and Suggestions," *Applied Social Psychology* (V. H. Winston & Sons, Inc., 1987), 286–307.

they have tentatively identified: G. F. Solomon, L. Temoshok, A. O'Leary and J. Zich, "An Intensive Psychoimmunologic Study of Long-Surviving Persons with AIDS," *Annals of the New York Academy of Sciences* 496, 1987: 647–55.

In the latest article I've read: Henry Dreher, "A Conversation with George Solomon," *Advances: Journal of the Institute for the Advancement of Health* 5 (1), 1988.

as of 1987 when Solomon reported on his case: Solomon and Temoshok, "Psychoneuroimmunologic Perspective on AIDS Research."

psychologist Suzanne Kobasa: S. R. Maddi and S. C. Kobasa, *The Hardy Executive: Health Under Stress* (Homewood, Ill.: Dow Jones–Irwin, 1984); S. C. Kobasa, "Stressful Life Events, Personality and Health: An Inquiry into Hardiness," *Journal of Personality and Social Psychology* 37 (1), 1979: 1–11.

Hans Selye, the endocrinologist: H. Selye, *The Stress of Life,* rev. ed. (New York: McGraw-Hill, 1976), 450.

he did animal studies: M.E.P. Seligman and S. F. Maier, "Failure to Escape Traumatic Shock," *Journal of Experimental Psychology* 74, 1967: 1–9.

Similarly, people may learn helplessness: L. Y. Abramson, M.E.P. Seligman and J. D. Teasdale, "Learned Helplessness in Humans," *Journal of Abnormal Psychology* 87(1),1978:49–74;M.E.P. Seligman, "Helplessness and Explanatory Style: Risk Factors for Depression and Disease," paper presented March 1986 at a meeting of the Society for Behavioral Medicine in San Francisco.

Seligman and his colleagues: D. Goleman, "Research Affirms Power of Positive Thinking," *New York Times,* February 3, 1987; D. Goleman, "Feeling of Control Viewed as Central in Mental Health," *New York Times,* October 7, 1986.

"I contemplated the physiologic wear and tear": G. E. Vaillant, "Health Consequences of Adaptation to Life," *American Journal of Medicine* 67, November 1979.

the results of a forty-year study: G. E. Vaillant, "Natural History of Male Psychologic Health: Effects of Mental Health on Physical Health," *New England Journal of Medicine* 301 (23), December 6, 1979.

a study updating the results on ninety-nine of those men: C. Peterson and M. E. Seligman, *Journal of Personality and Social Psychology* 55 (2), 1987: 237–65. Seligman's remarks are taken from D. Goleman, "Research Affirms Power of Positive Thinking," *New York Times,* February 3, 1987.

Recently I read an article: Ushanda io Elima, "Life With the Pygmies," *Mothering Magazine* 48.

Parents "should above all else": Elida Evans, *A Psychological Study of Cancer* (New York: Dodd, Mead & Co., 1926), 152.

"For the human spirit is virtually indestructible": Alice Miller, *For Your Own Good* (New York: Farrar, Straus & Giroux, 1983), 279.

CHAPTER 6

"Perhaps cancer is an experiment": Lockhart, "Cancer in Myth and Dream," 1–26.

Finally there are the words of a woman: Nancy Pappas, "Images of Healing," *Northeast/The Hartford Courant,* May 10, 1987.

wrote a master's thesis: The thesis is summarized in Sheila Campbell, "The Meaning of the Breast Cancer Mastectomy Experience," *Humane Medicine* 2 (2), November 1986.

Take the example of Ray Berté: B. S. Siegel with S. Schneider, "The Medicine Was Love," *Redbook,* December 1987.

It's been shown that married men: J. S. Goodwin, W. C. Hunt, C. R. Key and J. M. Samet, "The Effect of Marital Status on Stage, Treatment and Survival of Cancer Patients," *Journal of the American Medical Association* 258 (21), December 4, 1987. This article showed that married people diagnosed with cancer had five-year survival rates comparable to those of single people ten years younger than they. In a study by Dr. Harold Morowitz of Yale, reported in Kirk Johnson, "The Mind and Immunity," *EastWest,* November 1986, married men were shown to have lower death rates than single men regardless of whether they were nonsmokers or heavy smokers, and the single men fared better than men who were widowed or divorced. In fact, heavy smokers who were married had about the same death rates as nonsmokers who were divorced.

a doctoral student doing a related study: B. O'Regan, "Healing, Remission and Miracle Cures," *Institute of Noetic Sciences Special Report,* May 1987: 11 (paraphrased).

Dulcy also saw a psychiatrist: Siegel with Schneider, "Medicine Was Love."

He begins by telling how a friend's six-year-old son: M. Callen, "I Will Survive," *The Village Voice*, May 3, 1988. Reprinted in *Surviving and Thriving With AIDS: Collected Wisdom*, vol. II (New York: People With AIDS Coalition, 1988).

articles like the one in the *New York Times:* L. Altman, "AIDS Mystery: Why Do Some Infected Men Stay Healthy?" *New York Times*, June 30, 1987.

"1. Acceptance of the reality": Solomon, Temoshok, O'Leary and Zich, "Long-Surviving Persons with AIDS," 647–55.

"If I had to describe in one word": Callen, "I Will Survive."

"and guess what? My clients got better fast!": J. Segal, "Doing Good: Service in the Nineties," *AHP Perspective*, April 1987.

"Do you know what it's like to tie": "Rabbi Endures Pain to Teach Talmud," *New York Times*, January 4, 1987.

CHAPTER 7

Leonard Matlovich, an Air Force sergeant: Mike Hippler, "An American Hero," *Bay Area Reporter*, June 30, 1988.

"The most beautiful experience we can have": Albert Einstein, "The World As I See It," essay of 1931.

"religious nuts or psychiatric cases": Andrew Greeley, "Mysticism Goes Mainstream," *American Health*, January–February 1987: 47–49.

Reading List

Achterberg, Jeanne. *Imagery in Healing.* Boston: Shambhala, 1985.

Ader, Robert, ed. *Psychoneuroimmunology.* New York: Academic Press, 1981.

Bennett, Hal, and Mike Samuels. *The Well Body Book.* New York: Random House, 1973.

Benson, Herbert, with Miriam Z. Klipper. *The Relaxation Response.* New York: Avon Books, 1976.

Benson, Herbert, with William Proctor. *Your Maximum Mind.* New York: Times Books, 1987.

Borysenko, Joan. *Minding the Body, Mending the Mind.* Reading, Mass.: Addison Wesley, 1987; New York: Bantam Books, 1988.

Brennan, Barbara Ann. *Hands of Light.* New York: Bantam Books, 1988.

Campbell, Joseph. *The Hero With a Thousand Faces.* Princeton: Princeton University Press, 1968.

Campbell, Joseph, with Bill Moyers. *The Power of Myth.* New York: Doubleday, 1988.

Cousins, Norman. *The Healing Heart.* New York: Avon Books, 1984.

Delaney, Gayle. *Living Your Dreams.* New York: Harper & Row, 1981.

Evans, Elida. *A Psychological Study of Cancer.* New York: Dodd, Mead & Co., 1926.

Faraday, Ann. *The Dream Game.* New York: Harper & Row, 1976.

Frankl, Viktor. *Man's Search for Meaning.* New York: Touchstone, 1984.

Franz, Marie-Louise von, with Fraser Boa. *The Way of the Dream.* Toronto: Windrose Films Ltd., 1987.

Furth, Gregg. *The Secret World of Drawings: Healing Through Art.* Boston: Sigo Press, 1988.

Garfield, Patricia. *Creative Dreaming.* New York: Simon & Schuster, 1974; New York: Ballantine Books, 1976.

Gendlin, Eugene. *Let Your Body Interpret Your Dreams.* Wilmette, Ill.: Chiron Pub., 1986.

Green, Elmer, and Alyce Green. *Beyond Biofeedback.* New York: Dell, Delta Books, 1977.

Hertzler, Arthur. *The Horse and Buggy Doctor.* New York: Harper & Row, 1938.

Huxley, Aldous. *The Doors of Perception.* New York: Harper & Row, 1970.

Jung, Carl G. *Man and His Symbols.* New York: Dell, 1968.

————. *Memories, Dreams, Reflections.* Edited by Aniela Jaffé. Translated by Richard and Clara Winston. New York: Vintage, 1965.

————. *The Structure and Dynamics of the Psyche.* 2nd ed. Princeton: Princeton University Press, 1968.

Justice, Blair. *Who Gets Sick?* Los Angeles: J. P. Tarcher, 1988. Distributed by St. Martin's Press, New York.

LeShan, Lawrence. *How to Meditate.* Boston: Little, Brown, 1974; New York: Bantam Books, 1984.

————. *You Can Fight for Your Life: Emotional Factors in the Causation of Cancer.* New York: Evans, 1977.

Locke, Steven, and Douglas Colligan. *The Healer Within.* New York: Dutton, 1986; New York: New American Library, Mentor Books, 1987.

Menninger, Karl. *Love Against Hate.* New York: Harcourt, Brace & Co., 1942.

————. *Man Against Himself.* New York: Harcourt, Brace & Co., 1938.

Menninger, Karl, with Martin Mayman and Paul Pruyser. *The Vital Balance.* New York: Viking Press, 1963; Magnolia, Mass.: Peter Smith, 1983.

Mindell, Arnold. *Dreambody.* Boston: Sigo Press, 1982.

————. *Working With the Dreaming Body.* London and New York: Routledge & Kegan Paul, 1985.

Nouwen, Henri. *Out of Solitude.* Notre Dame, Ind.: Ave Maria Press, 1974.

Ornstein, Robert, and David Sobel. *The Healing Brain.* New York: Simon & Schuster, 1987.

Oyle, Irving. *The Healing Mind.* New York: Pocket Books, 1975.

Rosen, Sidney. *My Voice Will Go With You: The Teaching Tales of Milton H. Erickson, M.D.* New York: W. W. Norton & Co., 1982.

Rossi, Ernest L. *The Psychobiology of Mind-Body Healing.* New York: W. W. Norton & Co., 1986.

Rossi, Ernest L., and David Cheek. *Mind-Body Therapy: Methods of Ideodynamic Healing in Hypnosis.* New York: W. W. Norton & Co., 1988.

Samuels, Mike, and Nancy Samuels. *Seeing With the Mind's Eye.* New York: Random House, 1975.

Saroyan, William. *The Human Comedy.* New York: Harcourt, Brace, World, 1971.

Selye, Hans. *The Stress of Life.* Rev. ed. New York: McGraw-Hill, 1976.

Simonton, O. Carl, Stephanie Matthews-Simonton and James Creighton. *Getting Well Again.* Los Angeles: J. P. Tarcher, 1978; New York: Bantam Books, 1980.

Solzhenitsyn, Aleksandr. *Cancer Ward.* Translated by Nicholas Bethell and David Burg. New York: Farrar, Straus & Giroux, 1969; New York: Bantam Books, 1969.

Thomas, Lewis. *The Youngest Science.* New York: Viking Press, 1983; New York: Bantam Books, 1984.

Tolstoy, Leo. *The Death of Ivan Illich.* Available in various editions.

The Bible.

Copyright Acknowledgments

About the Author

Dr. Bernard S. Siegel, who prefers to be called Bernie, not Doctor Siegel, attended Colgate University and Cornell University Medical College. He holds membership in two scholastic honor societies, Phi Beta Kappa and Alpha Omega Alpha, and graduated with honors. His surgical training took place at Yale New Haven Hospital and the Children's Hospital of Pittsburgh. He is a pediatric and general surgeon in New Haven.

In 1978 Bernie started Exceptional Cancer Patients, a specific form of individual and group therapy utilizing patients' dreams, drawings and images. ECaP is based on "carefrontation," a loving, safe, therapeutic confrontation, which facilitates personal change and healing. This experience led to his desire to make everyone aware of his or her own healing potential.

The Siegel family lives in the New Haven, Connecticut, area. Bernie and his wife, Bobbie Siegel, have co-authored many articles and five children. The family has innumerable interests and pets. Their home resembles a cross between a family art gallery, a zoo, a museum and an automobile repair shop.

In 1986 his first book, *Love, Medicine and Miracles,* was published. This event redirected his life. He is now very involved in humanizing medical education and making the medical profession aware of the mindbody connection. Bernie travels extensively with Bobbie to speak and run workshops sharing his techniques and experience.

Woody Allen said if he had one wish it would be to be someone else. Bernie's wish, made several years ago, was to be a few inches taller. His work has been such a growth experience that he is now taller.

His prediction is that in a decade the effects of consciousness on man and matter will be an accepted scientific fact.

ECaP (Exceptional Cancer Patients) is the not-for-profit organization founded by Dr. Siegel in 1978. In the Connecticut area ECaP offers a clinical program with support group sessions led by psychotherapists. These are available to people who have cancer, AIDS or other life-threatening or serious chronic illnesses. In addition, each year ECaP sponsors several weekend workshops featuring Dr. Siegel that are open to anyone, with or without health problems.

ECaP has recently begun offering such services as professional training and consulting, intensive workshops and biofeedback and specialized groups such as art therapy for children.

ECaP has prepared packets with valuable information, including Dr. Siegel's national workshop schedule, medical information and support services and ECaP-like regional referrals where they're available. This set of materials can be ordered at nominal cost ($5 including postage and handling).

All of the videotapes and audiocassettes featuring Dr. Siegel can be ordered through ECaP. They also carry many other books and tapes that convey the ECaP philosophy. To place an order, request a catalog of books and tapes or get additional information, please write or call:

ECaP
1302 Chapel Street
New Haven, CT 06511
(203) 865-8392

Videocassettes available featuring Dr. Siegel:

Exceptional Patients   Inspirational stories of ECaP members, featuring Dr. Siegel (available August 1989)

The Art of Health and Healing: A Lecture by Bernie Siegel   A recent two-hour lecture presentation in which Dr. Siegel conveys a philosophy of healing body, mind and spirit

Fight for Your Life   Informative tape with Dr. Siegel and four cancer survivors, who deliver a message of hope and determination

Hope and a Prayer   Interview with Dr. Siegel that explores his philosophy of healing

Innervision   Tape on the many uses of visualization, featuring Dr. Siegel

Guided imagery audiocassettes available:

Opening to the Heart of Healing (1989)   Two-audiocassette set with a meditation and a lecture presentation tape

Getting Ready: Meditations for Surgery, Chemo and Radiation (available June 1989)   Four guided imagery sessions to prepare the mind for medical intervention

Meditations for Everyday Living (1988)

Healing Meditations (1988)

Guided Imagery and Meditation (1985)

Several lecture cassettes are also available, including:

Life, Hope & Healing (1988)   A new six-audiocassette set, featuring Dr. Siegel discussing in depth his philosophy and techniques for living to the fullest. Includes the stories of three survivors in their own words.

For an audio tape of *Peace, Love and Healing* or *Love, Medicine and Miracles* (abridged versions) performed by Dr. Siegel on two 90-minute cassettes, contact ECaP at the address above.